What othe

Reviews from Amazon

For starters, I am a Mormon and a Democrat (and an attorney). I was handed a copy of this book with the intent to never read it. Honestly, what arguments could there be... that I haven't already heard? The thing about this book is, although it is written for a conservative audience in mind, **I found it to be surprisingly objective in its handling of topics and forthright in its areas of subjectivity. I loved the book.** *... This book took to the issues that Mormons typically cite for being conservative, or more so, Republican, and struck straight at their core.* **If you want to know why Mormons skew conservative, read the book. If you want to read a thoughtful and careful review of current political and religious topics, read the book. Finally, if you want to enjoy a good debate, while coming to understand the Mormon psyche just a bit better, read the book.**

David Carr

This book is a breath of fresh air because it is so unassuming. In a sea of hate, misunderstanding and ignorance this book stands alone in its genre. *I hope it ends up not just on every Mormon's bookshelf but on the shelf and in the hands of every American. It seems it would do us all a bit of good. I hope that there will be a follow up that will be more secular in nature and address the much desired need for civility in our country.*

Hal Wonder

As a conservative, even many Republicans are too liberal for me. **I would recommend this book for anyone who wants to become more tolerant of those with a liberal point of view.** *It seems to me that so many books are one-sided and extreme. I get angry when I try to read a liberal book, and I just become more adamant about my point of view when I read a conservative book.* **It was nice to read something that didn't bash the other side or try to change my point of view. My mind was not changed, but my heart was.**

Stacy Self

I just recently started reading this book and already can't put it down. **The writing style is full of personality and the author is obviously a great combo of intelligent and fun!** *Issues are presented fairly and realistically–entertaining, not hostile or superficial. I've already bought 2 extra copies to give away–one to a republican friend of mine and one to a democrat relative–I'm sure they'll both love it!!*

Cami Nuttal

————

Instead of the usual finger-pointing and name-calling that you would find in political books, this book brings civil dialogue in a way that I have not seen in any other book. *The unique format of this book pits two opposing views against each other, from two people who seemingly share the same values and religious background. Instead of the typical rebuttal that you might expect, the two voices are then brought together to address what they agree on (which is often surprising to both parties). While covering a wide range of social and political issues,* **this book does not come across as preachy, and might offer insight to those both in and outside of the LDS faith that their idea of the stereotypical right-wing Mormon, is just that: a stereotype.** *A great read for all who may be even the slightest bit interested in politics, particularly those looking to restore a little civility in their political discourse.*

Tom Bogle

How Can You Possibly be a Mormon and a Democrat?

PERSPECTIVES ON ABORTION, ECONOMICS, THE ENVIRONMENT AND HARRY REID

First Edition

HOW CAN YOU POSSIBLY BE A MORMON AND A DEMOCRAT? inaugurates the non-fiction *How Can You Possibly*® book series, which consists of titles that ask hard, unusual, rhetorical or unasked questions and content that provides rational answers to these questions.

For more information, go to

www.howcanyoupossibly.com

Email: **possiblypublishing@gmail.com**

Other titles in the series:

How Can You Possibly be an
ANTI-TERRORIST MUSLIM?
A devoute Muslim answers this all-to-often rhetorical question

Forthcoming in the series:

How Can You Possibly be a
MUSLIM FEMINIST?

How Can You Possibly
DEFEND THE PREEMPTIVE WARS OF GEORGE W. BUSH?*

How Can You Possibly
BE A MORMON AND A REPUBLICAN?

How Can You Possibly
RESPECT THOSE POLITICIANS,
PUNDITS OR PINKO-COMMIES?

How Can You Possibly
SECURE THE BORDERS WITH OPEN IMMIGRATION?

How Can You Possibly
DEFEND PRICE GOUGING?

How Can You Possibly believe
SPIDER-MAN II IS SUPERIOR TO CITIZEN KANE?

How Can You Possibly
BUILD A HOBBIT HOLE IN YOUR OWN BACKYARD?
True stories of how it has been done!

*This the working title but (perhaps) not the final title of this book.

How Can You Possibly®
be a
MORMON
and a
DEMOCRAT?

PERSPECTIVES ON ABORTION, ECONOMICS, THE ENVIRONMENT AND HARRY REID

First Edition

by

Clinton Joe Andersen, Jr.

**Possibly
Publishing**

How Can You Possibly be a Mormon and a Democrat?:
Perspectives on Abortion, Economics, the Environment and Harry Reid
by Clinton Joe Andersen, Jr.

Possibly Publishing
www.possiblypublishing.com
www.howcanyoupossibly.com

ISBN-13: 978-0-6155309-4-9
ISBN-10: 061553094X
Publication Date: June 15, 2011

First Edition (POD)
Digital render date 8/22/2011 9:58 PM

1 3 5 7 9 10 8 6 4 2

Design & Composition: Possibly Publishing
Cover design: Possibly Publishing
Cover Photo of LDS Temple: Janet G. Andersen

To my wife, Karen,
who is so patient and longsuffering
and has been for so long
and for so many reasons.[1]

---

[1] Seriously. No, I mean really! Want proof? Just check out the "About the Author" for a mere taste of how longsuffering she must be.

Should You Feel Inclined to Censure

LDS Hymn #235

Should you feel inclined to censure
Faults you may in others view,
Ask your own heart, ere you venture,
If that has not failings too.
Let not friendly vows be broken;
Rather strive a friend to gain;
Many a word in anger spoken
Finds its passage home again.
Do not then, in idle pleasure,
Trifle with a brother's fame,
Guard it as a valued treasure,
Sacred as your own good name.
Do not form opinions blindly;
Hastiness to trouble tends.
Those of whom we thought unkindly,
Oft become our warmest friends.

Contents

A NOTE TO NON-MORMONS

Initially, I had not expected any non-Mormons to be interested in this book. Not so. A copy of this book seemed to pique the interest of plenty of people who are not LDS. In fact, the first two people who read the entire book were not Mormons.

I'm not complaining. But, like any book written to a Mormon audience, this one is laced with a certain amount of cultural lingo. More on that below.

As for how I argue my case, I do so much differently than most Christian/political works. I do not constantly appeal to the *Bible* (or even LDS scriptures) as an ultimate authority. When I use a quote, whether from scripture or not, I do so mostly on the merits of what the quote says. In any case, Mormons do not believe that God's revealed truth was ever limited to the *Bible*. It was Joseph Smith that declared that we "are ready to believe all true principles that exist, as they are made manifest from time to time." What sets us apart from other Christian religions is that we have an open canon, that is, scriptures in addition to the *Bible*.[2] It also makes us, as I see it, more open to truth from many different venues.

To be clear, I do consider the LDS scriptures to be sources of authoritative truth and reference them in this book. However, I do so sparingly. A scriptural reference is hardly proof to a non-believer. More importantly, trying to use scriptures to win political arguments is… boring, to say the least.

At this point I was going to provide a glossary of terms to help the non-Mormon reader. But I didn't want to give the impression of an authoritative declaration of Mormon doctrine. What is written on these pages are my own thoughts and views as a faithful, active Latter-day Saint. I am not an official representative of the LDS Church.

All the same, a couple of terms should, perhaps, be quickly clarified. For starters, when I refer to "the Church", I DO NOT mean the Catholic Church or the religious establishment. In this

---

[2] Includes the Book of Mormon, Pearl of Great Price, the Doctrine and Covenants (or "D&C")

book, "the Church" refers to the LDS Church, also known as the Mormon Church, officially known as The Church of Jesus Christ of Latter-day Saints. A "general authority" is a high-ranking LDS Church leader such as an Apostle. These general authorities are given the title of **Elder** as in "Elder Andersen".

Also, when I refer to someone as "President So&So", I either mean the President of the United States or I am referring to someone who is a member of the First Presidency (the highest governing body in the Church) or, in the case of President Boyd K. Packer, he is the president of the Quorum of the Twelve Apostles.

ON FOOTNOTES

I have been warned that too many footnotes might scare some readers. For example, the following is in the Preface of one of my favorite books by Thomas Sowell:

> In keeping with the nature of Basic Economics as an introduction to economics for the general public, the usual footnotes or endnotes are left out. However, those who wish to check up on some of the surprising facts they will learn about here can find the sources listed at the end of the book.[3]

I guess footnotes make a book look too academic or something. The last thing I would want to read is a book that felt like a textbook or, worse yet, like a research paper or an academic thesis. Boring!

However, I believe that anyone who cares enough about politics to read a book about political issues would want that book to demonstrate careful research. More importantly, as a reader, I would prefer to read a book that allows me to easily check all of the sources that went into it. Hence, I use footnotes and for two reasons:

First, they allow the reader to double check the stuff I write because, you know, you can't believe everything you read. When I quote someone, you can check to see if said quote was taken out of context. Or when I make some outlandish claim, you can at least see where I got my crazy idea.

Second, they help me keep track of my own sources. If there's one thing I've learned in writing this book, it's that I can't always believe everything I write.

What I mean is, while sketching out the content of this book, I would often make a claim, list a fact or quote something that I thought I had heard or read at some point in the past. I would write out the claim or fact or quote as best as I could. Then, I would insert a footnote that either said, "need to source" or something like "I think this was quoted in an article in *Time* magazine around 1983". Many times, upon searching for a

---

[3] Sowell, *Basic Economics 3rd Ed*, vii.

source, I would discover that it was, for example, from *Newsweek* in 1980 rather than *Time Magazine* in 1983. And there were times when I could not find any source at all for a claim.

More significant, however, were those times I discovered that what I had "known" was simply untrue. In a few instances, I had even gotten one or more "facts" backwards; meaning, it said the opposite of what I had been claiming for years.

Yes, it happens to the best of us. We come across something and didn't question it because we trusted the source or (more often, probably) we agreed or liked the claim. So, we believe it for years and even pass that "knowledge" onto others. Unfortunately, the claims that support our way of seeing the world, that prove that we are right in that vision, encourage us to recite their "proof" more often and with more vigor. The very act of "proving" makes our brains more certain than ever. But because we had never questioned the original source or even bothered to learn where our "facts" came from, we go on "knowing" a complete falsity. In fact, it is natural to avoid even questioning such previous assumptions. Our brains recoil from it.

No one should feel bad about this behavior, by the way. We *all* do this kind of thing. It's how every normal human brain functions. And that brain function is, believe it or not, part of what makes us humans so ingenious. Yet another part of human genius is that we have the ability to recognize our own limitations. Think about that: a brain that knows it does not know. Our brain, to put it figuratively, is capable of "biting its own teeth".

One reason we have a hard time questioning our assumptions is that questioning is often mistaken for doubting. What has been a tremendous help to my intellect while writing this book—and I recommend it to all—is that I did not need to **question** or **doubt** my claims and facts. I simply needed to **source** them and document those sources. This means that, without going through the psychological pain of self-doubt (a psychological reaction from which no human can escape), I was able to discover my false assumptions and better fortify the true ones by simply taking the time to source my claims.

If I did not leave an easy trail for the reader to follow (through footnotes) and if I did not show all of my sources (in the bibliography), I would feel like I were ripping off the reader. After all, a book is give and take: the author gives and the reader takes. Without showing my footnotes, I would feel as if half of my efforts, from all those hours of research, would go to waste. I would just be telling the reader what I think, rather than what I know, or at least why I think I know it.

PREFACE

BEGINNINGS AND ENDS

I think almost all the crimes, which Christians have perpetrated against each other, arise from this, that religion is confused with politics. For, above all other spheres of human life, the Devil claims politics for his own, as almost the citadel of his power.

C.S. Lewis

Sometime after the 2008 elections, I did a search and found around five or six books with titles along the lines of "How would Jesus Vote?" It's a catchy title to use for a book, chapter or an essay. But I was discouraged to see that every author actually claimed to know, without question, that Jesus would vote Republican.

Now, I have always been a right wing, Christian, free-market, conservative Republican and proud of it. But I was a little less proud after discovering such homogenized content in these books. Like C.S. Lewis, I feel there is something disturbing about the claim that God is on your side of politics.

There are certainly absolute truths. What they are, exactly, is one thing. What to do about them, exactly, is another. But I believe there is real danger in thinking you know, with exactness, what the problem is and how to solve it. That danger exists whether your claim is that God is most disappointed in liberals and would want you to vote Republican (as liberal readers roll their eyes) or whether your claim is that science tells us that global warming is happening and carbon dioxide reduction is the cure (now conservatives can roll their eyes).

This book is my contribution to the ongoing debate and the uncomfortable relationship between politics and religion.

Though it is from my own conservative point of view, this book is NOT at least, not intentionally partisan.

The following pages will tell you "the beginnings and ends", which is to say, the origins and goals of this book.

From Russia
with Love and Loathing

The government is good at one thing... it knows how to break your legs, and then hand you a crutch and say, "see if it weren't for the government you wouldn't be able to walk."

Harry Browne

It wasn't long after the fall of the Iron Curtain that I served as a missionary in Russia. When I arrived in the former Soviet Union, the "culture shock" was less shocking then I had expected. The lower standard of living was no surprise; I had always expected it. Rather, the most depressing part of the whole experience was witnessing firsthand what the communists had stolen from the Russian people. I do not mean so much the universal theft of private property. No. Something much more valuable had been withheld from these people. To this day, it remains difficult to put into words. The entire society seemed to wallow in one mass clinical depression. Not economic depression, mind you, but personal mental depression. One sign of this, I believe, was the plague of alcoholism. Some would describe the people as generally lacking any ambition. I've called it a lack of zeal or zest for life (or, rather, for living). Whatever it was, however you define it, it was definitely there, ever present. It made me sick to see so much life without liberty and the inability to pursue happiness.

Interestingly enough, the real culture shock hit me when I returned to the United States! In fact, when I arrived at the JFK airport, I remember actually relishing the sweet smell of... filtered cigarettes. That's right! I had grown so accustomed to the pungent mixture of soft-rolled cigarette smoke, vodka and vomit that filtered cigarettes had become a sweet welcome to my nostrils.

And so, it was my return to the States that made me see so many things that I had taken for granted. I was mesmerized by our streets. They were clean! They were well-maintained. So smooth, with bold yellow and white stripes! I vividly remember being so awe-struck when I made my first trip to the grocery store: talk about a land of milk and honey… and Honey-nut Cheerios and Captain Crunch and a hundred other brands of… of just breakfast cereal alone. The most mind-boggling thing was that cereal aisle. Oh, but then there was the checkout line… Speed! Had I really forgotten all this stuff?

However, the abundance and variety of consumer goods did not even compare to the quality of services offered in this country, particularly in the realm of customer service. It has been more than a decade since my return to the States and not once has an employee of any store snapped at me for asking a question. American customer service people make it a point–get this–**not to ignore** their customers. Even if they do not know the answer, they almost always try to help anyway. I'm afraid that the typical Russian customer service answer (if I even got an answer) was something along the lines of… "What's the matter?! Can't you read? It's right in front of you!"

Most Americans have no idea how lucky we are to be living in such a country with an abundance of goods and quality services. And while I rejoiced at returning home to rediscover more fully appreciate my good fortune, I lamented even more those coarse conditions that I had left behind. I got bitter. A few people misinterpreted my attitude as complete disdain for Russia itself. On the contrary, I came back with a great love for the Russian people and their culture. I was quite bitter toward the Communist government for what it had done to the people. They had sucked the life out of… living. It was like returning from visiting a friend's house that had been vandalized. Love my friend. Detest the vandal.

My Fellow American

Now here is where things get interesting. I thought that no one could possibly live in Russia without coming back a staunch conservative, overflowing with an appreciation for capitalism and a revulsion for anything that remotely resembled communism or socialism. And if any liberal-minded Democrats back here in the States dared attack American capitalism, I would let them have it! After all, I had been there. I had seen the results of rampant liberal thinking. "If you'd seen what I've seen," I could tell them, "you'd change your leftist politics in a heartbeat!" Yeah. That's what I wanted to say! I mean, how could you possibly have lived in Russia and still be a Democrat? Right? There was just one problem, one little snag in my plans to annihilate the opposition with my own eyewitness testimony.

You see, upon my arrival in Russia, one of the first people I met was a Sharmak (name has been changed), a fellow American and a complete genius at speaking and understanding Russian, as well as German... and Polish, Ukrainian, and Armenian as well, I believe. As a matter of fact, he seemed to have a knack for understanding the languages and cultures of almost every people who had suffered behind the Iron. There is no question that my friend Sharmak was far more in tune with the people, politics and culture of Russia and the former Soviet Union than I could ever hope to be.

So it was a bit of a surprise to me, at least, to learn that Sharmak was a lifelong Democrat. Even after witnessing the horrid handicap state of the Russian economy, Sharmak never had and never would have any interest in changing political parties. That's right! Neither capitalists, conservatives nor the Republican Party held any interest for him whatsoever. He remains as repulsed by capitalism as he was by the tyrannies of the U.S.S.R., perhaps more so. To this day, he remains a very staunch and liberal Democrat.

It is strange how two people can witness the same thing and draw such different conclusions. To him, the evils of the soviet socialist republic did not necessarily make socialism itself an evil. Wow! That kind of thinking was new to me and, I must admit, discomforting. Perhaps he just needed to read a bit of Cleon Skousen or acquaint himself with the works or words of Ezra Taft Benson. But of course, Sharmak was already well acquainted with President Benson, having sustained him as prophet, seer and revelator just as surely and sincerely as I had. Sharmak was a lifelong and fully active member of the Church, a man who had served in many callings, including leadership positions. In fact, it was our Church callings, which had caused our paths to cross.

My calling had, of course, brought me to Russia. And his calling had brought him to the airport to meet me when I first arrived. You see, Sharmak was my Mission President.

It should interest you to know that, to this day, this staunch Democrat continues to serve in the Lord's church as a patriarch.

How Wide the Divide?

Shortly after my mission, I came across a wonderful book called *How Wide the Divide: a Mormon and an Evangelical in Conversation* by Stephen E. Robinson (the LDS scholar who wrote *Believing Christ*) and Craig L. Blomberg (an Evangelical scholar). The back cover of this book reads as follows:

> Mormons and Evangelicals don't often get along very well. Unfortunately, much of what they say about one another simply isn't true. False stereotypes on both sides prevent genuine communication.
>
> Having discovered this sad state of affairs, [the authors] set out to listen to one another and to ferret out the genuine agreements and disagreements between them. In the conversation that develops, you will read what each believes about [four] key theological issues.[4]

Each chapter in this book is organized so that each side takes turns explaining his side of a specific theological issue, followed by a "joint conclusion" in which the two authors point out where there is consensus and agreement and where they must simply agree to disagree. Most helpful is when they discover simple but complete misunderstandings because the two religious cultures often work with a slightly different vocabulary, such as when both sides use the same word but mean two different things. Understanding, not debate, was the goal, as Robinson explains:

> It is our hope that with this book we will begin to tell and believe the truth about each other, the issue of who is ultimately right and wrong being set aside for the moment.[5]

---

[4] Blomberg and Robinson, *How Wide the Divide?*.
[5] Ibid., 12.

What a concept! What a wonderful and straightforward goal: First, seek understanding. Set aside any hopes of persuading the other side for the time being and concentrate on learning about each other. As simple an idea as this is, I am sure it was a rough ride for the authors to present their discussion in an organized manner. Nevertheless, it resulted in a great book. It was a long awaited step in the right direction.

It was while reading *How Wide the Divide* that I thought about how nice it would be to see a similar book written between a Republican and a Democrat of the same faith.

Instruments of the Lord's Peace

Elder Robert S. Wood gave one of my favorite General Conference talks in April of 2006 called "Instruments of the Lord's Peace". Finally, a talk on politics! I highly recommend that you read or listen to the entire talk on the Church's website. Here are some important and powerful excerpts:

> We appear to be living in an era in which many are speaking without thinking, encouraging emotional reactions rather than thoughtful responses. Whether it be on the national or international stage, in personal relations or in politics, at home or in the public forum, voices grow ever more strident, and giving and taking offense appear to be chosen rather than inadvertent.
>
> Have we who have taken upon us the name of Christ slipped unknowingly into patterns of slander, evil speaking, and bitter stereotyping? Have personal or partisan or business or religious differences been translated into a kind of demonizing of those of different views? Do we pause to understand the seemingly different positions of others and seek, where possible, common ground?
>
> It is far too easy sometimes to fall into a spirit of mockery and cynicism in dealing with those of contrary views.[6]

Elder Wood comes at this from a unique perspective. As the dean of strategic studies at the U.S. Naval War College and an advisor to several U.S. presidents and defense secretaries, he knows Washington politics up close.

---

[6] Wood, "Instruments of the Lord's Peace."

Elder Wood's conference talk was the final push that I needed to get this book underway, mostly because it finally helped me solve the problem I had with finding someone to write the liberal perspective on each issue. More on that will be covered in *Part I*, before we get into those topical "debate chapters".

The Goals of this Book

The issue isn't that these paradoxes are resolvable. It's that they must be transcended. And that's where the power comes. The paradoxes aren't resolved. They're not solved! You don't solve a paradox. You transcend it.[7]

Prof. J. Bonner Ritchie

I wrote this book with the following specific goals in mind:

1. Illustrate how people may hold quite different political positions while remaining faithful members of the Church.

2. Encourage respectful "labeling" but discourage "name calling". There is a vast and important difference.

3. Warn against passing judgments about the motives and intellect of those with differing viewpoints.

4. Provide multiple perspectives of a few politically-charged topics, specifically abortion, economics, environment.

5. Exhibit ways of understanding an opposing viewpoint. In fact, this book specifically demonstrates one particular tool for really getting into the mind of the opposite view.

6. Give hope that we can work together with civility, despite the hard fact that some views are irreconcilable.

7. Provide some practical advice on dealing with some of the controversies outlined in this book.

8. Show that there is good news, and a great deal of it, regardless of disparity and sometimes because of it.

9. Testify the true Gospel of Jesus Christ transcends the concerns of contemporary politics and religion.

May this book provide a broader perspective on politics, in general, while encouraging you to reconsider some specific political

---

[7] Ritchie, *Pillars of My Faith - 1992 Sunstone Symposium.*

assumptions, it does not seek to change anyone's political views. Above all, I hope this book will encourage a change in attitude.

You see. After this life, after the veil is finally lifted, when the big and little questions of life have been completely answered, we will all look back and see ourselves (our lives, our actions, arguments and opinions) from an eternal perspective. At that time, I believe, so many of our most serious and heartfelt arguments and deliberations will probably look more like the squabbling of children in a playground over a toy or whose turn it is on the swing. How we treated each other during the most passionate of these arguments will emerge as being far more important than the deliberations themselves.

Contents of this Book

Although Chapter 5 does cover some official statements from *The Church of Jesus Christ of Latter-day Saints* regarding politics, this book is neither a history of LDS politics, nor a survey of political opinions of Mormons.

This book is an attempt to represent contemporary political views of LDS members with honesty and intelligence. Part I contains discussions of specific political issues, which are of real and intense concern to members of the Church across the political spectrum. These controversial "hot topics" are:

1. Abortion: pro-life vs. pro-life [8]

2. Economics: free-market vs. capitalism [9]

3. Green Politics (or environmentalism)

These issues are certain to raise the blood pressure. Arguments are not sugar coated, though they are expressed with a reasonable measure of civility and respect (we hope). If there were no divergence of opinion, there would be no such thing as politics. The differences in opinion demonstrated in this book are stark and probably always will be. Strong convictions exist on all sides, but so might reasonable analysis. The point of demonstrat-

---

[8] That's not a typo. Both views are pro-life.

[9] That isn't a typo either. There is a difference between the two terms.

ing a strong unapologetic conviction for each side is not to stir up anger, although many readers are bound to experience frustration as they read. Such is a side effect of any passionate debate. This book attempts to show how you *can* possibly be a Mormon and a Democrat (or a Republican), not that you should or should not be.

Each of the three "hot topic" chapters will end with a joint conclusion, where agreements will be attempted, though not necessarily reached. In fact, just clarifying and understanding each other's position proved to be difficult. Even agreeing to disagree wasn't easy. Finding actual resolutions to these disagreements was never part of the program. In fact, it would be an unrealistic, even arrogant, expectation.

However, despite relentless misunderstandings and irreconcilable differences of opinion among members of the Church, there is a great deal of light at the end of each tunnel. You may find some of that light in the "joint conclusion" sections of the first three chapters. The most beneficial aspect of these joint conclusions is when they endeavor to transcend the issue. How is this done? Not by abandoning the debate or faking an agreement. Of course not. There are many means of transcending an issue. At least two ways are attempted in this book: discovering good news about each subject (even abortion) and offering up some practical advice in dealing with the issue.

Any good news about a controversial subject is a stress relief in itself and can help lift the burden of bitterness and frustration. As for the value of practical advice... well, ask yourself this question: Is there really any benefit in knowing about and debating a subject, if there is nothing to be done about it? What good are facts and flaring opinions if you cannot, will not or know not what you might do to improve the situation. "Knowledge is power," they say, but not by itself. Empowerment comes by doing.

With any luck, these little morsels of optimism and pragmatism will directly benefit the readers. However, the ultimate hope is that these discoveries will inspire the readers to find *their own* good news and practical advice–all this without necessarily having to solve and reconcile the tangle of differences.

Political Parties, Ideologies and PR Firms

Bear in mind that the views expressed here are not necessarily those of the average LDS Democrat or LDS Republican. It is certain that a number of Democrat readers will probably claim that the liberal perspective in this book is either too extreme or too diluted... or too inconsistent.

Likewise, many Republicans who read this book will claim that the opinions are not truly conservative. Unfortunately, the "mainstream LDS Republican" opinion and the "average LDS Democrat" opinion on any of the topics are both floating targets. Here are a few reasons why:

A friend of mine once remarked, "a political party is merely a public relations firm for political ideologies." This is a useful way of viewing political parties. Like a PR firm, a political party has clients: special interest groups driven by need or ideology.

Like any business firm, their clients change over time. Some clients lose their power or motivation and fade or lose influence. Some clients go out of business altogether, while other clients win their case and simply retire (abolitionists, for example). Sometimes a client will leave one firm and go to the other, like the southern Democrats who flocked to the Republican Party in the late 1960s.

In the end, the stated goals of a political party do not originate from one client alone but from multiple clients. They do not espouse a single ideology but several. Thus, many of these ideologies (and their subsequent goals) have nothing to do with each other. Accordingly, the stated goals of a firm are never consistent. Why should they be? Still, it is frustrating when your firm represents and advocates other agendas that you downright oppose. In the "real world" of business, you have plenty of options; the choice of several public relations firms. In the world of contemporary American politics, there are only two big shots and most people feel they need to cling to one or the other if they expect to have any chance of representation.

Unfortunately, many Republicans and Democrats (of any faith) continue to believe that their party has a relatively consistent ideology compared to that "other party." However, a serious look at the history of political parties tells us that many contradictory political positions are often a matter of incidental history or pure circumstance. I quote Orson Scott Card, from an editorial column called "The Insanity of Parties":

> Let's say you think abortion should be restricted to only those cases where the fetus is nonviable, and only when the pregnancy resulted from rape or incest, or when the life of the mother is at stake. That would be my position, too.
>
> So what rule of logic, what great universal principle then requires you also to think it's a great idea for assault weapons to be available to the general public, or for any clown to carry a handgun concealed on his person? How do these topics overlap?[10]

Likewise, consider the words of P.J. O'Rourke:

> Consider how much you'd have to hate free will to come up with a political platform that advocates killing unborn babies but not convicted murderers. A callous pragmatist might favor abortion and capital punishment. A devout Christian would sanction neither. But it takes years of therapy to arrive at the liberal view.[11]

That's the price we pay for a two-party system, so it is said. But, think for a moment if there really were several major political parties. These parties, like any group of people, could never avoid ideological hypocrisy because it is so difficult even for individuals to do so, as expressed by C.S. Lewis:

> Humans are very seldom either totally sincere or totally hypocritical. Their moods change, their motives are mixed, and they are often themselves quite mistaken as to what their motives are.[12]

If individual people find it difficult to remain consistent, why on earth should anyone expect groups of people to remain consistent?

---

[10] Card, "The Insanity of Parties - The Ornery American."
[11] O'Rourke, *Give War a Chance*, xxi.
[12] Lewis, *Letters to an American Lady*, 97, (28 March 1961).

Labels Over Time and Space

A person may be quite liberal in a political sense, but conservative when it comes to religious practice, and vice versa. There are plenty of Church members who believe in organic evolution, drink Pepsi, and support President George W. Bush and the war in Iraq. Such folks might be labeled "liberal" for tolerating evolution or drinking Pepsi. However, based on their support of President Bush alone, they would be considered politically "conservative".

Not only does ideology change, but language does as well. The language used to describe people, parties and ideologies changes over time and context. Yes, terms like "conservative" and "liberal" have different political meanings today than they did 100 years ago, not to mention terms like "gay" or "straight." I quote economist Thomas Sowell:

> If you have always believed that everyone should play by the same rules and be judged by the same standards, that would have gotten you labeled a radical 50 years ago, a liberal 25 years ago, and a racist today.

Whatever the historical definitions of ideology may have been in the past, this book was written in the context of the first decade of the 21st century. As such, let's not waste time quarreling about historical semantics.

For the sake of argument, we can acknowledge that the Republican Party, in general, currently represents conservatives and the Democratic Party represents liberals. Even so, this book will not typically use party affiliation as a guidepost for political ideology.

As the table of contents plainly shows, the "liberal" or "left-wing" perspective will be argued by Dan, while the "conservative" or "right-wing" perspective will be represented by Noah.

The joint conclusions are intended, primarily, to clarify the core disagreements, but not to resolve them. with the hope was to transcend the disagreement altogether, with practical advice, uplifting thoughts, and inspiring anecdotes.

A Note on Authority

Bear in mind that references to scripture and authoritative quotes by Church leaders are used much less in this book than you might expect. There are quite a number of quotes from a variety of sources, religious and secular. However, the contributors of this book have specifically tried not to use scriptures and leadership statements as explicit proof of a political view. There two reasons for this:

First, the persistent use of scriptures can quickly become tiresome. Readers soon learn to gloss over the scriptural references or quotes. Consequently, in this book, when such references are used, they are meant to be read.

Second, we wish to avoid appearing as if "God is on my side". Authoritative quotes and scriptures must necessarily be used as part of the reason for one's position. But please don't confuse the use of such references as an attempt to prove God's position.

Hugh Nibley once spoke of debates surrounding the authenticity of *The Book of Mormon*. What he said would certainly apply to the political arena, as well:

> The evidence that will prove or disprove [one side or the other] does not exist. When, indeed, is a thing proven? Only when an individual has accumulated in his own consciousness enough observations, impressions, reasonings, and feelings to satisfy him personally that it is so. The same evidence, which convinces one expert, may leave another completely unsatisfied; the impressions that build up the definite proof are themselves nontransferable.[13]

This book is not about proof. It is about possibilities.

---

[13] Nibley, *Since Cumorah*, xiii-xiv.

Part I

OPPOSING
AND
VIEWPOINTS

OPTIONAL INTRODUCTION

DIALECTIC: (Greek: διαλεκτική) in classical philosophy, is controversy, that is, the exchange of arguments and counterarguments respectively advocating propositions (theses) and counterpropositions (antitheses). The outcome of the exercise might not simply be the refutation of one of the relevant points of view, but a synthesis or combination of the opposing assertions, or at least a qualitative transformation in the direction of the dialogue.

Wikipedia

As stated quite clearly, this is an *Optional Introduction* to Part I of this book. As the name implies, these next few pages are *optional*, and the average reader won't miss much by skipping directly to where the action is: Chapter 1. The reason why it is optional is that it will be dealing with the topic of dialectics as described in the above definition. For those of you who are avid students of Murray Rothbard and dialectic libertarianism, these next few pages may interest you particularly.

Let's start with the standard deterministic permutations of modern dialectic theory and how it figures in with Marx's view of broader determinations as transposed with Hayek's view of liberty. I think anyone who has studied the techniques of debate in ancient Athens will agree with me that the Aristotelian model of the physical universe did have...

Psst! Are they gone?

Who?

Most of the readers, of course. Do you think most of them have moved on to Chapter 1?

Yea, I think so. Anyone left deserves to know, that's for sure.

Okay, let's tell them what's going on then.

Go ahead.

No. You do it.

Okay, I'll do it.

If you're still reading, I salute you. My deepest apologies for putting you through that last part. I had to do something to encourage most readers to skip ahead. I just hope I didn't lose anyone's attention permanently. But, that's a gamble you take when you're doing something like this.

Why am I trying to lose readers? Well, there's a secret about Part I of this book that I am about to reveal and it's what makes this book unique. I am aware this may cause me some criticism.

The secret is my method of exploring the topics. I call it *the schizophrenic method*. I haven't seen it used in any book that I have ever read. Here it is:

You see, this book is similar to *How Wide the Divide* because it is a debate (or conversation) between two different and mostly opposing sides of each issue. But, unlike *How Wide the Divide*, this book has only one main author: the one listed on the cover.

During the first three chapters of this book, I will provide arguments using two fictional alter egos named Dan and Noah. Dan projects the hypothetical perspective of a liberal-to-moderate Democrat. Noah represents what I view as a reasonable mainline registered Republican.[14], Dan and Noah will discuss/debate the issues of the next three chapters.

You might wonder why I didn't just use two actual people, a real Democrat and a real Republican? Why create fictional authors to debate the topics? For three reasons:

First, there is a pragmatic reason: control. Working with another real contributor would make it more difficult to keep the discussions contained and focused. Second, it is not easy to find two people with sufficient time, education, and the willingness to write this book in a coordinated manner. Third, utilizing these two alter egos (characters) saves me from constantly having to refer to them or their arguments as "a possible liberal opinion" or "the possible conservative position." That kind of observational rhetoric can wait for some graduate student's term paper. In short, Dan and Noah are a means of efficiently expressing these perspectives in a personable and readable way, with more life.

And now, to answer the question of why I have chosen to only reveal such a major aspect of this book here in this *Optional Introduction*:

You see, with a title as deliberately provocative as mine, it would be tempting for folks to assume that these staged discussions by one author are nothing more than a bunch of weak straw-man arguments, unfaithful to one position or the other or both. I suppose I have this little fantasy of readers skipping the optional introduction and going straight for the debates, all the while assuming that they were actually reading from multiple authors. Most likely, such folks will eventually find out the truth. Some will feel betrayed and others will just get a kick out of it.

That aside, there are also readers who either refuse to "play pretend" or have simply lost their ability to do so, no matter how plausible and realistic I present each perspective. For those who are simply incapable of playing pretend, I am doing them a

---

[14] IMPORTANT NOTE: Although I am a registered Republican and certainly consider myself a conservative, my own opinions are not necessarily always identical to Noah's.

favor. They can read the book thinking that Dan and Noah are real people and their arguments can be taken seriously.

I have taken great care not to build up straw men on either side. I am a conservative in most ways, but when portraying Dan's liberal arguments, I did my best not to sound like a conservative just trying to sound like a liberal. I had to make Dan and Noah real, in my mind, which (among so many other things) means creating a civil dialogue. Unreasonable fanaticism would be easier to write and would make for good drama. However, the goal of this book is not drama but productive dialogue. Even so, we do not plan to pull any punches, when possible... or punch lines, if possible.

How Can I Possibly Be Evil or Stupid?

Never challenge motive. Never challenge motive. Even though you may feel there is a motive there, never challenge motive.[15]
Milton Friedman

By using this schizophrenic method,[16] I removed two major roadblocks in understanding those with differences of opinion. Two common assumptions that we make about those with opposing views are that they are either stupid or evil. Let us look at those one at a time:

They are stupid (or ignorant): "If they knew what I know ...," we say. Or, "if only they had experienced what I have experienced or had read all that I have on the subject, they would agree with me."

Of course, if a person does have the same pool of knowledge or has had similar experiences, but still does not reach your conclusion, then they must be a moron, incapable of simple logic.

They are evil: "If they are intelligent and well informed," we say, "but they still claim to see things differently, they must have ill intentions or greedy motives."

---

15 Friedman, *Interview with Milton and Rose Friedman, by Bob Chitester.*

16 Technically, "schizophrenia" and "multiple personality disorder" (MDO) are not synonymous; not at all! But since most people don't know or care, I won't worry about it.

Hence, I have done my best to play both sides of each issue with virtuous intent, backed by as much knowledge as I have been able to assemble. I have done my best not to build up straw men.

The fact is, even if we are right about another person's stupidity or malicious intent, openly challenging their motives is simply unacceptable if you wish to engage in productive dialogue.

ABORTION

For those who are familiar enough with the 1973 Supreme Court case (and other subsequent cases), feel free to skip this brief overview of Roe v. Wade. But, believe it or not, we will scarcely bring up Roe v. Wade during this discussion on abortion.

What would it mean if Roe v. Wade was overturned today? Would that make all abortions in the United States illegal? The answer is no. The laws on abortion would simply revert to whatever the laws are in each respective state.

In general terms, the Supreme Court declared in Roe v. Wade that every woman had a *right* to choose for herself whether or not to have an abortion, but only during the first trimester.

Most people are unaware that, like the previous state laws on abortion, Roe v. Wade was also "trimester based." That is, the federal government removed the states' right to limit abortions for the first trimester and declared that a woman's right to choose an abortion was as much of a right (again, only during the first trimester) as the right to free speech. Roe v. Wade put specific limitations on the states' right to prohibit abortions for the second trimester. However, Roe v. Wade said nothing about abortion during the third trimester, which is why each state, as well as the U.S. Congress, has been free to enact laws regarding late-term abortions.

It may be useful to draw a comparison between abortion and slavery; specifically, to compare a slave to a fetus and a slave owner to a pregnant woman. Remember that this is a legal comparison, a metaphor to be used as a way of looking at Roe v. Wade as a states' rights issue.

The Civil War ultimately and eventually decided that owning slaves was *not* a right. But it went further than that. The federal government declared (via the 14th amendment) that every person had a legal right not to be owned by another. The federal government did not leave slavery up to the states, as it did before the Civil War

Keep in mind that overturning Roe v. Wade would not even take things that far. It would not "free the fetuses" as the slaves had been freed and given equal legal footing. It would not declare that every fetus had a legal right not to be aborted. It would simply leave it up to each state, as it did before Roe v. Wade.

Okay, now we've gotten Roe v. Wade out of the way and, essentially, out of the discussion from here on. This discussion involves abortion in general, regardless of trimester or level of government, whether federal, state or county.

RIGHT

The Biggest Issue
(Noah)

Why should people or nations regard human life as noble or dignified if abortion flourishes? Why agonize about indiscriminate death in Bosnia when babies are being killed far more efficiently and out of the sight of television cameras?[17]

Cal Thomas

Naturally, I oppose most of the positions of liberals, in and out of the Church, when it comes to the topics discussed in this book. However, for many members, abortion is *the* defining issue. All other differences of opinion on the economy or schooling or the environment are just that: differences of opinion. But our Church leaders have been clear about the immorality of abortion, except in cases of rape, incest or the endangered life of the mother.

President James E. Faust wrote a fantastic First Presidency Message, which can be found in the September 1995 issue of the *Ensign*. I recommend reading the entire message, which President Faust also gave at a BYU devotional, on November 15, 1995. He takes on many "liberal" causes, the first being abortion.[18]

President Faust declared abortion to be an "evil practice that has become socially accepted in the United State and, indeed, in much of the world." He then quoted Mother Teresa, who tied abortion to growing violence and murder in the streets:

> If we accept that a mother can kill even her own child, how can we tell other people not to kill each other?... Any country that accepts abortion is not teaching its people to love, but to use any violence to get what they want...

---

[17] Thomas, "Mother Teresa has Anti-Abortion Answer," A11.
[18] Faust, "BYU Speech: Trying to Serve the Lord Without Offending the Devil."

> [Concerns for orphan children] are very good. But often these same people are not concerned with the millions who are being killed by the deliberate decision of their own mothers. And this is what is the greatest destroyer of peace today—abortion...[19]

I can do no better on this subject than what has already been stated by those with more experience, more knowledge and more authority than I have. For this reason, I refer the reader to a well-known talk by Elder Dallin H. Oaks of the Quorum of the Twelve Apostles. This devotional, called "Weightier Matters," was given at BYU on February 9, 1999. I highly recommend that anyone interested in the subject of abortion (LDS or not) read this talk. Most of the points I will be making are based on this very devotional.[20]

The Welfare of the Child

Someone might ask the following: "What if the child cannot be taken care of? What if the means do not exist to provide a healthy stable atmosphere for the child once it is born?"

These questions do indeed bring up some real concerns and they need to be taken seriously. When a child of any age is tragically orphaned or abandoned, we certainly do need to sit down and discuss the options.

One of these options is adoption and there are plenty of willing parents out there, I assure you.

There is, of course, another option that is far cheaper, quicker and even painless if done correctly. We could just kill the child. I mean, why not? Better a quick and painless death than a life of misery, right?

Okay, okay. I was being a little facetious... and maybe a little bitter and snide. I was just trying to make a point. My point is that these "child's welfare" questions are often used to defend abortion. Well, when you apply these questions to a child that is out of the womb, killing is not considered an option. Why then, is it considered an option while the child lives within the womb?

---

19 Thomas, "Mother Teresa has Anti-Abortion Answer," A11.
20 Oaks, "Weightier Matters."

I really hope Dan comes up with a better argument than that one.

It is a valid concern that many women who find themselves accidental mothers do not have the means to take care of their child, or even the means of getting prenatal care or paying for the delivery. Adoption is a win-win-win solution because there are plenty of would-be parents who would be more than happy to pay for all of those costs.

So, rather than waste time and energy on abortion rights, let's work to make adoption much easier. I speak from direct experience, since my wife and I had to jump through a great deal of legal and bureaucratic hoops in an effort to adopt. Luckily, for us, LDS Family Services helped out, but for most adoptees, it is a much more difficult process.

The Choice of the Woman

The world so often argues for freedom while denying responsibility. The pro-choice stance of abortion is a classic case. Certainly, everyone has the right to choose what to do with his or her own body. However, the consequences of such choices are another matter.

When it comes to pregnancy, a woman must bear the responsibility for the one simple choice she made that led to that pregnancy, namely sexual intercourse. It is an awfully simple connection here. If a woman chose to have sex in such a way that resulted in pregnancy, she has a responsibility for the life that was created. She made her choice.

There may be accidental pregnancies but there is no such thing as accidental sex. It is either consensual or forced. When the act of sexual intercourse is consensual, abortion is not a matter of choice but an avoidance of responsibility for a choice already made. Why should the consequences of her actions be nullified in the name of choice?

The Choice of the Man

A pregnancy that is the result of rape or incest is an obvious infringement on the woman's right to choose. Such a pregnancy is not a result of her choice but of someone else's evil actions. Such violent actions should incur the harshest penalties that society can dish out. Of course, the liberals usually get in the way of that, as well. Why doesn't this unwavering compassion for the guiltiest among us translate into protecting the lives of the most innocent among us: a child in the womb? (The treatment of criminals will have to wait for another discussion, I guess.)

When a woman finds herself and her rights violated by rape, without question, she should be given the right to choose how then to deal with the pregnancy. To be forced to carry the pregnancy to term would compound the injustice already heaped upon her. There is no question that the law should give her the exclusive right of choice, to either abort or give birth.

Oddly enough it is much easier to protect a woman's right to an abortion than it is to protect her right to continue the pregnancy. I have often wondered how many abortions are performed against the desires of the mother. I am certain that Roe v. Wade, touted as a "woman's right to choose," has certainly been used as a convenient tool for the husband, the boyfriend, or the woman's father to evade the hassle, responsibility or embarrassment of a pregnancy. It is a fact that a woman is far *less* likely to consider abortion than a man is.

No doubt, many women are coerced into abortion by the selfish actions of an unrighteous dominant male in her life. There are women who have a great deal to fear (for herself or the child within her) unless they exercise their "woman's right" to abort. This is often done through those subtle threats and innuendos, the kind that would never hold up in court but would, nevertheless, haunt these women with fears of abandonment, divorce, violence or worse.

A woman's right to choose abortion–as interpreted by a wicked man–is *his* right to take her, break her and force that "choice" upon her.

The Choice of the Government

In Elder Oak's talk, "Weightier Matters," he referred to and rebutted one of the age-old arguments of the pro-choice movement: "While I am certainly anti-abortion in my personal life, in the public arena, I am for freedom of choice. It just does not feel right to force my morality on other people through legislation."

As far as the "public arena" and this fear of "morality by legislation," would you please identify a criminal law that is *not* based on morality? In his talk, Elder Oaks simply and directly answers those who believe that we, as citizens, have no right to "legislate morality":

> Those who take this position should realize that the law of crimes legislates nothing but morality. Should we repeal all laws with a moral basis so our government will not punish any choices some persons consider immoral? Such an action would wipe out virtually all of the laws against crimes.[21]

It is clear enough that the Church counsels that the only pretexts for abortion are the following:

- Pregnancy as the result of rape or incest
- Pregnancy that jeopardizes the health or life of the mother
- Pregnancy in which the fetus is so severely defective that it would not survive beyond birth

Keep in mind two things: First, these situations are extraordinarily rare. Second, while these situations may put abortion on the table as an option, they do not automatically justify terminating the pregnancy. Because the termination of a pregnancy is the termination of a life, the case is anything but closed. We are counseled to consider abortion only after the parents have consulted with their bishops and have received divine confirmation from the Lord through prayer.

THE DEMOCRATIC PARTY PLATFORM

It is not merely coincidental that most Democrats are pro-choice. The official Democratic Party platform states:

> [W]e stand proudly for a woman's right to choose, consistent with Roe v. Wade, and regardless of her ability to pay. We stand firmly against Republican efforts to undermine that

---

21 Ibid.

right. At the same time, we strongly support family planning and adoption incentives. Abortion should be safe, legal, and rare.[22]

Besides the obvious declaration of abortion as a "right," an additional source of frustration here is the clause "regardless of her ability to pay." This means, of course, that not only does someone have a right to an abortion, but also a right to my money (as a taxpayer) to pay for it? It's frustrating enough that the Democratic Party is so gung-ho for socialized medicine, but it's morally reprehensible that abortion is highest on their list of government-paid medical procedures! I wish there was a specific form I could fill out that demands that my money will go toward polio vaccines, bed netting for malaria, cleft palette surgery and so forth before it goes toward subsidizing someone's abortion.

Then the Democratic Platform tries to end nobly by stating that abortion should be "rare." How exactly do they expect it to be rare, when they have offered to pay for it (or have the taxpayer foot the bill)? Let's suppose the government declared that every American had "the right to choose to own a Lexus, regardless of the ability to pay." Does anyone really think that Lexus purchases would go down?

That they have the gall to expect me to pay for abortion then claim that one of their goals is for abortion to be "rare" is beyond belief! Please, Democrats, don't try to appease your consciences by stating that abortion "should be rare" after doing everything to encourage its continuation.

---

[22] Democratic Party, "The 2004 Democratic National Platform for America," 42.

A Non-Issue
(Dan)

We should avoid caricaturing the positions of others, constructing 'straw men,' if you will, and casting unwarranted aspersions on their motivations and character.[23]

Elder Robert S. Wood

First and foremost, using the term "pro-abortion" when referring to "pro-choice" folks is nothing short of slanderous. Please. I know of no one that would willingly carry such a label. Do you really expect that using the term "pro-abortion" will lead to productive dialogue? Perhaps this is exactly what Isaiah meant when he said that there would be those who "make a man an offender for a word, and lay a snare for him..." (Isaiah 29:21)

Pro-life Democrats?!

Let me first say that everything Noah has stated is nothing new to me. Furthermore, I agree with almost all of it. I am pro-life and, guess what? I am still a Democrat and a staunch one at that. Guess who else was a registered Democrat until the end of his days? President James E. Faust: the very man Noah quoted. That's right, a pro-life Democrat. We do exist...as do pro-choice Republicans.

If abortion is *the* issue for you, why are you letting the pro-choice Republicans remain in the party? Why not kick them out? The reason is simple: as was stated in the introduction to this book, few members of a political party will agree with every tenet and goal of their party's official platform.

---

[23] Wood, "Instruments of the Lord's Peace."

So you don't like that pro-choice is part of the Democratic Party platform. Well, neither do I. Do you hold fast to every single declaration made in the Republican Party platform? I hope not, for the sake of your own intellectual independence.

How do you propose to remove abortion from the Democratic Party platform, aside from eradication of the Democrats themselves? The fact is, as a Republican, you can't do anything about what is on the Democratic Party platform, can you? On the other hand, as a Democrat, I actually have influence in possibly changing such distasteful policies within my own party. So, what would be the point in becoming a Republican? If I changed parties based on the singular issue of abortion, I would lose all power to influence the current goals of the Democratic Party, which I agree with on most other issues. Therefore, I am going to remain a pro-life Democrat.

Here's a worthy question: As of 2008, who is the highest-ranking government official that is a member of The Church of Jesus Christ of Latter-day Saints?

Answer: Senate Majority Leader, Democrat from Nevada, Harry Reid.

Senator Reid is most definitely a controversial character, at least, among conservative members of the Church. The reason for this has to do with the fact that he simply holds many of the basic tenants of any self-respecting Democrat. It is then assumed that he must be pro-choice on the issue of abortion. But is he?

No. He is pro-life. He always has been. And his voting record shows it.[24] Here is a sample of his more recent voting record on reproduction related bills:

- NO on amendment indicating Congress' support of Roe v. Wade (Oct 1999)
- YES on banning partial birth abortions, including on military bases. (Oct 1999, June 2000 & March 2003)
- YES on criminal penalty for harming unborn fetus during other crime. (March 2004)

---

[24] ontheissues.org, "Harry Reid on Abortion."

- YES on notifying parents of minors who get out-of-state abortions. (July 2006)
- YES on prohibiting minors crossing state lines for abortion. (March 2008)

Reid does not get a perfect score from many pro-life groups for the simple reason that he is so anti-abortion that he is interested in preventing abortions, even to the extent that he will allow Federal Funding to pay for contraception or to groups that provide contraception.

This is why it's risky to base your opinion of someone's voting record on another group, whether the NRLC or the NRA. Rather, to make an accurate assessment, I recommend looking at each bill one at a time.

In any case, how many of you conservatives out there have assumed that Harry Reid was pro-choice on abortion? My guess is, most of you. I know Noah did. I am making a generalization of conservatives, of course, but it is based on my own experience. Most conservatives that I have talked to really did think they knew that his position was "pro-choice." Many conservatives are both delighted and surprised to find out that his position has always been "pro-life."

Far too many conservatives, however, seem determined to despise Senator Reid. For more about him, see the last chapter.

Republican Impotence in Overturning Roe v. Wade

A political science scholar and a friend of mine, Professor Brian Dille, Ph.D., had this to say about Republicans and abortion:

> Abortion policy in America is a Republican Party creation. Most of the laws governing abortion were drafted by Republican legislatures (state and federal). Granted, Democrats usually fought for a more liberal version of the laws that were passed, but the laws that exist are those that survived the debate.
>
> The more compelling argument is that the Supreme Court is a Republican court and has been for decades. The Roe v. Wade decision was written by a Nixon appointee in a court operating under a Nixon appointed Chief Justice. Six of the nine current justices are Republican appointees, and all nine have been appointed since Roe v. Wade. Two thirds of the federal judiciary is composed of Republican appointees, and

most of those are Reagan or George W. Bush appointees. Republicans have controlled the Presidency for 23 of the 37 years since Roe. They controlled all three branches of government for 6 years from 2000 to 2006. It has been demonstrated historically to be simply untrue that electing Republicans will change abortion policy.[25]

It is quite unfortunate that Republicans bring out the abortion issue during election time for the sake of getting the votes but have not performed as promised. Republican voters should be wary.

Pro-Choice Church Members?

Many readers may have thought that in this chapter I would try to argue in support of a pro-choice position. Instead, I hope I have shown what should be plainly obvious, that Democrat does not equal pro-choice. If I accomplish nothing else in this book, I hope to eradicate this one myth. On the road to eradicating other myths and stereotyping, this would be a nice place to start. However, I cannot help but list a few reasons why some people (even Church members) might find themselves sympathetic towards a pro-choice position. I do this with a bit of a shudder.

In fact, before I actually play the devil's advocate for a moment, I wish to first make my position quite clear regarding late-term abortions: I view them as a disgusting and completely unnecessary practice. By "late term", I do not necessarily mean the age of the fetus in months or weeks or heartbeats. When I use the phrase "late term" I am talking about viability. When a fetus can survive outside the womb (even if needing respiratory assistance), I do not understand how any woman can claim the right to kill it. It is difficult for me to fathom how any doctor can go through with it as well.

Having said that, there are some pro-choice arguments that I would like to cover. You might ask why I would even present such arguments. Why put up any kind of defense that could be used in defense of the "choice" to abort a life? Once again, the answer is simple: to build bridges of understanding. In fact, I

---

[25] Dille to Andersen, "personal email regarding abortion (2010)."

must tell you that I actually feel moved by the Spirit to, at least inform the reader as to how anyone could possibly be pro-choice. There are strong and levelheaded reasons why even some members of the Church have sympathized with or even held a pro-choice position (i.e. Mitt Romney) rather than attacking it on every level (i.e. Harry Reid). Therefore, I do this in the spirit of defending the character of a pro-choice person rather than to defend the pro-choice political position.

I want the practice of abortion as a form of birth control, wiped out! However, adults understand that you can fight for a worthy cause without vilifying those who oppose you. So, after some real hesitation, here are a few points in sympathy of a pro-choice position on abortion:

The Gray of Conception

The biology of abortion or of life or conception is just a pain to study. The questions are emotionally exhausting to ask (or answer). Try the following exchange:

"When does life begin?"

"At conception!"

"You mean the moment a zygote (a united sperm and egg) comes into existence?"

"Yes. At that point, it is a unique independent life."

"So anything that prevents that life from continuing down the road to an embryo is murderous?"

"Yes, things like abortion or the morning-after pill."

"Oh, so things like using an IUD (inter-uteral device)."

"I didn't say that."

"Why not? IUDs don't always prevent an egg and sperm from uniting into a zygote or preventing that zygote form multiplying into an embryo. In fact, 10% of the time, IUDs do not prevent conception, but instead, they prevent the conceived embryo from rooting itself into the wall of the uterus. So, once again, when does sacred life begin?"

Plenty of Church members seem comfortable using an IUD but the morning after pill is considered as abortion. But, from the point of view of a fertilized egg, I see little difference between the two. Do you?

At the very least, I hope this helps the reader to sympathize with Catholics for not using contraception, not to mention some LDS Church leaders who preached against birth control a few years back.

Defining Life Through Neural Activity

Ever heard of brain death? You can legally kill a person who is brain dead, you know. A person whose brain activity has completely flat-lined is considered dead, even if the rest of their organs are functioning just fine. In fact, a body with healthy organs and a dead brain is great news for all those folks who need new healthy organs.

Well, if a lack of neural activity is the key to defining death (and dismemberment), perhaps you can see why there are some people who do not consider an embryo to be alive at least until its brain has developed to a point of "minimal consciousness."

Incidentally, this is as close as we're going to get to discussing embryonic stem cell research. The official Church position on embryonic stem cell research is clear enough and here it is:

> The First Presidency of The Church of Jesus Christ of Latter-day Saints has not taken a position regarding the use of embryonic stem cells for research purposes. The absence of a position should not be interpreted as support for or opposition to any other statement made by Church members, whether they are for or against embryonic stem cell research.[26]

The Grim Reality of FaBBAaBs

Once again, the recent conservative Republican presidential candidate, Mitt Romney, shows us the way. In his debate with Ted Kennedy for governor of Massachusetts, Romney was asked about his position on abortion. He skillfully answered by first talking about how the state of Massachusetts was a pro-choice state and he would uphold that position. He then mentioned a tragedy in his own family: one of his relatives had apparently died from a *"fatally botched back-alley abortion"*, occasionally referred to as FABBAAB[27].

---

26 LDS Church, "Embryonic Stem-cell Research."
27 FABBAAB is just an acronym that I made up just for this book.

Personally, I think Romney should have stuck with the state's rights answer, which was concise, logical and a better reflection of how he handled abortion while governor. I think his story about the tragic death of a relative was an appeal to emotion. After all, politicians have to show that they "feel your pain".

In any case, how many women has Roe v. Wade spared from a FABBAAB? Who knows? But let's overshoot the estimate using a high mortality rate of 1%, which means that the 1.2 million abortions that occurred in 2005 would have saved 12,000 women. Again, I think this is an unrealistically high number.

Nevertheless, let's ask the question: Are 100 fetuses worth the life of one woman? Hard-line conservatives would answer, "Absolutely not!" (And, perhaps, so would I.) "A life is a life. No one worth more than the other." But, ponder this one: What if the woman who died already had six children? Now, we've got six most likely impoverished children growing up without a mother. As cold and calculating as it might sound, that mother of six is starting to tip the scales a bit.

Now I'm starting to sound like a conservative economist, or worse yet, a eugenicist. So let's humanize this picture, more along the lines of what Romney was getting at, and imagine that the woman saved was someone you were close to? Your mother? Your sister? Your daughter? Your wife? Hmmm, oddly enough, this "thought experiment" does not draw much sympathy even from me. The trouble is, while I do have a wife, a daughter, several sisters and a mother, they are all currently alive and well. How can I truly put myself in Mitt Romney's position when I have yet to suffer the death of any of these women in my life by any means? I'm not even interested in trying to imagine their death.

Half of the population of China could die tomorrow, but I would surely lose more sleep tonight over the sudden death of a close loved one who was (just yesterday) a living breathing person, an imperfect person, with a unique laugh, unique experiences and sentient thoughts. These are qualities possessed by all those hypothetically dead Chinese folks but such qualities are not yet possessed by an embryo.

What it comes down to is the fact that I cannot help but feel differently about the loss of a close friend or family member than I might about any number of unseen and undeveloped embryos.

Forgiveness for Abortion within the Church

Abortion is certainly deplorable, but as far as the official Church position goes, abortion is not and has never been treated as equivalent to murder.

Prospective converts who have had abortions are not treated in any was as if they have committed murder or even a crime.

As far as I am aware, for any member who has an abortion, disciplinary counsels are *not* mandatory, but each situation is subject to the judgment of the bishop. If the Church considered abortion to be murder, a person who has an abortion would have a much tougher time escaping Church discipline.

Also, if you are determined that abortion is, hands down, always murder, then what difference does it make whether the conception is the result of rape?

In the Meantime...

What does the future hold for abortion law in the United States? There are two possibilities: The federal government will either remain pro-choice or it will not. In my mind, the chances of overturning Roe v. Wade in the near future are slim at best. And even if it does happen, most states would probably opt for pro-choice anyway.

Once again, I do not consider pro-life to be a lost cause and I will continue to fight the good fight, particularly for the fundamental right to life of the viable (even borderline viable) fetus, which is no different from a premature infant.

However, it is a misconception (on both sides) that overturning Roe v. Wade will result in the nationwide illegalization of abortions. The battle would merely shift ground to the states. This may satisfy the purely states' rights conservatives while the true anti-abortion conservatives would take up their position in their respective states with a variety of strategies, protests and litmus tests for politicians. Essentially, the battle to outlaw abortion would go on as it did before, just as it has for almost four decades.

What I am getting at is that the pro-life movement should look beyond Roe v. Wade. Moreover, conservatives should realize that battling abortion should not be solely confined to outlawing it. Republican politicians, for example, are so aggressive (especially around election time) about outlawing abortion that they seem to have little energy left for preventing and reducing abortions.

There are around 3,300 abortions (at minimum) occurring each day in this country. That's a full half of the number of deaths that occur from any and all causes.

Here is my point: these abortions continue every single day, despite 35+ years of rallies, money, prayers, propaganda, abortion clinic bombings, peaceful protests and all manner of politically motivated and sincere efforts to outlaw abortion! For a pro-life but otherwise "liberal", like myself, what does the Republican party offer besides rhetoric? This rhetoric is effective at demonizing liberals and Democrats but it is demonstrably impotent at outlawing abortion.

On the contrary, preventing and reducing abortions seems to be the exclusive work of Democrats! For example, in 2005 the life-long pro-life Senator Harry Reid not only launched an anti-abortion initiative, known as the "Prevention First Bill", but he also managed to secure Hilary Clinton as a co-sponsor. Reid explains:

> Whether you are pro-life or pro-choice, our amendment advances goals we should all share: reducing the number of unintended pregnancies, reducing the number of abortions and improving access to women's health care.[28]

So, how did the bill do? The vote was 47-53, against. All of the nay votes came from the Republicans.

Although Senator Reid's goal was, in part, to reduce abortions, he did have a couple of serious liabilities with regards to gaining any Republican support. I don't know which was worse

---

[28] Myers, "Prevent Pregnancy, Prevent Abortion: Harry Reid proposes legislation."

in the eyes of the Republicans: Was it the fact that his bill seeks to improve access to women's health care? Or would supporting the bill mean reaching across the aisle to the likes of Hillary Clinton? Is that what Republicans are so afraid of?

In the meantime... 3,300 per day.

The Lesser of Two Evils

Frankly, I don't like the idea of handing out condoms at high school. But, unfortunately, in our current cultural climate, too many people actually think that abstinence is impossible! That is a lie, of course. I really miss the days when teenagers actually understood that they could control themselves and, consequently, managed to avoid pregnancy by avoiding intercourse. That time-tested method of abstinence really worked back in the 1950s. I hope, someday, our culture will latch onto it again.

For now, if you think abortion is murder, isn't it high time to start supporting measures to reduce abortions, even if such measures include promoting birth control methods by way of education and, yes, by providing contraception at the taxpayers' expense?

Often conservatives will say that they are not interested in having their tax dollars go toward "subsidizing sexual promiscuity." But an abortion is not necessarily the result of promiscuous sex. Just look at Third World countries where families have trouble feeding their existing children. They often choose abortion (or even infanticide) as an alternative to possible starvation. These are horrors, to be certain, but they are not necessarily the result of promiscuity. Throughout history, severely impoverished but committed married couples have elected primitive abortion methods as a form of birth control. Today, in many places, abortion persists merely because the parents are either unaware of or unable to obtain other more civilized methods of contraception.

I completely understand the objection to using tax dollars to fund abortions. I am against that myself. Still, when it comes to funding U.S. foreign aid packages, Republicans refuse to include *any* form of birth control, as a matter of principle. This can have the unintended consequence of higher abortion rates!

Abortion, after all, is an ancient practice. Even the original "Hippocratic oath" includes a vow not to perform abortions. Modern medicine and technology not only brought about safer abortions (at least, for the mother) but also reliable means of preventing pregnancy in the first place. Such twentieth century innovations are what the Third World lacks.

A lack of reliable birth control is certainly a major cause of poverty and even infanticide. This is the most optimistic way to look at one of President Obama's first actions in office regarding the reversal of "the Global Gag Rule" or "Mexico City Policy" regarding the use of foreign aid for organizations that promote "family planning".[29] Yes, this means taxpayer dollars going toward birth control, which unfortunately includes money for abortion as a means of birth control. While that is tragic, the ultimate goal of the Obama administration was never to increase abortions! On the contrary, the hope here is to reduce abortions by preventing pregnancies. You cannot have an abortion if you are not pregnant in the first place. By allowing our foreign aid to go through organizations that provide birth control, we help prevent unwanted pregnancies, thereby reducing the number of abortions as well as the number of children born to impoverished conditions.

Even if we were talking about providing contraception to the promiscuous and virtuous alike, if the result is a net reduction of abortions, then why is there even a discussion? You have promiscuous safe sex on one hand and murder by abortion on the other. Let's pick the lesser of two evils! It may ease your conscience to proclaim yourself "pro-life" from the rooftops and picket abortion clinics (and, by all means, continue to do so!), but until that day when Roe v. Wade is overturned or abstinence becomes the newest fad (let us pray), we should be working together to reduce the number of abortions whenever and however possible.

---

[29] "Obama Reverses 'Global Gag Rule' (Medical News Today)."

Jimmy Carter on Reducing Abortion

One of the most honest presidents we've ever had was Jimmy Carter. He is a man who has given his life to God and to serving his fellow man. He continues to do so to this day.

In his book, *Our Endangered Values,* he talks about abortion. Although he is decidedly pro-choice, he makes some important points concerning abortion and the views of supposedly "compassionate conservatives."

> Many fervent pro-life activists do not extend their concern to the baby who is born, and are the least likely to support benevolent programs that they consider "socialistic." They ignore the fact that once a doubtful mother decides *not* to have an abortion, she and her family usually have a number of needs: continued education for the mother...an adequate minimum wage; and tax credits to help the employed mother and her child have a decent life.[30]

What he is highlighting here is obvious: the hypocrisy of too many conservatives who are so adamant about defending the life of a fetus but seem to drop their concerns about this helpless individual the minute they are born.

I realize that I am now getting into economics, which will be debated in another chapter. However, even if you are a conservative and not a fan of government-sponsored programs, I urge you to look inside yourself and think about whether or not you have equal concern for the born as well as the unborn.

Want to reduce abortions?

> It has long been known that there are fewer abortions in nations where prospective mothers have access to contraceptives, the assurance that they and their babies will have good health care, and at least enough income to meet their basic needs.[31]

For every neuron you fire in anger at the idea of abortion, how many do you fire off in an effort to help those that need your help; that you have been commanded to help? Try to ask yourself where your priorities are? What do you work for each day?

---

30 Carter, *Our Endangered Values,* 73.
31 Ibid., 74.

To purchase a nice 'n shiny SUV? Or serving your fellow man: "the least of these"?

JOINT

A Bright Side to Abortion?

For all the conflicting views on this issue, it speaks well of our country that we recognize abortion as a problem. The law may call it a right, but no one ever called it a good, and, in the quiet of conscience, people of both political parties know that more than a million abortions a year cannot be squared with the good heart of America.[32]

Mitt Romney

Agreements

The first thing Dan and Noah can agree on is that using the term "pro-abortion" is not only unfair but completely unproductive. It is nothing more than name-calling and does nothing to promote civil discussion of the issue. (The same goes for the term "pro-war".)

Regarding abortion, Democrats and Republicans can agree on much. Many people have been delighted to learn that plenty of Democrats are, in fact, pro-life. In that regard, the conservatives probably have the most to learn from this first exchange. Noah admits and rejoices in the fact that one can certainly be a pro-life Democrat. And when it comes down to actually casting a vote on abortion, party lines do not dictate the matter. Both President Faust (a member of the Democratic Party and Church leader) and Harry Reid (a member of the Church and a Democratic Party leader) are testaments to the fact that a person's stand on abortion is his choice and not at the mercy of his political party.

Abortion is too important an issue for the kind of simplistic thinking that leads to the assumption that all Democrats are pro-choice and all Republicans are pro-life. In fact, during the 2008

---

[32] Hewitt, *A Mormon in the White House?*, 109.

Presidential elections, initially one of the leading Republican presidential candidates, Rudy Giuliani, was pro-choice. At the same time, Senator Reid, one of the highest-ranking Democrats in Congress, was pro-life.

Agreeing to Disagree

On the issue of abortion, Dan and Noah are both pro-life. Yet they have managed to find a few things to disagree about. Dan pointed out the impotence of the Republican Party on overturning Roe v. Wade. This might be because of the many Republicans who are themselves pro-choice or sympathetic to the pro-choice cause (but slipped under the conservative radar) or because the party simply doesn't know how to organize itself.

Indeed, while Noah agrees that the Republican majority (always a slim one) has failed to make this a pro-life country or, rather, give abortion rights back to the states, he does not believe this is entirely due to Republican weakness or disorganization.

It could be said that the Republicans have never had absolute control of Congress because even when they had a majority, it was always a slim one. Much of the responsibility can be laid on the shoulders of the pro-choice legislators (Democrats and Republicans) for doing everything within their power to interfere with a pro-life agenda, including the blocking of openly pro-life judges.

This difference in views may find resolution in some empirical study that may already exist or has yet to be done. Such a study should look at what each publicly elected official (legislative, judicial and executive) has done since 1973 with regards to abortion. Did they vote pro-life? Did they abstain from making a decision? Did they vote pro-choice? Answers to these questions–which have nothing to do with party affiliation–should tell us who the responsible people are.

Another issue that Noah and Dan must, for now, agree to disagree about is Obama's reversal of the "Global Gag Rule" on foreign aid.[33] Noah likes to call Dan's explanation the "fund

---

[33] "Obama Reverses 'Global Gag Rule' (Medical News Today)."

abortions to reduce abortions theory" and he is not at all convinced.

While Dan has sufficiently explained why even a pro-life individual may wish to support this order, the question that must be asked is not what anyone's intentions were but whether the act will, in fact, cause a reduction in abortions. Until the time when empirical evidence can demonstrate a net reduction (or a net increase) of abortions as a result of this executive order, Dan and Noah must agree to disagree. In the meantime, their disagreement is a matter of what each *thinks* will happen, not on what either of them knows at this point.

Political Suggestions

If abortion really is THE defining issue for you, do your best to elect only pro-life candidates, regardless of party affiliation. In general, for any issue, make certain to base your vote on a candidate's position, not on his party. Better yet, base your vote on a politician's actual voting record. For example, while running for governor of Massachusetts, Mitt Romney made a shrewd political move by sympathizing with the pro-choice position during a debate with Ted Kennedy. Nevertheless, conservatives can take some comfort in the fact that, as governor, his record appears to be, at best, pro-life and at worst neutral. Using veto power, he did not allow abortion to extend its reach, but I cannot find whether he ever had a chance to restrict abortions.

The bottom line is this: politicians are in the job of getting elected and can often appear more (or less) of an ally than their actions might eventually indicate. In matters of pure policy, vote for them based on what they do, not on what they say. This is typical advice; however, voters have an amazing advantage over past generations. In this age of information, the votes of a politician are easily tracked, tallied and readily available for your scrutiny.

Personal Advice

Dan and Noah also agree, wholeheartedly, that Christlike compassion for the mother is *never* out of place. We should withhold our judgments (as in "that scumbag is going to hell") towards those who feel the need to consider an abortion. We should counsel against abortion, but true counsel is characterized by effectiveness, not just blowing off steam.

We all know how to counsel effectively but, all too often, forget when the actual situation presents itself. Effective counsel usually means doing so "with kindness, and pure knowledge... without hypocrisy and without guile..." (D&C 121:42)

There are times when counsel must be given with a certain degree of sharpness. However, such situations are rare and should only be within your stewardship and, even then, only as prescribed by the Lord, in scripture, which gives guidance for when stern counsel is needed, as articulated in the following verses from section 121 of the Doctrine and Covenants (slightly modified to apply to abortion):

> *When moved upon by the Holy Ghost; and then showing forth afterwards an increase of love toward [her] whom thou hast reproved, lest [she] esteem thee to be [her] enemy; That [she] may know that thy faithfulness is stronger than the cords of death [even of the unborn].*

In today's political and social climate, for some women, it can be a brave choice to carry her baby to term. Often, the choice not to abort may go against the advice, wishes and even threats of her friends and relatives. It often takes a brave and courageous woman to endure those months of pregnancy...and scorn. No one knows the frequency of these kinds of situations and only a small number of people would know the details. Therefore, in *all* cases, encouragement and praise are appropriate, helpful and Christlike.

As for women who use abortion as birth control and think little of it, please withhold your judgment. Keep in mind that their culture and upbringing probably have a lot to do with it. Joe served his mission in Russia and almost every female convert he encountered had undergone an abortion at some point (paid for by the government, of course). Their practice of abortion ended with their conversion to the Gospel, not angry screams from protestors or judgmental diatribes.

And as for the woman who aborts a child and should know better... well, how rarely it is that we know her actual circumstances or the state of her mind (or anyone's, for that matter). Still, if her abortion was, in fact, an act of blatant selfishness against a greater light and knowledge, does she not deserve the most pity and the most prayer?

THE GOOD NEWS

Abortion is a sad story and it is difficult to find anything good regarding the subject. However, after some diligent searching, I do believe we can end this chapter with some kind of upswing.

First, we can take some solace from the fact that abortions in America have been declining steadily for a number of years, falling in 2000 to the lowest number since 1978[34] and falling even lower in 2005[35] (even with a growing population).

Also, as of 2009, both the Senate Majority Leader and the Senate Minority Leader consistently vote pro-life. This would not be the case without a Mormon Democrat in Congress: Harry Reid. If abortion is the most important issue to you, then Harry Reid is your man.

How about a Small Miracle?

Norma McCorvey was a ninth-grade dropout and spent time in reform school. She was abused as a child, raped as a teenager and beaten by her husband (whom she married at age 16). She was involved in alcohol and drug abuse and experienced with lovers of both sexes. She had three children whom she never met. They were all adopted. In short, Norma had a rough life.

However, at some point, she managed to pull her life together. She became an active feminist and an influential abortion-rights activist. Although she never had an abortion herself, she worked in abortion clinics and was heavily involved in the

[34] Easterbrook, *The Progress Paradox*, 53.
[35] Stein, "Abortions Hit Lowest Number Since 1976," A01.

pro-choice politics. In 1994, she wrote a book about her experiences.

A year after publishing her book, a mostly Catholic pro-life group called "Operation Rescue" (O.R.) moved their offices right next door to the women's clinic where she worked. Her need for periodic smoking breaks prompted her outside several times a day, where she had no choice but to "face the enemy" (those O.R. volunteers).

These volunteers organized protests only on days when the clinic actually performed abortions. On the "non-protest days," she could take her smoking breaks in peace. As a result, she managed to strike up a few civil conversations with one of the O.R. volunteers, a priest named Phillip Benham.

This seemingly uptight Catholic priest had morphed from enemy to friend, all because he had mentioned the Beach Boys at some point. It is often the simplest things that can finally help us see the enemy as human. In this case, for Norma, it was the simple fact that Rev. Benham had not only heard of the Beach Boys but had actually attended a concert.

That is when things began to change for Norma. Other O.R. volunteers began to reach out to her, with scriptures, advice, words of wisdom and simple conversation. They would share snippets of the Gospel and she would explain her crystals and book of runes.

"It wasn't exactly Elijah and the prophets of Baal," she said, "but in both of our minds it was clearly a case of *may the true God win.*"

Possibly the most influential of these people was a 7-year-old girl, Emily, the daughter of an O.R. volunteer named Ronda. Norma even took to inviting Emily into her office as she made appointments. One time, during one such visit, Norma lost her temper during a phone call and exclaimed, "I'd just as soon see you in hell as see you in here!"

"You don't have to go to hell, Miss Norma," said Emily. "You can pray right now and Jesus will forgive you."

Later, Norma remarked:

> This childlike faith cut open my heart, making me receptive to
> the truth... I wasn't won over by compelling apologetics. I had
> a ninth grade education and a very soft heart. While the O.R.
> adults targeted my mind, Emily went straight for the heart.[36]

Norma eventually conceded to go to Church, not out of any real
desire but simply because she was exhausted from having to say
no to the persistent invitations by the 7-year-old Emily. In that
first Church meeting, she found peace and forgiveness. She
found the Savior. And, as you might expect, shortly after her
conversion, Norma began to question her own views on abortion, especially as she maintained her relationship with Emily.

> And over time, Emily began to personify the issue of abor-
> tion—especially when Ronda broke down and told me that
> Emily had almost been aborted.
>   I felt "crushed" under the truth of this realization. I had to
> face up to the awful reality. Abortion wasn't about 'products of
> conception.' It wasn't about 'missed periods.' It was about
> children being killed in their mother's wombs. All those
> years...I was wrong. Working in an abortion clinic, I was
> wrong. No more of this first trimester, second trimester, third
> trimester stuff. Abortion—at any point—was wrong. It was so
> clear. Painfully clear.[37]

Rev. Benham baptized Norma a member of the Catholic Church
in 1995. "I'm one hundred percent sold out to Jesus," said
Norma, "and one hundred percent pro-life. No exceptions. No
compromise."

In 1998, Norma co-authored a book about her conversion
story called *Won by Love*. What a contrast this new book was to
the other one she had published just four years earlier, dealing
with her life as a pro-choice activist.

By the way, the title of that first book that Norma wrote is
quite significant: *I Am Roe: My Life, Roe v. Wade, and Freedom of
Choice*.

That's right. Norma McCorvey is none other than "Jane Roe,"
the anonymous plaintiff in that historical case in 1973.

---

[36] McCorvey and Thomas, "Roe v. McCorvey."
[37] Ibid.

She now joins the ranks of such unexpected converts as the Apostle Paul and Alma the Younger. Like those beings sent to Paul and Alma, little Emily first disarmed, then testified and finally invited. No word could describe her better than "angelic."

I have no doubt that this angel was sent by God, for when she spoke, Norma understood.

When God wants a great work done in the world or a great wrong righted, he goes about it in a very unusual way. He doesn't stir up his earthquakes or send forth his thunderbolts. Instead... God puts the idea into a mother's heart, and she puts it into the baby's mind. And then God waits. The greatest forces in the world are not the earthquakes and the thunderbolts. The greatest forces in the world are babies.[38]

E.T Sullivan

---

[38] Wallis, *Treasure Chest*, 53 (quoted in Pres. Hinckley's final First Presidency Message).

CHAPTER 2

ECONOMICS

When a military medical team arrives on a battlefield where soldiers have a variety of wounds, they are confronted with the classic economic problem... Almost never are there enough doctors, nurses, or paramedics to go around, nor enough medications.

If the medical team does not allocate its time and medications efficiently, some wounded soldiers will die needlessly, while time is being spent attending to others not as urgently in need of care or still others whose wounds are so devastating that they will probably die in spite of anything that can be done for them. It is an economic problem, though not a dime changes hands.[39]

Thomas Sowell

Economics is not about money- who has it or how to make money. It is not even about wealth, per se. In its simplest terms, economics is the study of the many ways that limited resources are (or can be) put to use. The principles of economics are the same under socialism or capitalism and might concern medicine, food, land or such non-physical resources like knowledge, time or even risk tolerance.

In a more academic definition, economist Lionel Robbins defined economics as "the study of the use of scarce resources, which have alternative uses." There would be no need for the science of economics in the Garden of Eden, which was a place without scarcity. Everything was in abundance. Likewise, during the Exodus, it would have been meaningless to study the

---

[39] Sowell, *Basic Economics (Hardcover)*, 3-4.

economics of manna because God ensured that it was exactly abundant enough for its one and only use: consumption as food.

In today's world, however, there is never an infinite quantity (supply) of any given resource, and there is always a variety of uses (demands) for a given resource. In other words, there are many types of demand for any given supply.

At the mere mention of "supply and demand", most people start to doze off or even grow nervous that terms like "gross national product" will start to invade the text. Relax! This chapter was written in a way that avoids (as much as possible) all those boring academic terms that you "memorized" in high school.

In any case, volumes can and have been written regarding the disagreements between liberals and conservatives when it comes to economic issues. This chapter has been limited to discussing the role of government intervention in the marketplace, whether local, national or international.

Freedom is a Free Market
(Noah)

Labor gets a minimum wage, so agriculture seeks a price support. Consumers demand price controls, and industry gets protective tariffs. In the end, no one is much further ahead, and everyone suffers the burdens of a gigantic bureaucracy and a loss of personal freedom.[40]

Ezra Taft Benson

I think it's helpful to liken an economy to your own living, breathing human body. A free market, price driven economy is a body in its most natural state. In this state, the body's various systems are free to react with each other through an infinite variety of chemical and electrical signals. Imagine trying to micro-manage your sweat glands, pulse, neural activity, lymphatic system, endocrine system, digestive track, and on and on. You could certainly go to a doctor who , by any number of therapies, drugs or surgeries, could alter the behavior of a part of your bodily system. But any one change to the system will create effects in almost all other systems.

Government interference is like performing surgery or prescribing drugs. Sometimes certain treatments are necessary, even life saving. Still, a body in its natural state is more self-regulating than we can ever be aware. Any interference with that natural state should generally be treated with caution and as a last resort or in an emergency.

If you start getting the odd notion in your head that drugs and surgery are natural and should be a regular part of life, well, you can just imagine how problems can develop: so many sur-

---

[40] Benson, *An Enemy Hath Done This*, 136.

geries and so many drugs, each one promising relief from every ailment or relief from the side effects of the last prescription or incision. Eventually, you can hardly recognize how the natural state of the body should behave and there are many pills to take.

This argument constitutes much of the reason why conservatives want smaller government. It does not encompass everything, of course. But… you know what? I'm a bit weary of continuing at this point. To conservatives, this stuff is old hat. But I am trying to convey my position to liberals.

How to Persuade a Liberal?

It's not as if the progressives haven't heard this stuff before. I know they have; which is why I consider it such a monumental undertaking to present the conservative perspective on economics in such a way that a liberal might actually pay some attention. I'm not trying to convert anyone to my way of thinking. I'm only trying to persuade the liberal to stop thinking of me as a greedy moneygrubber who worships the dollar.

I could continue to go through the standard right wing, free-market reasons for supporting a more laissez-faire approach. Those arguments will be presented at some point, as I certainly believe and hold to them myself. They are much of the foundation of my own conservative attitude. But, I'd like to do more.

My goal is to help the willing liberal to think a little outside the box; outside their box, that is. I will assume that I have an audience of open-minded progressives with real curiosity and actual intent to learn.

SHOCKING DOCTRINE

Klein tells great stories. Whether they have much to do with actual realities of globalization is another matter.[41]

Allan Wolfe

I must express my frustration with many on the left who give great praise to slanderous or libelous works, regardless of actual truth, so long as such books express their worldview. The worst

---

[41] Wolfe, *The Future of Liberalism (Vintage)*, 271.

example of this would be Naomi Klein's book *Shock Doctrine*. What a piece of work it is! The most shocking thing about this book is that I keep running into people who actually take it seriously! They have it on their shelves and refer to it as a seminal work.

I have many left wing books on my bookshelf, but Klein's is, perhaps, the worst of them all. I'd go so far as to say that, with regard to what it says about Milton Friedman, Shock Doctrine is a completely false book.. I won't waste your time with every one of the numerous misrepresentations; but here are a few of them articulated by Johan Norberg:

> Klein also blames Friedmanite economics for the Iraq war, for the International Monetary Fund's actions during the Asian economic crisis of the late 1990s, and for the Sri Lankan government's confiscation of fishermen's property to build luxury hotels after the deadly tsunami of 2005. In a 576-page book about such evils, why wasn't there room to mention that Milton Friedman opposed the Iraq war, thought the IMF shouldn't be involved in Asia, and believed governments should be prohibited from expropriating property to give it to private developers?[42]

For more details, read that entire article. I also recommend the complete book review of *Shock Doctrine* from the Cato Institute[43] called *The Klein Doctrine: The Rise of Disaster Polemics*.

If Milton Friedman's actual views are so wrong, why did Klein feel the need to distort them into something else entirely? I've heard it rationalized that although her observations about Friedman may not be spot on (a.k.a. lies), the book has much more to offer. I have two responses to that:

First, the rest of the book is almost entirely anecdotal. It paints the picture she wants to paint and does little more, even where she could have gathered some evidence. Apparently, the scholarly approach would have taken work, or something. Even a liberal such as Alan Wolfe (see above) recognizes that Klein does not demonstrate her worldview empirically, but argues it dramatically.

---

[42] Norberg, "Defaming Milton Friedman."
[43] Norberg, "The Klein Doctrine: The Rise of Disaster Polemics."

In short, most of *Shock Doctrine* is fluff. I mean, Al Franken's book *Lies and the Lying Liars Who Tell Them* may have its share of unfair attacks, but at least the bulk of the book is packed with fact after fact; and at least Al Franken is funny while he's striking his low blows.

Second, I find it hard to ignore Klein's lies about Friedman when the very title of the book is one of the most distorted and disgusting. The title of the book is referring to a completely nonexistent Chicago style economic theory known as the "shock doctrine". She got this "doctrine" from a simple observation made by Friedman. It's as if Friedman were to observe that lightening storms cause fires and Klein comes out with a book called *Lightening Doctrine*, where she claims that Friedman is a proponent of forest fires caused by lightening storms.

It really is that bad. As one Amazon reviewer put it,

> Klein makes a straw man's argument against a phantom opponent whose ideas don't resemble anything Friedman actually believed or wrote. This would be obvious to anybody who actually read his works, in which he makes a case for individual liberty free of government intrusion, elimination of government handouts for corporations, and organized democratic process that reflects the will of the people, while maintaining individual rights.[44]

Naomi Klein's pathetic rhetoric is usually the purview of anti-Mormon evangelicals. My anti-Mormon friends in high school would have had much more luck convincing me of the error of my religious ways, had they given me material that actually proved accurate about what I knew of my own beliefs. I'm not talking about seer stones and Nauvoo polygamy. I'm talking about the "You don't believe in Jesus or his atonement or his resurrection, but you should!" argument.

If my own understanding of current Mormon doctrine is wrong, why distort it into something else entirely in order to knock it down? By presenting me with such ignorance regarding my own beliefs, they made me much more skeptical of anything else they brought to my attention. Even more frustrating was

---

[44] Amazon.com Customers, "Customer Reviews of The Shock Doctrine."

that there wasn't a chance they would listen to me when I tried to tell them that *their* facts were wrong about *my* religion and about what *I* believed. It was like pulling teeth to get them to listen to that. They didn't care. I was wrong. They were right.. Besides, I was "brainwashed", they'd say.

So it is with readers and admirers of *Shock Doctrine*. It is like pulling teeth to get people to get a clue.

How can the two sides even have a discussion if liberals are so eager and ready to endorse slanderous material that seems to fit their worldview? These foolish and incorrect ideas perpetuate among liberals who don't bother questioning their assumptions. For instance, in a recent review from "The New Yorker", on the book *Freefall* by Joseph Stiglitz, a liberal reviewer praises Stiglitz for showing how

> Wall Street, under ideological cover from the Chicago school, conspired with Washington, first to peel away the regulations that might have prevented the mortgage bubble, and then to shield the financial sector from losses once the bubble ruptured.[45]

Here we go again: perpetuating a straw man! It is so frustrating. But liberals apparently need their hand held on this one. So, let me be clear about this:

The ideology of the Milton Friedman/Chicago School of Economics does indeed embrace deregulation. At the same time and for the same reason, they have always been firmly against bailouts! They have always been against subsidies. They have always fought against government shielding of any sector from losses; whether from bad accounting or a bursting bubble. The "Chicago Boys" are against government collusion of any kind. That is why (again) they are against regulations *and* subsidies. Now, is there anything unclear about that?

How can we build bridges when demonizing is more important than truly being informed?

All right, let's get back to business, specifically big business.

---

[45] "Review of the book 'Freefall' by Joseph E. Stiglitz."

BIG BUSINESS

[Obama] doesn't trust big business. From where I sit, the biggest business–and might I add, the most corrupt business of all–is the government.[46]

Dennis Miller

Aside from the analogy above, which compares a price-system free-market to a human body, by far the biggest reason why I hold a conservative free-market view of economics is because, more government inevitably means more collusion with big business.

Maybe this view will surprise liberals but free market conservatives like me do *not* trust big businesses and are quite suspicious of the economic power that they can and do wield. Yes, we free-marketeers have a long tradition of fighting against the power of these "special interests".

Adam Smith, the father of laissez-faire economics, referred to the corporate powers of his day as "mercantilism". He said,

> People of the same trade seldom meet together, even for merriment and diversion, but the conversation ends in a conspiracy against the public, or in some contrivance to raise prices... [The law] ought to do nothing to facilitate such assemblies, much less to render them necessary.[47]

Call it "corporate collusion" or "mercantilism" or "corporate cohortism," for all I care. John Stossel recently referred to it as "crony capitalism",[48] which is probably my favorite term because you can't get it mixed up with something else.

In continued efforts to build on common ground, let me ask this: Don't both liberals and conservatives believe that those in powers (corporate or government) will do what they can to fix the system to their own advantage? And won't they do it by whatever means they are able? When a large corporation wants to protect their market share (fairly or unfairly), they always prefer to do so through legal methods. They do this by lobbying

---

46 Miller, "Miller Time! on The Factor on Oct 7, 2009."

47 Smith, "The Wealth of Nations, Book 4, Chapter 8," 49.

48 Stossel, "Crony Capitalism."

to bend the government to the will of the corporation, not by molding their business to the shape dictated by government. That's "crony capitalism" in a nutshell: buying the protective services of the government to suit your own economic needs.

And the big joke (on pro-regulation liberals) is that all these corporations have to do is call these protective services "regulation" and not only do liberals fall for it, they embrace it.

To free-market conservatives, the bigger the government and the wider its reach and power, the more easily it can be used as a tool of big corporations. Only these large corporations have the resources to utilize all those government rules, regulations and bureaucracy against other competitors, large or small, with indifference to the little guy.

This is precisely why conservatives are suspicious of big government; not because they trust big business more but because they acknowledge that a bigger government is just more opportunity for corporate collusion. Milton Friedman phrased it simpler still:

> I am for less government because when you have more government, the industrialists take it over. Most monopolies can only prevail because government supports them.[49]

Am I building a small bridge of understanding? I'm trying. I mean, we conservatives may be wrong about government-corporate relations; but what is it about this view that makes me "greedy" and you pro-regulation progressives the more compassionate ones?

From Regulations to Crony Capitalism

A liberal friend once told me that what we really need is "a regulator to save us from the greedy destructive corporate unaccountability and machinations."

Hah! Government regulation is precisely one of the most effective mechanisms to facilitate the government to big business "partnership". There are numerous examples, but let's look at just one:

---

[49] Friedman, "Charlie Rose Interview (Dec 26, 2005)."

The Interstate Commerce Commission (ICC) was created in 1877 to regulate railroad companies. These big businesses couldn't be trusted to act fairly in the ruthless free-market arena; not individually nor collectively. We all know these railroad tycoons would conspire together to rip off the public with their price-sharing rackets and market sharing agreements. These shifty railroad practices were nothing more than cartels. Anti-capitalists, concerned citizens and competing businesses all argued that the railroads could only truly be held in check by a government regulatory agency. Thus, the ICC was born!

At last, "a regulator to save us from the greedy, destructive, corporate unaccountability". But as Milton Friedman explains,

> As the campaign against the railroads mounted, some far-sighted railroad men recognized that they could turn it to their advantage, that they could use the federal government to enforce their price-fixing and market-sharing agreements and to protect themselves from state and local govern-ments.[50]

So, who do you think was the first commissioner of the ICC?

Perhaps it was one of the activists who had supported the creation of the ICC. Maybe. Although, typically,, once a victory like this has been achieved, such activists usually move onto other causes and other victories.

Perhaps the fist commissioner was a professor from an ac-claimed university; a noble character that had long supported government regulators that saved consumers from the greed of those railroad barons. While there is certainly no shortage of such well-meaning folks, I suspect that most academics would not have the qualifications to fill such a role. And, looking at it from the professor's point of view, I can't imagine why anyone would leave a fulfilling job like teaching to be a government regulator. Boring!

No. The first commissioner was none other than Thomas Coo-ley. A lawyer who had previously represented the railroads, of course! (I just know that some readers are laughing.)

---

[50] Friedman, *Free to Choose*, 196-197.

Six years after the ICC was created, Attorney General, Richard J. Olney, wrote to one of the railroad tycoons, saying that the ICC can be made...

> of great use to the railroads. It satisfies the popular clamor for a Government supervision of railroads, at the same time that that supervision is almost entirely nominal. Further, the older such a commission gets to be, the more inclined it will be found to take the business and railroad view of things. It thus becomes a sort of barrier between the railroad corporations and the people and a sort of protection against hasty and crude legislation hostile to railroad interests... The part of wisdom is not to destroy the Commission, but to utilize it.[51]

Milton Friedman explains some further developments of the Interstate Commerce Commission, originally created to regulate the railroads:

> The artificially high freight rates maintained by the ICC for railroads enabled the trucking industry to grow by leaps and bounds. It was unregulated and highly competitive. Anybody with enough capital to buy a truck could go into the business. The principal argument used against the railroads in the campaign for government regulation—that they were monopolies that had to be controlled to keep them from exploiting the public—had no validity whatsoever for trucking.
> But that did not stop the railroads from agitating to have long distance trucking brought under the control of the Interstate Commerce Commission, And they succeeded. The Motor Carrier Act of 1935 gave the ICC jurisdiction over truckers—to protect the railroads, not the consumers.
> ... The ICC became as much an agency devoted to protecting the trucking industry from the railroads ... as to protecting the railroads against the trucks. With it all, there was an overlay of simply protecting its own bureaucracy.[52]

The Natural History of Government Intervention

The ICC illustrates what you might call "the natural history of government intervention":

1. A real or fancied evil leads to demands to do something.

---

[51] Josephson, *The Politicos*, 526.
[52] Friedman, *Free to Choose*, 197-198.

2. A political coalition forms consisting of sincere, high-minded reformers and equally sincere interested parties.

3. Incompatible objectives of the coalition (low prices to consumers and high prices to producers) are glossed over by fine rhetoric about "the public interest" and "fair competition".

4. The coalition succeeds in getting the legislature to pass a law. The preamble to the law pays lip service to the rhetoric while the law itself grants power to government officials.

5. The high-minded reformers experience a glow of triumph and turn their attention to new causes.

6. The interested parties go to work to make sure that the powers are used for their benefit.

7. Problems, which are inevitable, are always met by broadening the power of the government, never by lessening it.

8. Bureaucracy takes its toll so that even the initial special interests may no longer benefit.

9. The eventual effects are often precisely the opposite of the original objectives.

I hope you liberals can begin to see why we free-market conservatives laugh when you express your naïve fantasy that "regulation will save us from greedy corporations". You've been saying that forever. But you're always forgetting about last year's regulations, which created the problem in the first place. Never would you consider repealing legislation because that is what is known as... you know... deregulation. Relax. I know you liberals hate that word, but I had to use it.

The entrenched corporations have got you so duped! And you make it so easy for them by your infatuation with the word "regulation" and your fear of the word "deregulation". Besides, who wants to look back (at their mistakes) to repealing old legislation? It's much easier to support some wonderful new legislation that will finally, this time, somehow, protect us all from those greedy corporations... and a new cycle of government regulation begins. Ah, the circle of life!

As Thomas Sowell once said of liberal intellectuals:

> They imagine that... if it has not worked in the past, it is only
> because they have not had the right people doing it. In other
> words, Communism would have worked if it had not been for
> Stalin.
>   But of course, once you have a system like Communism,
> people like Stalin are the ones who will come to the floor.[53]

THREE CHEERS FOR LAISSEZ FAIRE

Conservatives generally oppose government-enforced compassion such as minimum wage, rent control laws, tariffs, a welfare
state, corporate bailouts, handouts or subsidies, etc. The reasons
why conservatives prefer a free-market approach to our economy all boil down to three principles: the moral, the legal and
the practical. Let's look at them one at a time.

THE MORAL PRINCIPLE

**What right has any private man to take by force the property of
another? The laws of all nations would punish such a man as a
thief. Would thousands of men engage in the same business
make it more honorable?**[54]

John Taylor

Is any law moral so long as it is created through the democratic
process? Of course not. After all, it would not be just for a majority of the citizenry to vote for the extermination of the rest,
would it? So then, by what principle is a law just or unjust,
moral or immoral? Conservatives (and libertarians) will often
use what I call *Bestiat's Rule* to judge whether a law is moral or
immoral. (Frederick Bestiat was a French philosopher and
economist born in 1801.)

Similar to the above quote by John Taylor, Bestiat's Rule says
that the moral rights of a government are derived from preexist-
ing individual rights. In the words of Bestiat himself:

> See if the law takes from some persons what belongs to
> them, and gives it to other persons to whom it does not be-

---

[53] Sowell, "Uncommon Knowledge Interview: Thomas Sowell (October 21, 2008)."
[54] Taylor, *The Government of God*, Chapter 3.

long. See if the law benefits one citizen at the expense of another by doing what the citizen himself cannot do without committing a crime.[55]

In other words, if it is morally wrong for me to steal my neighbor's cow (for whatever reason), it is morally wrong for me to vote for a law that gives the government the power to steal my neighbor's cow. Such a law would constitute "legal plunder".

I could go on forever on the topic of legal plunder. But for a real thorough treatment on the subject, I refer the reader to the book *An Enemy Hath Done This* by Ezra Taft Benson.

Liberals will, of course, use something like the following scenario to justify legal plunder:

Suppose ten children are starving to death and they live next door to a man who owns 100 healthy cows. This man refuses to share. Is it not the moral obligation of the society to use the power of the government to take from the greedy man and give some of his obvious surplus of cows to the starving children?

Actually, if the children were under my charge, I wouldn't wait for society or the government to take action. I'd be slaughtering me some cows, but only after exhausting all other options. However, I would still consider it stealing. Yes, it may have been a necessary evil, but an evil nonetheless. It should be seen as an emergency.

Because the minute I start to believe that I have a right to that man's property and once I delegate that sense of entitlement to the government, all kinds of dumb things result. After all, I live right next to the greedy cow owner. My plundering is, at least, efficient. Government bureaucrats, on the other hand, when they feel entitled to citizens' property, start doing weird stuff.

---

[55] Bestiat, *The Law*, para. L.64.

LEGAL PRINCIPLE

The powers not delegated to the United States by the Constitution, nor prohibited by it to the states, are reserved to the states respectively, or to the people.
10ᵗʰ Amendment of the U.S. Constitution

Conservatives like to see strict constructionists on the Supreme Court. Any federal law that violates the limits spelled out in the Constitution should be stricken down, regardless of how great an idea the law might be. Among the most ignored parts of the constitution is the 10ᵗʰ Amendment. The meaning of the 10ᵗʰ Amendment is quite clear: the federal government *only* has claim to powers that are explicitly given in the Constitution and no more. Then again, we haven't paid serious attention to the 10ᵗʰ Amendment ever since FDR's New Deal, a good eighty years or so ago.

The Supreme Court originally struck down New Deal laws but they were eventually muscled through by taking advantage of a simple clause in the Constitution. The Interstate Commerce Clause gave the federal government the power to regulate the buying and selling of goods that crossed state lines. This slippery slope snowballed into an ugly idiotic avalanche of immoral laws that defied common sense as well as the Constitution. Once FDR crossed that line, the Interstate Commerce Clause was used as a blank check that gave the federal government the power to do... well, you name it.

The biggest of the New Deal interventions were the *Agricultural Adjustment Act* and the *National Industrial Recovery Act* . They controlled prices, wages and output, with absolutely ridiculous results, as you will see.

The Agricultural Adjustment Act (AAA)

Such legislative packages as the Agricultural Adjustment Act were certainly motivated by the sincere desire to improve people's lives. The persistent problem is that these congressional decrees almost always morph into something else entirely. Thomas Sowell makes it clear by lamenting that

in the twenty-first century, [the government is] paying agricultural subsidies to millionaires and billionaires because of a
program created during the Great Depression to help small
farmers who were having a hard time. Again, once you have
opened the floodgates you cannot tell the water where to go.
Programs set up to help one constituency acquire new constituencies and take new directions.[56]

Why does Ted Turner get money from the government just by
owning land and doing nothing with it? For one thing, repealing
laws is simply more difficult than not enacting them in the first
place.

The National Industrial Recovery Act (NRA)

It's hard to imagine more asinine laws than the ones in the National Recovery Act; which was just another one of FDR's "do
somethings" that prolonged the Great Depression for an entire
decade. The endless list of arbitrary rules given in the NRA was
impossible for anyone to follow. And yet, people were treated
like criminals for missing out on its 557 basic codes of business
requirements.

Large corporations were more likely to have the resources
and bureaucratic infrastructure to comply with all of the rules.
They would also have a team of lawyers ready to defend their
actions. But what about the small business owners? How do you
think they fared under such a regulatory onslaught? So much for
helping the little guy.

Let's look at a few specific cases of how the central plans of
the NRA and its enforcers spread their "compassion", by putting
citizens in jail. Here are a couple of their supposed "crimes":

- Charging too little for dry cleaning
- Allowing customers to select their own poultry
- Growing your own grain… to feed your own livestock

Look at that. People were jailed and fined for charging too little
(and in other cases, charging too much, of course), allowing

---

56 Sowell, *The Housing Boom and Bust*, 136.

customer choice and growing your own food. What heinous crimes!

Jail Time for Dry Cleaning

The National Industrial Recovery Act fixed prices for almost every sector. This wonderfully "compassionate" federal mandate actually made it a crime to increase production; you know, the kind of production that produces more goods and services. I do not understand how placing limits on output, in any industry, is supposed to lead to recovery. Oh, and while it was ensuring that people could not produce more, it also made it a crime to cut prices. Do you know what the results were? A 49-year-old immigrant dry cleaner was actually jailed for charging 35 cents instead of 40 cents to press a pair of pants![57]

No Pickin' Your Own Chicken

This was another real genius of an idea to get the economy going, not to mention compassionate. Thanks FDR.

> In the poultry industry, the relevant line of code had barred consumers from picking their own chickens. Customers had to take the run of the coop, a rule known as "straight killing." The idea was to increase efficiency.[58]

In fact, a family of poultry salesmen, the Schechters, were fined and jailed for several months for not conforming to the NRA rules or price regulations. What a travesty. Amity Schlaes explains:

> The authority of the NRA ranged widely... Under the NRA Ickes had authority to set production quotas an authority he used to curtail supply in the name of driving up price. In other industries, the NRA rules were equally specific. NRA code determined the precise components of—macaroni; it determined what tailors could and could not sew. The idea was to increase efficiency.[59]

---

[57] Powell, *FDR's Folly*, xii.
[58] Shlaes, *The Forgotten Man*, 151.
[59] Ibid.

Next thing you know, some poor farmer would land himself in jail for feeding his own livestock with his own feed, grown on his own land.

The Supreme Court Case of *Wickard v. Filburn*

Oh, you haven't heard about the farmer that was prosecuted for growing grain on his own farm in order to feed his own poultry? Sounds like I'm just speaking in hyperbole, doesn't it? Can you imagine a farmer not being able to feed his cows with his own corn that he grew on his own land? That would be ridiculous, wouldn't it? Yes, it would. And yes ,it was ... absolutely ridiculous. I am not making this one up.

This idiotic law was challenged as unconstitutional in a case called *Wickard v. Filburn*. It was brought before the Supreme Court in 1942, which was, by then, packed with New Deal judges. How do you think the United States Supreme Court ruled in this case?

The Court actually ruled that this Ohio farmer named Roscoe Filburn could not grow wheat on his own land to feed his own poultry. The Court defended its position as follows:

> ...home-consumed wheat would have a substantial influence on price and market conditions... Homegrown wheat in this sense competes with wheat in commerce. The stimulation of commerce is a use of the regulatory function quite as definitely as prohibitions or restrictions thereon. This record leaves us in no doubt that Congress may properly have considered that wheat consumed on the farm where grown, if wholly outside the scheme of regulation, would have a substantial effect in defeating and obstructing its purpose to stimulate trade therein at increased prices.[60]

Does this make any sense? Does the 10th Amendment mean anything? More importantly, does common decency mean anything? When it becomes a federal crime for a man to grow his own wheat for his own livestock... well, I got nothing. I would like to say something like, "Hey, next thing you know a man won't be able to grow his own feed for his own..." Wait! There is nothing next! These laws make no sense.

---

[60] *Wickard v. Filburn (317 U.S. 111).*

If that doesn't get your blood boiling, think about this: Filburn would not have been in any kind of legal trouble if he had grown absolutely nothing on his land. In retrospect, he should have done just that and let his livestock die. It would have been cheaper, when compared to his lost time, effort and legal fees.

This law makes no compassionate sense! It makes no economic sense! It is utterly unconstitutional. It makes no moral sense. And yet we "strict constructionists" are the ones who are accused of being without compassion.

PRACTICAL PRINCIPLE

Today it is so widely accepted that the federal government must "do something" to cope with recessions and depressions that the actual consequences of government interventions tend to receive relatively little scrutiny in the media or in politics.[61]

Thomas Sowell

At the end of the day, what matters most regarding any economic policy are the results. Does government intervention do the good that it claims? The answer depends on the particular incentives created by the economic law or policy. Conservatives seem to stand alone in asking such a question. Liberals seem content with whatever the law was intended to do. The preamble to a law can claim anything. Regardless of how wonderful a law may sound, it doesn't magically accomplish the goal just by saying it. History is littered with laws that seek economic fairness, but produce economic tragedy.

FDR's New Deal, for example, is still credited for ending the Great Depression. But have people ever bothered to take an empirical look at the issue? Thomas Sowell gives part of the answer:

> [A] plausible case can be made that either the market or the government was responsible for the severity and duration of the Great Depression. What must be done is to go beyond plausibility and scrutinize the facts more closely.
> Because the stock market crash occurred first and the government began to intervene on a large scale some time later,

---

61 Sowell, *The Housing Boom and Bust*, 131.

we can trace what happened before and after the federal interventions...

Two months after the stock market crash in October 1929, unemployment rose and peaked at 9 percent, after which it began a generally downward movement over the next several months and [by June 1930] subsided to a level of 6.3 percent... [which was] not even half of the unemployment rate that would begin, and persist for years, after major federal interventions in the economy.

The first of these major interventions began in June 1930, when Congress passed the Smoot-Hawley tariffs...

[T]he double-digit unemployment that began after the Smoot-Hawley tariffs continued for every month throughout the entire remainder of the decade of the 1930s.[62]

One thing is certain about the 1930's. No decade saw a greater expansion of federal interference in the economy and no decade has ever had a worse depression or longer lasting unemployment. Am I villain for seeing a simple cause and effect here?

Ending the Great Depression

Many say that World War II brought us out of the Great Depression. Actually, the end of the New Deal is what finally brought about the end of the decade long Great Depression. Thomas Sowell explains:

FDR said that "Dr. New Deal" was replaced by "Dr. Win-the-War." The Roosevelt administration abandoned its anti-business stance...

In short, the war ended the New Deal—and the end of the New Deal saw the economy recover, as it had recovered from depressions on its own throughout the history of the country prior to the 1930s.[63]

WHY LAISSEZ-FAIRE?

I once received an email asking, "How on earth could anyone be against minimum wage laws, rent control or laws against price gauging?" My answer was that I was not so much being against these things, but more in favor of the following:

---

62 Ibid., 135-136.
63 Ibid., 138,139.

- I am in favor of gainful employment, which is hindered by minimum wage laws.
- I am in favor of available housing, which is hindered by rent control.
- I am in favor of food, while price controls have historically led to mass starvation.

PRICE CONTROLS

The most dramatic way to appreciate a free market is to observe an economic system that does not allow prices to fluctuate; that is, where price controls exist. If there is one consistent fact in the history of economics, it is the repeated tragedies of price controls, from the Roman emperor Diocletian in fourth century A.D. to Italy in the 1600s to India in the 1700s and again in the 1800s. Let's look at those briefly, one at a time:

In the year 302, Emperor Diocletian commanded that there "should be cheapness." "Our law shall fix a measure and a limit to... greed," he said. The result? Starvation.[64] Luckily, some avoided starvation when a black market arose. Sure, it was against the law; but if your kids were starving, you'd pay your life savings to feed them.

In the year 1628 when a local harvest shortfall occurred in Italy, the locals (understandably ignorant of basic economics) demanded that the government magistrates take action. The results:

> The magistrates did do something: fixed the maximum price for various foodstuffs, threatened to punish those who refused to sell, and other edicts of the sort. Since such measures, however vigorous, do not have the virtue of diminishing the need for food, growing crops out of season, or attracting supplies from areas of surplus, the evil lasted, and grew.[65]

But, at least the magistrates who enacted these laws *felt* nice and compassionate.

The most enlightening example is that of two different local food shortages in India. In the 1700s, the local government in

---

[64] Bowman, Garnsey, and Cameron, *The Cambridge Ancient History*, 178.
[65] Tilly, Ardant, and Politics, *The Formation of National States in Western Europe*, 381.

Bengal cracked down on the rising price of rice. The results? You guessed it: widespread starvation in some parts and an overabundance of rice in other parts. However, when another famine struck a century later, India was under British colonial rule. Thanks to Adam Smith's *The Wealth of Nations*, the British understood the dangers of price controls during a time of food scarcity. Instead, they did do something quite useful:

> [T]he Government, by publishing weekly [food prices] in every district, rendered the traffic easy and safe. Everyone knew where to buy grain cheapest and where to sell it dearest and food was accordingly brought from the districts, which could best spare it and carried to those, which most urgently needed it.[66]

Oh, I should mention that, at this time in India, the British were so laissez faire that they even allowed people to feed their own homegrown grain to their own livestock. Bastards!

Rent Control: More Destructive than Bombing

I was going to argue against rent control with more historical anecdotes. Instead, I refer the reader to Thomas Sowell's excellent book *Basic Economics: a Citizen's Guide to the Economy*.

Before moving on, however, something should be said about the dangers of rent control. Perhaps the liberal reader will listen to a couple of central planners on the topic of rent control. The first is Assar Lindbeck, a Swedish economist and socialist:

> In many cases, rent control appears to be the most efficient technique presently known to destroy a city—except for bombing.[67]

This also rings true according to Vietnam's own Foreign Minister, Nguyen Co Thach, who said that Americans

> couldn't destroy Hanoi, but we have destroyed our city by very low rents. We realized it was stupid and that we must change policy.[68]

---

[66] Schuettinger and Butler, *Forty Centuries of Wage and Price Controls.*
[67] Block, "Rent Control Article from The Concise Encyclopedia of Economics."
[68] Seligman, "Keeping Up."

If these people, a socialist and a communist, can understand and accept the destructive consequences of price controls on housing, perhaps the liberal reader could give this perspective a chance as well.

CONCLUSION

[Liberals] find it very hard to believe that someone else could honestly, sincerely, and intelligently reach a different conclusion. They talk about how complex the world is but it never seems too complex enough that other people can have read the same evidence they looked at and come up with a different conclusion.[69]
Thomas Sowell

So, you pro-regulation liberals see things differently than we free-market conservatives. You see government as a check on the growing power of rich corporations. And we see government regulation as an aid to powerful corporations and that is why we generally oppose regulation. We recognize that rather than keeping corporations in check, regulation is often used as a tool for big businesses to protect themselves from being left to "the whims of the market".

By far, the biggest and grossest misunderstanding that liberals have about conservatives is that greed drives us to support a free market. And just because I am against certain laws that "provide" things to citizens, this does not mean I am against people having such things. Quoting Bestiat once more:

> Socialism, like the ancient ideas from which it springs, confuses the distinction between government and society. As a result of this, every time we object to a thing being done by government, the socialists conclude that we object to its being done at all... We object to a state religion. Then the socialists say that we want no religion at all. We object to a state-enforced equality. Then they say that we are against equality. And so on, and so on. It is as if the socialists were to accuse us of not wanting persons to eat because we do not want the state to raise grain.[70]

---

[69] Sowell, "Uncommon Knowledge Interview: Thomas Sowell (October 21, 2008)."
[70] Bestiat, *The Law*, para. L.107.

Conservatives don't want people starving or suffering or lacking basic necessities. We want people who need healthcare to get healthcare. I'm certain that liberals and conservatives can agree with the following statement by Friedman:

> My major problem with the world is a problem of scarcity in the midst of plenty... of people starving while there are unused resources... people having skills, which are not being used.[71]

So, how to solve this problem? Well, just wanting the solution is not enough. And merely passing a law intended to solve the problem does not mean it will happen. Intentions are not results!

But I suppose I understand why it is so hard for liberals to understand the conservative penchant for a hands-off approach. Charity, it would seem, is pro-active, not laissez-faire. Indeed "faith in the market" would seem more like apathy than charity. But the market is a pretty reliable thing to put one's faith in.

In fact, I shall exercise my faith in the market right now by going to a store for some #2 pencils.

Fifteen minutes later... I'm back. My faith rewarded. There were plenty of pencils there, and without any law to ensure that they would be. I bought a 10-pack for $1.26.

How to Make a Pencil

Milton Friedman often illustrated the miracle of a free market by holding up a #2 pencil and pointing out the fact that no single person could succeed in making a pencil. That is, even the pencil manufacturer knows little about how to make the red and yellow paint or the graphite inside the barrel, etc. All the manufacturer need know, in a price-driven economy, is who supplies the wood, graphite, rubber, paint and metal, and the prices of each.

> In order to make a pencil, you have to get wood for the barrel. In order to get wood, you have to have logging. You have to have somebody who can manufacture saws. No single person knows how to do all that.
>
> There are probably thousands of people who have cooperated together to make this pencil. Somehow or other, the people in South America who dug out the graphite cooperated

---

[71] Friedman, "Commanding Heights Interview with Milton Friedman in October of 2000."

with the people in Malaysia who tapped the rubber trees, co-operated with, maybe, people in Oregon who cut down the trees.

These thousands of people don't know one another. They speak different languages. They come from different religions. They might hate one another if they met. What is it that enabled them to cooperate together?

The answer is the existence of a market.[72]

Another economist, Walter Williams, used the example of a baker. What does a baker know about processing flour, growing wheat, sugar, yeast, vanilla or raising dairy cows for milk?

What's called the market is simply a collection of millions upon millions of independent decision makers... Who or what coordinates the activities all of these people? Rest assuredly it's not a bakery czar.[73]

There are a number of ways to allocate goods and services. They include first-come-first-served, gifts, violence, dictatorship or lotteries. I prefer the market.

Corruption and Power

Government is a bunch of people with a variety of motives, dispositions and agendas; a human organization, with power and authority. We have been warned that

it is the nature and disposition of almost all men, as soon as they get a little authority, as they suppose, they will immediately begin to exercise unrighteous dominion. (D&C 121:39)

So, because people run government, it is as corruptible as any large corporation is, but far less accountable. Some say that the scariest thing about government is its monopoly on the *legitimate* use of force. But just as scary, for me, is the government's ability to change the rules of the game. The most twisted and dishonest practices of government are, by definition, law.

Only Congress can run a deficit for years without anyone being hauled before Congress (the irony!) for defrauding investors. Congress can weasel their way out of sloppy bookkeeping by

---

[72] Friedman, "The Pencil Story."
[73] Williams, "Economics for the Citizen Series (Part 9 of 10)."

making up their own accounting rules and definitions and changing them when it suits them. They can make it perfectly legal to "rob Peter to pay Paul". Social Security IOUs and government employee pension funds come to mind. And, who can argue? It's legal by definition.

While there is no question that Enron was corrupt, what a joke to watch federal legislators in Washington pronounce moral condemnation upon Enron and other corporations for *their* accounting practices. If Enron could have fixed its accounting practices the way Congress does–with the stroke of a pen and the bang of a gavel–it surely would have.

The Last Question

I have one final challenge to liberals. You're so confident in the centralization of government power. You think it perfectly constitutional. Fine. But are you just as comfortable and confident in your friend, big government, when you know, very well, that the next election could shift the power into the hands of Republicans, conservatives and capitalists?

It is your wish to centralize. Yet, it is your constant complaint that Republicans screw it up. Yet you must know they will always be part of government. Do you still trust your centralized government when Republicans are in charge?

I just don't get it.

And that, in a nutshell, is why I don't understand big government left-wing Democrats.

Consecration is NOT Capitalism
(Dan)

I wish we didn't live in a world where buying and selling things (especially selling) seems to have become almost more important than either producing or using them. [74]

C.S. Lewis

I'm a little disappointed with Noah. He was so caught up in disparaging Democrats for their economic foolishness, that he leaves the impression that economic ignorance is a characteristic of liberals, while understanding economics is part of conservative ideology.

Such is the conservative paradigm and I am glad that Noah demonstrated it because this is one paradigm that I have been eager and interested in smashing. Economic ignorance plagues the country as a whole, not just liberals. In fact, in a few pages, I will give empirical evidence that the average economist is a moderate Democrat.

Many readers may be surprised to know that, regarding economics, I agree with most of what Noah has said on the subject. However, I am not a capitalist. While I acknowledge most of the facts Noah brought to light, I vehemently disagree with many of his conclusions. But, before I get to that, I must...

Redeem Naomi Klein... a bit

Noah sure did slam Naomi Klein, didn't he? I'm afraid I do agree with him that *Shock Doctrine* "really is that bad," at least as far as Klein's misrepresentation of Milton Friedman and his

---

[74] Lewis, *Letters to an American Lady*, 50, (19 Dec. 1955).

views. I even agree that the philosophies of Friedman are treated in similarly to LDS doctrine. As a Catholic sociologist once said,

> The Book of Mormon has not been universally considered by its critics as one of those books that must be read in order to have an opinion of it.[75]

So it goes with Milton Friedman. Too many progressives, like Klein, have no idea how much they have in common with his views. I might even go so far as to say that *Shock Doctrine* spends half it's time misrepresenting Friedman and the other half preaching his views (though not in a way that Friedman would have presented them). The invasion of Iraq is the best example. Klein spent pages and pages on Iraq. Not once did she mention that Friedman was against the invasion. Nor did she acknowledge how much her own post-invasion views of military-industrial collusion were in line with Friedman's. I don't think she even knew, which is why I don't think she lied. *Shock Doctrine* is just bad scholarship. For that reason, I would never recommend it. However...

I would highly recommend Naomi Klein's earlier book *No Logo: Taking Aim at the Brand Bullies*. It is written in the same dramatic style as *Shock Doctrine*. Her assumption of guilt is as headstrong as ever and there is an immoral conspiracy around every corner. *No Logo* lacks the blatant misrepresentation found in Shock Doctrine, and is actually quite fun!

I'm not sure how conservatives would enjoy it, but I do think they should read it. It clearly shows the means by which corporations can engage in real control, not just of things, but of thinking. Such control may not be by the "legitimate use of force," or government, but the book does show how real those corporate powers can be. It's also a great indictment on commercialism.

While I still consider Klein to be a bit "whiny" in her narrative, she is clearly more in her element. For such a pessimistic book, I thought it was quite fun.

Now, let's tear down some capitalist fantasies, shall we?

---

75 O'Dea, *The Mormons*, 26.

The "Natural" State of Things

History is full of amazing varieties of social constructs and economic systems. However, an entirely "free market," unregulated by some form of coercive power, whether a nation-state or a small tribe, has never ever existed. The free market is a myth. It's not even an ideal to strive toward, and I'll tell you why.

Noah opened his comments by comparing an unregulated economy to a living body in its natural state. This makes for a good argument, but only if you buy into the analogy as an accurate representation of reality. I suspect that most liberals do not see that analogy as a reflection of reality.

Anthropologists and historians have difficulty identifying the subtle and complex cultural inheritances that allow our economic system to be as free as it is. Humanity has created an innumerable variety of economic systems, each with its own quirks and cultural inheritances. However–and here is my point–none of these economic systems seem very "natural" to me.

The current economic and social miracles conferred upon citizens of the United States is just that: a miracle. Rather, it's a series of miracles over hundreds of years, resulting in social norms, customs and legal conventions that are difficult for the typical American to appreciate. This lucky state of things, however, is not natural. I'll even quote Friedman to make the point:

> We who have been lucky enough to have been born in a free society, take freedom for granted as if it's a natural phenomenon. But let me ask you... what fraction at any moment of time ever lived in free societies?
>
> It is true that the normal condition of mankind is tyranny and misery. We've escaped. We've been extraordinarily fortunate to escape into an island of freedom and prosperity. If we do not maintain that island of freedom, of prosperity, if we do not maintain the essential features of this society, which made that freedom, and prosperity possible, there isn't a wide range of alternatives. We go to misery and tyranny, to the normal state of mankind.[76]

---

[76] Friedman, "The Open Mind 1977 Interview 'A Nobel Laureate on the American Economy'."

While Noah draws a parallel between economics and a living breathing body in its natural state, I see an economic system more like a garden. And a garden in its "natural state" is no garden at all. It is a weed patch! The free market is an idyllic myth, an irrelevance. We live in a world of tangible realities.

In order to function in the society in which it operates, an actual economic system must adapt. Should it adapt itself, as in the case of freely fluctuating prices? Or, should government adapt it, the way a vine is pruned and trained by the gardener?

Why not both?

Liberals Are NOT Economic Illiterates

I am eager to show those on the right wing of the political spectrum that they DO NOT have a monopoly on the understanding of basic economics. This may come as a surprise, but I'm ready to prove it. Empirically.

I freely admit that Noah made some solid and convincing arguments regarding economics. And yet, here I am: a Democrat who understands basic economics. How can this be? Am I just some kind of weird anomaly? A political mutant?

Let it be known, here and now, that the average economist (in the US?) is actually a moderate Democrat! Seriously, I'm not making this one up. In fact, not only do Democrats understand economics, they have taken action on such knowledge. You can read about it in the book *The Myth of the Rational Voter* by economist Bryan Caplan or check out his interview with Russ Roberts on EconTalk.[77]

Most economic progress is a bipartisan affair, though conservatives are never willing to give Democratic politicians their due credit. Republicans like to claim credit for deregulation of the airlines and lowering of the tax bracket.

However, according to Brink Lindsey, vice president for research at the Cato Institute, exclusive credit for these economic changes should not be given to Republicans alone:

> Better policies were not foisted on us by conservatives but were recognized as good ideas across the political spectrum.

---

[77] Roberts, *Caplan on the Myth of the Rational Voter (EconTalk Podcast)*.

Much economic deregulation started under Jimmy Carter. Ted Kennedy was the author of airline and trucking deregulation, and cheering him on as an activist was Ralph Nader. The last three major rounds of global trade talks were concluded by Democratic Presidents... [Johnson, Carter and Clinton].

Of course, we associate tax cutting with Republicans. Famously, Reagan did lower the top rate from 70% to 50%. But then it went all the way down to 28% thanks to a bill sponsored by two Democrats: Bill Bradley in the Senate and Dick Gephardt in the House.

I see this economic deregulation has been fundamentally bipartisan movement.[78]

Another example, that the right cannot deny, is President Clinton's support for the North American Free Trade Agreement (NAFTA). Wise or not, this policy aligns itself with current conservative "free trade" values. Conservatives should at least give Clinton and Gore credit for that. Notably, they both paid a political price for their support of NAFTA.

WHAT I DO NOT DISPUTE: PRICES

Some people say that prices convey knowledge, not greed. I would say, while prices do convey knowledge, they can also be an indicator or greed. And despite what die-hard, conservative, free-marketers say, greed is not good. I don't understand how a Christian could ever consider greed a good thing.

In an affluent, consumer-driven economy, the dollar sign becomes so involved, and people have a tendency to start seeing little difference between a price tag and a "for sale" sign. That is where the moral danger lurks. But, for the moment, let's discuss the different way the left and the right view prices.

As someone who is familiar with economics (at least as familiar as Noah), I do understand the importance of free flowing prices. However, where free-marketeers believe that prices *are* an accurate and true reflection of the demand and the cost of a product, I believe that prices *should* reflect the demand and the cost of supplying the product. The difference may seem subtle at first but it is absolutely crucial in understanding the difference

---

[78] Roberts, *Brink Lindsey on The Age of Abundance (EconTalk Podcast)*, ~57:45.

between how us pro-regulation folks see the world and how free-marketeers see it.

Free-marketeers believe that prices *are* a reflection of reality, while pro-regulation folks believe that prices *should* reflect reality. There is a term that all who study basic economics must be familiar with: externalities. Externalities are costs born by third parties, costs that *are not* reflected in the price of a product. Externalities are an undisputed economic reality, and really throw a wrench in the theoretical concept of "the free market". The existences of externalities are a major reason that I am not a capitalist and why I am leery of just letting the market do its work. If we were to strive for the government-less ideal of a free market, so espoused by conservatives, the full cost of producing something would not always be reflected in its price.

Let me make it absolutely clear that, despite my so-called liberal view on economic issues, I fully acknowledge the incredible damage that direct price controls have done over thousands of years of human history. I do not believe in price caps in the form of, for Often example, rent control laws. It is an economic fact of life and history that price caps can be more devastating than war and as deadly as plague, as Noah has demonstrated. For this reason, and perhaps to the chagrin of many fellow liberals, I oppose laws against "price gouging", especially in areas suddenly hit by famine or natural disaster, areas where lives are at stake. Getting the necessary goods to people in such areas is a moral imperative and anti-price gouging laws prevent goods from arriving as quickly as possible.

The only people who appear to benefit from price controls in emergencies are politicians and the media, who benefit because "greed" stories bring more viewers. However, when such emergencies strike, liberals (from politicians to voters) are never alone in their rash actions with respect to price controls. Conservative voters and politicians are just as eager in condemning the gougers and proliferating harmful price control laws.

I tried to explain the issue of price controls to a co-worker once and he commented, "Hmm, interesting theory." Listen. This is *not* theory. This is history. Please do not take my word for it. Study the history of price controls for yourself. There are ample examples, both recent and ancient! Of course, if you are too busy or lazy to study the history of price controls, then do a favor for the starving and homeless and take my word for it: price controls kill people, particularly in emergencies. Exceptions are rare.

Obviously, the government is still crucial during times of disaster or emergency. The market alone will not save us.

WHAT I DO DISPUTE: A LOT

Where Noah sees iron clad doctrine, I see room for exceptions. After all, without first learning the general rules, we could never dispute the exceptions.

"Faith-Based Econometrics"[79]

Although economics is a science, it is too often used to promote ideology (more often by the right, it seems to me). I think that economists, like many professions, are too often ignored; and yet, at the same time, are often taken way too seriously.

Economist Russ Roberts himself explains:

> I've started asking economists if they can name a study that applied sophisticated econometrics to a controversial policy issue where the study was so well done that one side's proponents had to admit they were wrong. I don't know of any. One economist told me that in general my point was well taken, but that his own work (of course!) had been decisive in settling a particular dispute.
>
> The defenders of modern macroeconomics argue that if we just study the economy long enough, we'll soon be able to model it accurately and design better policy. Soon. That reminds me of the permanent sign in the bar: Free Beer Tomorrow.
>
> We should face the evidence that we are no better today at predicting tomorrow than we were yesterday. Eighty years after the Great Depression, we still argue about what caused it and why it ended.[80]

---

[79] Leamer, *Macroeconomic Patterns and Stories*, 4.
[80] Roberts, "Is the Dismal Science Really a Science?".

Bestiat's Rule Revisited

Noah placed much emphasis on "Bestiat's Rule":

> See if the law takes from some persons what belongs to them, and gives it to other persons to whom it does not belong. See if the law benefits one citizen at the expense of another by doing what the citizen himself cannot do without committing a crime.[81]

Perhaps it is wise and prudent that "Bestiat's Rule" be one of the first considerations in evaluating a new law. However, it should not be the last! After all, the most basic of economic principals is that we live in a world of trade-offs, not absolutes. No society or government has ever existed in full harmony with Bestiat's litmus test. To expect the world to be so simple is, well, dangerously simplistic.

Free-market conservatives and libertarians too often see society as nothing more than the sum of its parts. They see a society or a community as merely a collection of individuals, without valuing the community itself. However, the community, through laws and traditions, gives the physical and cultural infrastructure that allows the individuals to have their freedoms in the first place.

For example, you have the freedom to drive to whichever store you wish (near or far) to buy your groceries. That "freedom", is possible, in part, because there is a network of streets that connect these supermarkets to your home and to each other. These streets are built and maintained through the cooperation of private and public entities (not to mention the numerous other unacknowledged traditions, standards, laws and cultural assumptions), making your trip to the grocery store possible.

Beware of Externalities

I quote Thomas Sowell:

> The cost of coal is more than dollars and cents. It is also danger and lives. So are the costs of other ways of producing power for our homes and industries...

---

[81] Bestiat, *The Law*, para. 64.

> [T]he mark of maturity is weighing one thing against another in an imperfect world.
>
> An adult weighing trade-offs cannot demand that nuclear power be "safe" because nothing on the face of this earth is 100 percent safe. The only meaningful question is: Compared to what? Compared to digging for coal or burning oil? Compared to hydroelectric dams? Compared to running out of electricity and having blackouts?[82]

Sowell makes an excellent point when he asks, "Compared to what?" Such a question should be asked more often and would give better perspective to policy debates.

"We pay too many taxes!"

Too many taxes compared to what? The United States has the lowest tax rate of any industrialized country, doesn't it?

"Welfare costs are too high!"

Well, what are the costs of not having a welfare system? Higher crime rates?

"Government sponsored healthcare costs too much!"

Again, too much compared to what? Higher medical bills due to unpaid care is currently passed off to paying customers.

Sowell is correct. Put arguments in perspective, compare, and factor in externalities. There are costs and benefits to every government program. There are costs and benefits of not having government regulations, as well.

I'll even quote Bestiat to make the point:

> There is only one difference between a bad economist and a good one: the bad economist confines himself to the visible effect; the good economist takes into account both the effect that can be seen and those effects that must be foreseen.
>
> Yet this difference is tremendous; for it almost always happens that when the immediate consequence is favorable, the later consequences are disastrous, and vice versa. Whence it follows that the bad economist pursues a small present good that will be followed by a great evil to come, while the good economist pursues a great good to come, at the risk of a small present evil.
>
> The same thing, of course, is true of health and morals. Often, the sweeter the first fruit of a habit, the more bitter are its later fruits... When a man is impressed by the effect that is

---

[82] Sowell, "At What Cost?".

seen and has not yet learned to discern the effects that are not seen, he indulges in deplorable habits, not only through natural inclination, but deliberately.[83]

Externalities, again, are missing from so many capitalist views on economic questions. The producer of a good or service is not the only one that pays for it. Additional costs, whether from ignorance, negligence or criminal avoidance, are not always reflected in the price of that good or service.

One of the most obvious externalities that a company or an individual might push onto others is environmental damage, such as pollution or overharvesting resources. The benefits of poor environmental practices are reaped by the polluting businesses. The costs may be borne by future generations or unfortunate individuals who live downstream (or downwind, hence the term "downwinder"). The cost may be spread out over an entire population that is either uninformed or too unorganized to do something about it. This is where the government comes in.

GOVERNMENT REGULATION

When the right balance between market regulation and market freedom is found, our economy prospers so much and so long that we have enough surplus to feed the poor, make the rich richer, sustain the infrastructure, pay for government waste, and even fight a war or two.[84]

Orson Scott Card

Let's take a look at three types of government regulations that I find appealing and appropriate: renters' rights, the FDA and usury laws.

Renters' Rights

We take for granted that a landlord cannot evict somebody without cause or notice, leaving them on the street the next day. Likewise, a landlord cannot waltz into your apartment and in-

---

83 Bestiat, *Selected Essays on Political Economy*, chap. 1.
84 Card, "Government and the 'Free Market'."

vade your privacy whenever he wants. They must notify you a certain amount of time beforehand.

It is government laws that prevent this kind of treatment, not courtesy or tradition. Do such rights raise the price of renting? Of course, and they certainly should. No one ever said rights were free.

Another cost that raises the price of rents is property taxes, which can go towards funding things like the local fire department. And I believe that this insurance against fire, , should be enforced by law despite the fact that it forcibly raises the cost of rents and housing. Free-market purists would throw such laws out. Silly!

The Food and Drug Administration (FDA)

Scores of people in the United States have died from diseases like beriberi, iron deficiency anemia and pellagra. These are all vitamin deficiency diseases; the results of a free market, I'm afraid. So, in the early 1900s, milling companies began to bleach their flower. This was not, altogether, a bad thing. Bleached flour has a longer shelf life and will not go rancid as quickly as un-bleached flour. However, the process of bleaching flour had the unfortunate side effect of removing essential vitamins and minerals. The result was an increase in nutrient deficiency diseases.

Diseases like pellagra claimed the lives of tens of thousands in 1915.[85] However, in 1942, the FDA used its legitimate use of force to direct flourmills to add certain vitamins and minerals to bleached flour. This was an inexpensive national health initiative and another example of the benefits of a government that does not strictly heed "Bestiat's rule".

The FDA also protects the public from snake-oil salesmen by ensuring that drugs and certain medical procedures are safe and effective. Thus, only drugs that have gone through the most rigorous tests are allowed on the market to compete.

Do these regulations raise the price of rents, drugs and bread? Yes, of course. The increase is marginal in some cases and size-able in others. As with anything, when taken too far, the benefits

---

[85] Ettlinger, *Twinkie, Deconstructed,* 29-30.

may outweigh the costs. There are always trade-offs. That is fundamental to economics.

Usury Laws

One very powerful thing that can affect the accuracy and efficiency of an economy that depends on a free-flowing price system is the economy's money supply. This was demonstrated in the book *A Monetary History of the United States, 1867-1960* by Milton Friedman and Anna Schwartz. Incidentally, this book (with its 800 pages, foldout graphs, half-page footnotes and other meticulous attention to detail) is truly as boring as it sounds. Nevertheless, this must be the standard by which a Nobel Prize in Economics is earned and this is how Friedman won his. I wouldn't recommend it to anyone other than a professional economist. Instead, I recommend Friedman's *Money Mischief.*

A significant aspect of money supply in our current economy is the ease by which we can obtain credit. When gas prices go up and you are already in a little credit card debt, it is easy to keep driving the same distances and paying with the card. If, instead of credit cards, we had to pay with the cash that we actually had on hand (or in the bank), then we would actually start making trade-offs right away. The demand for gas would immediately drop, which would then affect the price of gas itself. Unfortunately, the role that prices play, namely economic triage, is gummed up by the presence of such easily obtainable credit. I will talk more of credit and the absolute necessity of usury laws in a moment.

The ease of obtaining credit may be the most dangerous game we play in this modern economy. But, perhaps that is what "the market" dictates. Of all things to regulate, I believe that usury laws are still lacking in this country. It disturbs me that a credit card company can change your interest rate with them because you missed a car payment. This does not happen when you take out a loan from the bank or a mortgage. The interest rate is agreed upon ahead of time. Why should credit cards be able to change the interest rate willy-nilly?

Besides the obvious problem of corporations use predatory lending practices to lull people into debt, more general problems arise from our poorly regulated credit system.

To put it simply, as a commodity, credit is fraught with danger because it has such a profound effect on the money supply. The supply and demand of commodities is one thing but the supply and demand of credit affects and troubles our society in untold ways and is largely responsible for our turbulent economic times. I could write pages and pages on this topic. Instead, I refer the reader to the PBS Frontline episode called *The Secret History of the Credit Card*.[86] Watch it online.

Life without Regulation

One basic function of government is to give individuals and businesses incentives not to inflict harm on their fellows. Regulations are meant to discourage gaining wealth by hurting the public good. Orson Scott Card:

> We absolutely know that reasonable regulations... are essential for our country to function because history has shown us what America is like without them. Back when strikes were illegal, back when sweatshops kept children in slave-like conditions, back when patent medicines could sell you tapeworms as a weight-loss method or put cocaine in bubbly drinks, back when people could work twelve-hour days and still starve, we hated it so much that we elected politicians to change things.
>
> All these regulations came about because conditions without them were intolerable. We throw them away now at our peril.[87]

By demanding an end to all regulation, we would actually curtail the free market by allowing it to turn into a "race to the bottom" or, by my analogy, allow the noxious weeds to have free reign over the productive plants of the vegetable garden.

And yet, there is another cost to deregulation, articulated by James K. Galbraith:

> Thus, the economic world of "flexible" wages and prices is a world where a manufactured form of complexity is a major

---

[86] Frontline, *The Secret History of the Credit Card.*
[87] Card, "Government and the 'Free Market'."

implement of private power. The ability for a consumer to prosper in this world depends to a large degree on one's ability and willingness to search—to find the needles of good value hidden in the very large haystacks of dross, scam, and flummery. Without reliable standards, without clear guidelines as to what is safe and reasonable and what is not, the overall efficiency of the market declines because search and transaction costs rise beyond all reasonable limits. The efficiency of the market becomes limited by the fear of fraud. Shopping, far from being the exercise of market freedom, becomes itself an endless absorber of time and attention, whether one is discussing clothes, electronics, cell phone contracts, a mortgage application, or airline seats from New York to Pittsburgh.[88]

That quote is from the book The Predator State: How Conservatives Abandoned the Free Market and Why Liberals Should Too. Good read. I highly recommend it.

THE REDISTRIBUTION OF WEALTH

What improves the circumstances of the greater part can never be regarded as an inconveniency to the whole. No society can surely be flourishing and happy, of which the far greater part of the members are poor and miserable.[89]

Adam Smith

What's so wrong with redistributing the wealth? Oh, I don't mean government wealth redistribution. I am talking about voluntary giving here.

I remember, some years back, a conservative friend of mine actually got upset when he heard that J.K. Rowling (author of the Harry Potter books) gave away millions of dollars to combat poverty.

"That defeats the whole point of being rich," he said, to my confusion. To him, her philanthropy was anything but virtuous.

Would it have somehow been more wise or virtuous for Rowling to spend her money on buying a fleet of million dollar yachts for herself? Free-marketeers will tell you that, because people are paid to construct those yachts, by way of purchasing the yachts, she is actually enriching to the economy.

---

88 Galbraith, *The Predator State*, 182.
89 Smith, "The Wealth of Nations, Book 4, Chapter 8," 96.

I can certainly see more value in people working their trade and earning their pay rather than just having money fall from the sky. On the other hand, at the end of the day, the final product is just a personal fleet of yachts; more stuff for J.K. Rowling. Why would more stuff make her any happier or make the world a better place? Instead, why not utilize the skills of those yacht-building artisans for something else: for building a thousand low-cost fishing boats for people who need them after a hurricane or a tsunami.

Perhaps that potential yacht money could go toward building a thousand houses or a medical center or to fund research to find a cure for a disease. That is exactly what Rowling did with her money. Scientists and artisans would be paid, the economy was enriched, and the end product would help others, rather than being hoarded by Rowling herself. Rowling said, "I think you have a moral responsibility when you've been given far more than you need, to do wise things with it and give intelligently."[90]

This is what annoyed my conservative friend so much. How can that kind of attitude possibly be in harmony with the most basic teachings of the Savior?

Progressive Taxation

Let's talk taxation; more specifically, the "progressive tax". Conservatives see progressive taxation as being tantamount to socialism. At the very least, they fear it's a slippery slope toward socialism. I acknowledge that excessive taxes (flat or progressive) will, of course, kill the golden goose of productivity and sink everyone's boat. Liberals, in general, believe that it is simply logical to tax the rich at a greater rate than the poor and see nothing unjust in a simple and predictable progressive tax. I quote a well-known economic theorist:

> The luxuries and vanities of life occasion the principal expense of the rich, and a magnificent house embellishes... all the other luxuries and vanities which they possess. A tax upon house-rents, therefore, would in general fall heaviest upon the rich... It is not very unreasonable that the rich should con-

---

[90] Memmott, "J.K. Rowling's fond look back at Harry Potter - USATODAY.com."

tribute to the public expense, not only in proportion to their revenue, but something more than in that proportion.

Who am I quoting? FDR? Hilary Clinton? Sounds like a British scholar from long ago, doesn't it? Maybe John Stuart Mill? No, it's gotta be Friedrich Engels or Karl Marx, right? Wrong again. It so happens that this call for a sensible progressive tax was by none other than Adam Smith, the patron saint of classical economics, the father of laissez-faire. And it is not from some obscure letter to a friend. Read it (and weep) in *The Wealth of Nations*, chapter two, paragraph six.

Incidentally, this is one of many examples, which illustrate that Adam Smith was *not* a capitalist. He was in favor of both government regulations and redistribution of wealth, at least as modern conservatives would interpret the above quote.

A Flat Tax I Do Support

There is a flat tax, of sorts, that I do support. I would like all types of income to be taxed equally. I believe that incomes–from rental income, wages, stocks, lotteries, pro ice hockey salaries, windfall profits for CEOs and, yes, even Christmas bonus checks–should be taxed at the same rate. The higher the total annual income, the higher the tax rate. What does it matter how the income is obtained? Why should the income from, say, a mostly retired consultant engineer who works ten days out of the year be taxed at a different rate than, say, the income of a totally retired TV repair man who has chosen to build a portfolio of stocks that actually pay dividends?

Think about it. Dividend originated money doesn't buy better food than the same amount of consultant-engineering earned money. We pay our tithing on 10% of our income, regardless of how we obtain that income.

Just imagine two people, John and Phil, who make equal income. Let's simplify the story by assuming that all of their expenses (mortgages, cars, food, etc.) are relatively equal. The twist in this story is that they make equal income for doing practically the same kinds of jobs. However, in our current tax system, John pays far more in taxes than Phil. John owns and maintains an apartment complex where he spends his time as plumber, electrician, and landscape maintenance guy. Phil, on the other hand, spends his day doing the same tasks for a resort and lets say, for one of Oprah's mansions as well. Phil gets his income in the form of a salary, while John's source of income is from rent payments. Even though John works way more hours and gets no vacation days, they both end up with the same net income. By what logic should the government impose more taxes on John's income because it's from rental property? Why should Phil be taxed less because it's a wage? Again, I ask, what does it matter how that money is obtained?

So, yes, I support a particular kind of flat tax, a flat rate on income of the same amount of money. But I still agree with Adam Smith in his support for progressive tax rates: higher taxes for higher incomes (regardless of the source of income) and lower tax rates for lower incomes (regardless of the source of income).

The funny thing is, there's little point in arguing for a progressive tax when we can't even get the tax flattened so that the rich pay a percentage that is, at least equal to the rest of us. The rich, especially the super-rich, pay less of their income in taxes than the rest of us. Don't believe me? Ask Warren Buffett.

Warren Buffett's Bet

When asked about what he thought of a flat tax, he said that he didn't think our present system was flat enough and that it disproportionately placed the burden on people with lower incomes. He proved this by asking for the average tax rate of some 15 people who worked in his office, including the receptionist. Their personal income tax rates were all higher than his personal income tax rate!

It is quite comforting that Buffet, the third richest man in the world, feels that he does not pay his fair share in taxes. But he took things to another level when, during an interview with Tom Brokaw, he said,

> I'll bet a million dollars against any member of the Forbes 400 who challenges me that the average (federal tax rate includ-

ing income and payroll taxes) for the Forbes 400 will be less than the average of their receptionists.[91]

No one has ever taken him up on this bet, though three of the Forbes 400, close friends of Buffet's, said they made the same calculations and the results were the same.[92] The reason for this discrepancy is that we tax some kinds of income at a lower rate than others

All I ask is equal payment; an equal percentage for the same amount of income, regardless of the source of the income. I can't believe conservatives would oppose this.

Social Security Solution

The first place we should apply this flat tax is on Social Security, which conservatives decry as just another redistribution of wealth scheme. Far from it. Social Security, as it presently functions, is "a transfer from the less well-off to the better-off," to quote one conservative icon (actually two).

That's right. Even according to Milton and Rose Friedman, Social Security steals form the poor and gives to the rich. I'll quote them more fully, lest I be accused of taking their words out of context:

> In addition to the transfer from young to old, Social Security also involves a transfer from the less well-off to the better-off. True, the benefit schedule is biased in favor of persons with lower wages, but this effect is much more than offset by another. Children from poor families tend to start work—and start paying employment taxes—at a relatively early age; children from higher income families at a much later age. At the other end of the life cycle, persons with lower incomes on the average have a shorter' life span than persons with higher incomes. The net result is that the poor tend to pay taxes for more years and receive benefits for fewer years than the rich—all in the name of helping the poor!"[93]

My wife pointed out that, as far as lifespan goes, so what? It's not like the government was killing off the poor. I mean, women

91 Buffett, "Warren Buffett and NBC's Tom Brokaw."

92 Crippen, "Warren Buffett's Fellow Billionaires Don't Bite..."

93 Friedman, *Free to Choose*, 106-107.

live longer than men do. Should we tax women more, then? No. I'm just asking for equal payment!

Right now, Social Security is only paid on the fist $100K, or so, of a person's income. After that, no more money is paid into Social Security.

"It's going to go broke any minute!" say conservatives. "Get rid of it!"

To this, I simply reply that it could be totally solvent if those who made above $100K paid the same percentage of their incomes (at least!) to Social Security.

THE TROUBLE WITH TRADE

As a rich man is likely to be a better customer to the industrious people in his neighborhood than a poor, so is likewise a rich nation. [Trade restrictions], by aiming at the impoverishment of all our neighbors, tend to render that very commerce insignificant and contemptible.

Adam Smith

One example of the general economic literacy (or illiteracy) in this country is how trade is viewed. This ignorance is shared by liberals and conservatives alike. Take terms like "trade deficit," "budget deficit" and... oh, perhaps "average household debt accrual". People (i.e. stockbrokers, journalists and politicians) who should understand these basic terms and the differences between them often do not even realize their own ignorance. How many "financial experts" out there use the terms "trade deficit" and "budget deficit" interchangeably? These words are nowhere near being synonyms.

Regarding the economics of international trade, it is hard for me to believe that politicians, at least on the federal level, are simply as ignorant as the public appears to be. I am inclined to believe that our Washington politicians, at some point, either learn these basic facts or refuse to learn them. Even when politicians are learned in the realm of economics, they will inevitably encounter two dilemmas. The practical dilemma is that basic economics usually does not sell to their constituents. The other is the simple and obvious dilemma of being corrupted by the powers that be. The result is the same: even politicians who do understand economics must push that knowledge to the back of their minds.

Unlike many free-trade purists, I believe that tariffs have their place. However, I also believe that enriching the domestic fat cats seems to be the primary purpose of tariffs today.

Sugar tariffs are a prime example of government corroboration with big business. First, the artificially higher price of sugar (from sugar beets and/or sugar cane) is partly what has caused food industries in the U.S. to switch to corn syrup in many of our products.

Second, the prices that American consumers pay are of little concern to me because it's a small amount per American. What does concern me is that, with our tariffs, we effectively close off Third World sugar farmers from doing business. This is not charity. Even a socialist like Stephen Lewis agrees that U.S. tariffs are one of the cruelest things we can impose on the Third World.[94]

Third, the U.S. government hurts the Third World, yet again, in subsidizing all kinds of agriculture by buying up surplus products. I don't believe they destroy it (or as much of it) as they used to. Instead, they export it to Third World countries; "dumping it" at below market value (or perhaps for free). This puts local farmers in these countries out of business. It's an awful practice, all for the fat cats back here in the U.S.

Fourth, since Noah was willing to refer all the way back to the Great Depression and FDR to bash on today's Democrats, I must point out a few historical examples of how Republicans have played against a free-market. One of the most anti-free-market laws in history was co-written by Republican senator from Utah, Reed Smoot (also an Apostle); namely the Smoot-Hawley Tariff, which jump-started the Great Depression. There was also the high Republican opposition to Woodrow Wilson's efforts to lower tariffs to a 50-year low. Lincoln, himself, was a huge protectionist.[95]

---

[94] Lewis, *Stephen Lewis in the Munk Debates 2009.*
[95] Dilorenzo, *The Real Lincoln,* 69-70.

Granted, today's protectionists seem to have moved more into the Democratic Party. But I must protest any notions that put Republicans on a free-market pedestal.

Trading Guilt and Garbage

In any case, globalization and international trade is thick with problems as well as opportunities. I believe that both the government and the private sector have the power to solve many of the problems created by rapid rampant trade. What are these problems? The two broad categories that most concern me are environmental damage (including outsourcing garbage to places like China) and slave labor abroad. We'll look at environmental damage in the next chapter. So, let's look at slave labor:

U.S. citizens have much concern over child slavery when it occurs on our own land. However, it seems they have no problem outsourcing it to other countries. Out of sight out of mind, I guess. Child labor is not out of the sight of the corporations that outsource cheap labor. They don't seem to have a conscience about it. Says labor activist, Charles Kernaghan:

> Companies know a lot about copyrights, property rights and intellectual property rights. But they know almost nothing about human rights.[96]

Companies can make their goods much cheaper outside of the United States because there are fewer regulations and rules that they have to follow. Instead of paying more to follow the rules and employ age appropriate workers here, they have it done where they can pay the lowest amount. China has no regulations on child labor. Children might work 12 hour days in factories as early as age 12 to pump out Sponge Bob after Sponge Bob. These children are used up until they are no longer useful or no longer as profitable. Then they are kicked out on the streets with no prospects of earning a living, as they have no other workable skills or learning.

I believe their plight can be improved without becoming a party to the exploitation process, as many "free trade" conserva-

---

[96] Kernaghan, *Ending Child Labor and Sweatshop Abuses (2005 Chautauqua Lecture).*

tives would have us do. I also believe these problems should be addressed without abandoning and shutting out the poor; namely, without shutting down trade, as many "fair trade" protectionists (the Lou Dobbs-types) would have us do.

Unfortunately, the World Trade Organization (WTO) couldn't even agree to ban the trade of goods made by children sold into slavery, saying that it would hinder free trade. The United States is only one of two countries that have not signed the United Nations convention to end child labor. The other country is Somalia!

FINAL THOUGHTS

When you see that trading is done, not by consent, but by compulsion–when you see that in order to produce, you need to obtain permission from men who produce nothing–when you see that money is flowing to those who deal, not in goods, but in favors–when you see that men get richer by graft and by pull than by work, and your laws don't protect you against them, but protect them against you–when you see corruption being rewarded and honesty becoming a self-sacrifice–you may know that your society is doomed.[97]

Ayn Rand

That is from Ayn Rand's own magnum opus, *Atlas Shrugged*. I'm sure that, with this quote, she was specifically decrying the communism of her native country (Russia). Many conservatives see Chinese and Soviet communism as the ultimate examples of liberalism gone awry. I see them as the ultimate expressions of capitalism, a view shared by many economic progressives, such as Orson Scott Card:

> If you want to know what America would look like without anti-trust protection, you have only to look back at the old Soviet Union. The USSR never had communism... The actual economic system was state-owned monopoly. It was as if Microsoft ran every business.[98]

---

[97] Rand, *Atlas Shrugged*, 390.
[98] Card, "Government and the 'Free Market'."

You see, the mantra of the United Order is "What's mine is yours. What's yours is mine." The mantra of pure capitalism is "What's mine is mine. What's yours is mine... if, by any means, I can help it."

"It's the System!"

I don't like complaining about "the system". It sounds like a copout. Still, there is something a bit wrong with some of the laws we have in place. For example, there is what is termed "breach of fiduciary responsibility." Henry Ford was sued by stockholders for breaching "fiduciary responsibility" because he raised workers wages.[99] Either something's wrong with the system or with the hearts of the people. It's usually both. It certainly seems like there is something wrong with the hearts of conservatives who proudly wear the title "pro-selfishness" or even "pro-greed." Too often, consumerism or commercialism is confused with a free market. Conservatives defend disreputable commercialism–a form of idolatry–as if it were virtuous! It's like celebrating pornography as a right to free speech!

The words of Orson Scott Card again:

> The enormous economic power of the United States came about because we tamed the free market to work for the benefit of all the people, not just a few.
>
> America is astonishingly free of corruption, both in government and business, precisely because most people believe in and practice fairness in their business dealings. [Regulations are] a creation of that American insistence on fairness... While these are in balance, trust continues and the economy thrives.
>
> ... It ain't broke. So put away your chainsaw and your sledgehammer, and keep the dogmas of your "free market" religion to yourself.[100]

A Federal Candidate

On February 18, 2010, The Deseret News ran a letter to the editor from Eric Samuelson, which was sure to get (and it did) the highest number of reader responses that day:

---

[99] Diamond, *Collapse*, 483-484.

[100] Card, "Government and the 'Free Market'."

In 1844, an Illinois big-city mayor announced his candidacy for president of the United States. His platform marked a complete repudiation of the limited government, states rights' orthodoxy of his day. He wanted to nationalize jails and prisons, give prisoners job training and set them free. He wanted to expand the reach of the federal government to infrastructure, building roads, levees, dams and other internal improvements. His biggest proposal was compensated emancipation... Had this passed, it would have marked the largest expansion of the federal government in history, with a huge bureaucracy required to run it and a major expansion of revenue sources...

The name of this radical candidate? Joseph Smith, Jr.[101]

If you don't buy this federal expansionist interpretation of Joseph Smith's politics, please examine his platform for yourself.[102]

Keep in mind that I am not referring to the Prophet's candidacy or his platform as a means of proving my progressive views as doctrines of the Church. I'm not so sure that was Samuelson's point either (though I cannot speak for him). Nevertheless, it does not appear that Joseph Smith's political views are exactly "in sync" with the strict constructionist/states' rights perspective that drives today's conservative movement. It would seem unwise, then, to claim that one's political views are exclusively founded upon the principles of the gospel.

The gospel is much bigger than that.

---

[101] Samuelsen, "A Federalist Candidate," A14.

[102] Smith, "General Smith's Views... of the Government of the United States (1844),"
    http://olivercowdery.com/smithhome/1840s/1844Smit.htm.

JOINT

Capitalism vs. the Free Market

Keynes was a great economist. In every discipline, progress comes from people who make hypotheses, most of which turn out to be wrong, but all of which ultimately point to the right answer. Now Keynes... set forth a hypothesis, which was a beautiful one, and it really altered the shape of economics. But it turned out that it was a wrong hypothesis. That doesn't mean that he wasn't a great man![103]

Milton Friedman

It has been said[104] that John Maynard Keynes was the most influential economist of the first half of the 20th Century, while Milton Friedman was the most influential economist of the second half of the 20th Century.[105] The economic views of these two figures could hardly be more different. Keynes was the government planner, greatly influencing the New Deal, for example. And Friedman is the patron saint of the free-market.

We would not know what Keynes thought of Friedman since he died (in 1946) before Friedman's influence started to take hold. But the above quote tells us exactly what Milton Friedman thought of John Maynard Keynes. How refreshing it is to see Friedman praising Keynes as a great man and also praising him even for a theory that turned out to be (in Friedman's view) dead wrong. This is the kind of attitude that should be emulated.

And now let's move on with this Joint Conclusion by first discussing that which Dan and Noah have agreed on.

---

[103] Friedman, "Commanding Heights Interview with Milton Friedman in October of 2000."

[104] Summers, "The Great Liberator."

[105] It may seem like a bit of an oversight that neither Dan nor Noah mentions Keynes, while they both quote Milton Friedman. The reason is simple: a discussion of Keynesian economics means discussing monetary policy, which neither side was comfortable debating.

AGREEMENTS

All economics can do is make you aware of the consequences of your choices. It cannot tell you what your philosophy or your priorities should be, though it can reveal inconsistencies between goals.[106]

Thomas Sowell

The scriptures, say many things that can be analyzed by economists. However, the primary message of the scriptures involves behavioral and spiritual values given to us as we relate to God and to each other. Such values, or the values of any religion, do not conflict with economics any more than they conflict with, say, math. Economics is just a tool for weighing one value against another. The tool of economics is used by both sides, effectively and ineffectively.

The Danger of Capitalism

Capitalism can and does usurp a free market. Noah and Dan agree that there are many means by which capitalists can disrupt the workings of a free market, both through the government and by other devious means. They agree that Adam Smith, himself, was NOT a capitalist. Walter Williams, an economist, offers to give any student an A if they can find one positive comment in the works of Adam Smith that is at all kind to businessmen. Economists, from Marx, to Smith to Friedman agree that businessmen will work the system if they can. Pro-business is not equal to pro-free market, or vice versa.

Dan and Noah are also both sickened by the human rights violations in other countries, particularly when the citizens of those countries are forced at the point of a sword to make stuff for us. The existence of such evils, as well as the problem of global inequality, is not in dispute. How we go about solving such problems is, indeed, an area disagreement.

---

[106] Sowell, *Basic Economics (Hardcover)*, 344.

How to Trust in Economics

While it is true that those who do not learn from history are condemned to relive it, those who *do* learn from history still cannot predict it! So it goes with economists. As with physics, the study of economics can provide some predictions. There are laws of economics as there are laws of physics. Although we used Newton's laws to reach the moon, Newton himself could have never predicted such an event. Therefore, an economist cannot predict the future any better than a historian can. The best economists will usually refrain from making predictions of an absolute nature. Economist Russ Roberts explains:

> I've come to believe there are too many factors we [economists] don't have data on, too many connections between the variables we don't understand and can't model or identify.[107]

Nevertheless, economists can advise the public and policymakers and their counsel should be taken seriously.

It's like a group of expert doctors trying to diagnose and cure an incredibly complex disease. Would you expect these doctors to agree with each other on how to treat this complex disease? No. And yet, such a situation would not negate the field of medicine, nor would the lack of consensus mean that these doctors were unqualified.

You, most likely, would not hear the phrase "keep 'em hydrated," because that consensus view would already be assumed, already agreed upon. On the other hand, there's a sentence you definitely would not hear: "Looks like you could use a good bleeding!"

I continue with the words of Russ Roberts:

> If economics is a science, it is more like biology than physics. Biologists try to understand the relationships in a complex system. That's hard enough. But they can't tell you what will happen with any precision to the population of a particular species of frog if rainfall goes up this year in a particular rain forest. They might not even be able to count the number of frogs right now with any exactness.

---

[107] Roberts, "Is the Dismal Science Really a Science?".

We have the same problems in economics. The economy is a complex system, our data are imperfect and our models inevitably fail to account for all the interactions.

The bottom line is that we should expect less of economists. Economics is a powerful tool, a lens for organizing one's thinking about the complexity of the world around us. That should be enough. We should be honest about what we know, what we don't know and what we may never know. Admitting that publicly is the first step toward respectability.[108]

President Truman lamented that he wished he could find a "one-handed economist" because economists were always giving him answers that included the clause, "on the other hand..."

Lessons Learned For Conservatives

For Noah, the most jarring paradigm shift was learning that one could have an understanding of basic economics and yet remain a Democrat. Also surprising was the apparent fact that the average economist is a moderate Democrat![109]

While all economists acknowledge the importance of basic economic principles (such as the benefit of trade, immigration and the danger of price controls), moderate Democrats remain skeptical of the "free-market," as many conservatives define it.

Much is taken for granted by many conservatives who, by default, campaign for a free-market in any and all circumstances. However, a true "free-market economy" is an ideal that has never existed. Also, conservatives might claim that economics is on their side, but economics is a science and understanding the intricacies of economics is comparable to understanding physics, biology or any other science. It takes years of study and the average person is neither a physicist nor economist. So, the average conservative is as ignorant of the intricacies of the science called economics as he is of modern physics. Conservatives should be cautious in believing that any economy can or should be "freed up" and then to expect economic miracles to follow.

---

108 Ibid.

109 Caplan, *The Myth of the Rational Voter.*

Lessons Learned For Liberals

Dan has learned that conservative support of a free-market can be (or perhaps most likely is) driven by actual Christlike charity: concern for individuals and the society as a whole. Adam Smith, the founder of classic economics, was a huge philanthropist. Being an "economic conservative" does not equate to "worshiping the dollar." That's just standard name calling.

At the least, liberals should not pre-suppose that greed is the driving force behind a conservative's desire for a free market. With as much "thou shalt not judge" rhetoric as liberals espouse, passing judgments of greed is no more Christlike than passing other kinds of judgment. The time to be most wary of your own hypocrisy and pride is when you find yourself constantly assuming that the other guy is full of hypocrisy and pride.

Something else that has been brought to light is that, while conservatives wrongly claim a monopoly on economic understanding, liberals too often distrust economics altogether. Too many dismiss it as a field of study that is not scientific, but a tool of the right-wingers. No other group of scientists are as ignored as economists (except, perhaps, evolutionary biologists). As with every science, there are numerous disagreements among economists, to be sure. However, there are certain fundamentals that almost all economists agree on, regardless of political persuasion. Economists can warn the public of economic disasters just as surely as an astrophysicist can warn the public of a meteor strike.

Whether conservative, Libertarian, Republican, liberal, Democrat, "classical liberal" or progressive, every citizen would do well to treat economics as the science that it is. Like any science, it is constantly evolving. At least, economists should be acknowledged as scientists. Most importantly, the opinion of non-scientists (in economics, physics, biology, medicine, etc.) should not be acknowledged as expert opinion, especially when that non-scientist is… well, you, the reader, or me, or Dan, or Noah.

LESSONS FOR BOTH: ECONOMICS VS THE FREE MARKET

All too often, liberals and conservatives alike have equated the term "economics" with "the free market." Comparing these two terms isn't like comparing apples to oranges; it's more like comparing apples to botany or comparing oranges to cooking. Economics is a branch of science devoted, not to the study of money, but to the study of people's needs and wants, as well as what people provide and produce.

As mentioned in the introduction, economics is at play on the battlefield, just as medics must make heart-wrenching decisions about how and when to use their limited supply of time and medical provisions. Economics plays out in the socialist and capitalist systems in modern times, but did so among Aztecs and aboriginal Australians in ancient times as well. The only place where the study of economics was irrelevant was in the Garden of Eden.

Paradigm Shift #1:
The Average Economist is a Moderate Democrat!

According to an interesting study in the book *The Myth of the Rational Voter* by Robert Caplan, the average economist is a moderate Democrat.[110] Never would have guessed that! Here's an enlightening excerpt from the book:

> Economists are richer than non-economists, but millionaires without economics degrees think like other people, and economists who drive taxis think like other economists.
>
> Ideologically moderate, politically independent economists are totally at odds with ideologically moderate, politically independent non-economists. How can this be? Economics only looks conservative compared to other social sciences, like sociology, where leftism reigns supreme. Compared to the general public, the typical economist is left of center. Furthermore, contrary to critics of economics profession, economists do not reliably hold right-wing positions. They accept a mix of "far right" and "far left" views. Economists are more optimistic than very conservative Republicans about downsizing or ex-

---

110 Roberts, *Caplan on the Myth of the Rational Voter (EconTalk Podcast)*.

cessive profits—and more optimistic about immigration and welfare than very liberal Democrats.[111]

This kind of stuff really upsets both liberals and conservatives. After all, liberals tend to poo poo economics or at least economists.

What will upset conservatives is simply the fact that they have always assumed that they dominate in understanding the science of economics. It was none other than Thomas Sowell who had the following to say:

> Conservatives have no monopoly on skepticism about government intervention during an economic downturn. It was none other than Karl Marx who referred to "crackbrained meddling by the authorities" that can "aggravate an existing crisis."[112]

Paradigm Shift #2:
If You Think You Understand Economics, Think Again

While much of basic economics is intuitive and fairly easy to grasp, both the left and the right must understand how little they really know about economics.

If you think you understand economics, the following should shake your foundations a bit. Allow me to point out at least one example of a current conservative icon whose past political and economic views will break your paradigm.

Although a conservative talking head of tremendous influence, this man has never been a registered Republican. In fact, he was a registered Democrat until the 1970s (when he switched to independent). He was even a Marxist in college. What is most surprising is that he remained a Marxist even while perusing a post-graduate degree at the Chicago School of Economics. He took classes from the likes of Milton Friedman and George Stigler.[113] He successfully earned himself a PhD in economics from

---

[111] Caplan, *The Myth of the Rational Voter*, 82-83.
[112] Sowell, *The Housing Boom and Bust*, 140.
[113] Sowell, "Q&A with Thomas Sowell (2005)."

Chicago, all the while remaining a Marxist![114] Not exactly one of your typical "Chicago boys", was he?

Who was he? None other than Thomas Sowell. Dr. Sowell obviously isn't a Marxist any longer, but the point here is that he would never have graduated from Chicago without a clear and comprehensive understanding of basic economics. And, to underscore the lesson for conservatives, if there can exist a Marxist who understands economic principles, then it is no stretch to accept that Democrats can also have a firm understanding of economics.

The bigger lesson for me is that, if a Marxist can get a Ph.D. from the Chicago School of Economics, no matter how much I think I understand economics, I don't. How could I claim to understand economics when Sowell graduated from Chicago as a Marxist? This fact keeps me aware of my own ignorance. Keeps me humble.

There are, of course, Democrats who have little understanding of economics, as there are Republicans. There are politicians from both sides who, though they may understand economics, choose political expediency instead. Nixon's price controls come to mind.

A Joint Proposal

Before moving on to take a closer look at the disagreements between Dan and Noah, let us first look at one more specific agreement, discovered over the course of writing this book. That agreement concerns subsidies and is articulated here by Thomas Sowell:

> Government subsidies would be drastically reduced, starting at the top. That is, there would be a prohibition against giving a dime of government money to anyone whose annual income or total assets exceed one billion dollars. Why should agricultural subsidies be going to Ted Turner and David Rockefeller...
>
> Who could object to cutting off subsidies to billionaires? Once that was done, however, the next step would be to cut off millionaires. Then we could proceed on down the income

---

[114] Sowell, *A Personal Odyssey*, 126.

scale until people making a hundred grand a year could no longer expect to be subsidized with the taxpayer's money.[115]

Why such a thing has not occurred yet is... well, it's just pathetic.

MORE THAN AGREE TO DISAGREE

Government can be a friend.

Sen. Harry Reid

A little government and a little luck are necessary in life, but only a fool trusts either of them.

P.J. O'Rourke

Like so many others, Dan and Noah have their differing opinions on economics and those opinions aren't going away any time soon.

Perhaps it boils down to the degree in which government plays a part in our lives, economically. Modern liberals favor a great deal of government influence on the economic system. Modern conservatives want a lot less government interfering with economic decisions. But why? Both sides want the world to be a better place. And each side sees the other as hindering progress.

Here are a couple of ways of explaining why these competing views may never be recognized. 1) the "Competing Values" model and 2) the "Conflict of Visions" model.

COMPETING VALUES

One way to explain the differences between liberals and conservatives is by acknowledging the fact that economic values are often in conflict. Here is a list of such economic values:

1. **Freedom**
   The freedom to choose how to use the resources you have on what you value the most, without institutional force.

---

[115] Sowell, "My Platform."

2. **Growth**
A societal increase in the average standard of living. Not all in society benefit equally from economic growth, but all benefit in one way or another.

3. **Stability**
Minimization of fluctuation in the economic cycle, minimization of the influence of inflation, price stability.

4. **Security**
The ability to take economic risk without fear of economic damages, public safety nets.

5. **Full Employment**
Exactly what it implies, at least 95% use of all factors of production: labor, land, capital, entrepreneurship, and technology (by most definitions).

6. **Equity**
Fair economic justice, viewed as either equal economic opportunity, or equal economic outcomes.

7. **Efficiency**
Maximizing output per input.

It appears that free-market conservatives may place higher priority on economic efficiency and growth freedom, while economic progressives place a higher priority on economic equity, security, stability and employment. The trouble here is that these values here are, by nature, set against each other. Growth can only come at the expense of stability and security. Equity can only come at the expense of freedom. An economy is most efficient when it does not allow for full economic employment. Will these two views ever be reconciled? Not in this book.

A CONFLICT OF VISIONS

One of the most helpful perspectives that I have run into is found in a book by Thomas Sowell called *A Conflict of Visions*. This book is unlike most of his other books. It's very tedious and academic but, given what he is tackling, it actually needs to be. In this book Sowell proposes that the reason why these two sides so often oppose one another goes further than how they prioritize their values. In fact, it may explain why their economic values are prioritized differently.

In this book, we're going to refer to the two visions as the "tragic" and the "utopian". The tragic vision[116] is the more conservative perspective. The utopian vision[117] is the more liberal.

The difference between the two opposing viewpoints is not that they have different end goals or even priorities, but that the two sides see the world working differently. The following paragraphs, from *A Conflict of Visions*, seem to show the crux of the matter:

> [Conservatives see] market economies as responsive to systemic forces–the interaction of innumerable individual choices and performances–rather than to deliberate power shaping the ultimate outcome to suit particular individuals or organized decision makers. A competitive market, as thus conceived, is a very efficient system for "the transmission of accurate information," in the form of prices. These prices not only bring information as to changing scarcities, technological advances and shuffling consumer preferences, but also provide "an incentive to react to the information," according to Milton Friedman.
>
> [Liberals argue] that this is NOT how the economy operates, that it is currently obeying the power of particular interests and should therefore be made in future to obey the power of the public interest. Deliberate price setting exists in most basic American industries, according to this view. The answer is for "an angry public" to appeal to its political government. Thus, "the market gods are increasingly brought within control of humanely exercised power."
>
> **The point here is not to resolve this contradiction** but rather to indicate **how completely different are the worlds envisioned** by those who see the role of power differently. [Power] is in one case scattered among millions, in the other concentrated in a few large corporate hands...[118] (emphasis added)

Although each side dismisses the other's vision as a myth, each vision is sincerely believed. And so, each side sincerely fights on. Which "myth" or "vision" do you lean towards? And how does

---

[116] Sowell calls it "the unconstrained vision"

[117] Sowell's name for this one is the "constrained vision"

[118] Sowell, *A Conflict of Visions*, 155.

the world really work? My answer is that the world works both ways... or neither way.

The Tragic View

If the conservative view were true, we would be complacent, closing our minds to improvements on the larger societal level (i.e. government or culture). We could trust that market mechanisms will generate the best–though never ideal–outcomes. In this view, it is mighty tempting to turn away from the poor because of the temptation to think that the free market would provide anyone wanting to work with the opportunity to do so. Hence, if they are on the street, it is their own fault. But, King Benjamin tells us the fallacy of this attitude.

The Utopian View

However, if the liberal view was truly how the world worked, then we would need to merely find the right leaders, the right laws, and trust that such measures would improve the lot of the poor. The danger here is that too often laws, sincerely enacted to help the poor, can backfire. The danger of this vision is that there would be less incentive to ensure that progressive reforms actually help rather than hurt. So long as our efforts are virtuous and sincere, the outcome would be secondary. For example, it churns the stomach of liberals/progressives to allow price gouging. Yet, the forbiddance of price gouging may result in massive injury and starvation. Yes, the people who bring generators, water, ice and medicine into an area struck by catastrophe may be driven by greed, but would you rather there were less generators, water, ice and medicine in such an area?

So, the world certainly does not work completely one way or the other. Nevertheless, by understanding that people see the world differently, we can assume better motives from the opposing side. In the meantime, each side can strive to understand how the other perspective sees the world. Thomas Sowell's book *A Conflict of Visions* offers a way to understand such perspectives, not only regarding economics but also all types of political and social issues. I highly recommend it.

SOME PRACTICAL ADVICE

So, here we are, in a fallen world, full of scarcity, greed, and a bunch of hairless primates running around thinking we have all the answers. Only, everyone has a different answer. We're constantly fighting each other in an effort to make the world a better place… for each other. What more could you ask for from a "lone and dreary world"?

So, blame this paradox on Adam and Eve. It appears that good people fighting each other may even be part of the plan. In the meantime, pray to the Lord to lift the burden of bitter feelings toward those you disagree with. And… fight on.

The Limits of Economics

Although it takes years to become an accomplished scientist in the study of economics, any economist will tell you that understanding basic economics is not as difficult as your high school economics course made it seem. In fact, economics classes, as taught in many high schools today, have probably done more harm than good. Far too much time and effort have gone into memorizing lists of economic terms. Such terms are useful only if you plan to major in economics. Indeed, memorizing vocabulary has scared far too many students into being repulsed by otherwise interesting topics. Nowhere is this truer than in the study of economics. Understanding basic economics is truly necessary for every voting citizen.

So argues Thomas Sowell:

> Most of us are necessarily ignorant of many complex fields, from botany to brain surgery. As a result, we simply do not attempt to operate in, or comment on, those fields. However, every voter and every politician that they vote for affects economic policies. We cannot opt out of economic issues. Our only options are to be informed or not informed when making our choices.[119]

While we can acknowledge that individual economists do not think alike, "the dismal science" is still a science, as Russ Roberts explains:

---

[119] Sowell, *Basic Economics 3rd Ed*, vii.

Facts and evidence still matter. And economists have learned some things that have stood the test of time and that we almost all agree on—the general connection between the money supply and inflation... Nearly all economists accept the fundamental principles of microeconomics—that incentives matter, that trade creates prosperity—even if we disagree on the implications for public policy.[120]

Know Some Basic Economics

Even journalists who use basic economic terms, often times do not understand them. It is up to us, the reader, to remember the ignorance of the media. Journalists do their best, but they can't know everything; and it is not incumbent upon them to know it all. It is incumbent upon us to view everything with a healthy skepticism, but follow that up with a general self-education.

Here are a few book recommendations:

- *Basic Economics: A Citizen's Guide to the Economy*
  by Thomas Sowell

- *Marxism*
  by Thomas Sowell

- *Naked Economics: Undressing the Dismal Science*
  by Charles Wheelan

- *The Paradox of Choice: Why More is Less*
  by Barry Schwartz

- *The Progress Paradox:*
  How Life Gets Better While People Feel Worse
  by Gregg Easterbrook

- *How to Lie with Statistics*
  by Darrell Huff

- *Affluenza: The All-Consuming Epidemic*
  by John DeGraaf, David Wann and Thomas H. Naylor

---

[120] Roberts, "Is the Dismal Science Really a Science?".

- *Giving: How Each of Us Can Change the World* [121]
  by Bill Clinton

Think Things, Not Words

When it comes to economics, Justice Oliver Wendell Holmes said, "Think things, not words". Let's try it out. For example, "the weakness or strength of the U.S. dollar" may mean something to the mind. But, the stomach cares nothing about the "strength" or "weakness" of pieces of paper. The stomach cares only about being full.

Let us say a man is given an allowance of $2 per day. He buys a loaf of bread in the U.S. for $2 and eats the loaf. The stomach is full and happy.

The next day, he gets his $2 allowance and does something different. He finds himself in Europe and decides to convert the 2 dollars into Euros. Unfortunately, he finds that the exchange rate gave him only 1 Euro for his 2 dollars. His mind feels cheated.

While his mind is agonizing over this issue, his stomach calls out for nourishment, So, he goes out and finds the equivalent of the loaf of bread that he bought yesterday. To his amazement, he discovers that the loaf of bread is, seemingly, cheaper because it only costs 1 Euro, rather than the $2 that it cost back in the U.S. What a deal! So, he buys the bread, eats it and his stomach is full and happy.

Now he has a full and satisfied stomach, but his mind grows frustrated that the exchange rate of the dollar is, seemingly, "weak" and that the bread is, seemingly, "cheaper" in Europe. His mind feels doubly outraged. However, his stomach cannot understand why his mind is so angry. His stomach is just as full and satisfied today as he was yesterday. And on both days, his entire $2 allowance was spent on the same amount of sustenance. What's the problem?

When pondering economic issues, think of tangible goods and services, rather than abstract words and "values." And keep in

---

[121] Bill Clinton's *Giving* is agreed by all in this book to be an optimistic and even useful book. However, while Dan recommends the entire book, Noah (the conservative) would exclude the last 2 chapters, as they are a bit more skewed to the left than the rest of the book.

mind that money itself is somewhat abstract. Our modern world is full of wealth. But that wealth has nothing to do with how much money is in it. Friedman makes the point while giving us something to be grateful for:

> The rich in ancient Greece would have benefited hardly at all from modern plumbing—running servants replaced running water. Television and radio—the patricians of Rome could enjoy the leading musicians and actors in their home, could have the leading artists as domestic retainers. Ready-to-wear clothing, supermarkets—all these and many other modern developments would have added little to their life. [B]ut for the rest, the great achievements of western capitalism have rebounded primarily to the benefit of the ordinary person. These achievements have made available to the masses conveniences and amenities that were previously the exclusive prerogative of the rich and powerful.[122]

CONCLUDING THOUGHTS: TWO LESSONS FROM CHINA

Will China become an economic adversary or a friend in the near future? I'm not about to attempt to answer that one. Let me just say that we'd rather have wealthy trading partners than poor ones. China's growth is good for its citizens and it can be good for us. I'm not bringing up China to talk about trading goods but, rather, trading ideas.

For centuries, we have learned from China. Countless technological contributions that came from the Chinese are part of the foundation of western civilization. Among these are gunpowder and printing. I believe there is yet more we can learn from China.

Words of Wisdom from Shanghai

A member of my stake, who is from Shanghai, recently brought this to light. He said the following say about how Chinese and American labor markets work:

> China and United States are super powers in the world and both are large countries. Certainly, my personal opinion can only reflect and represent my own experience and under-

---

122 Friedman, *Free to Choose*, 148.

standing. One thing for sure is that currently United States overall is a more specialized society than China. As a natural consequence, employers tend to look for workers with specialized trainings and skills. On one hand this social phenomena is constructive as each individual specializes in their own job responsibility and teamwork brings about greater productivity. On the other hand, it has negative impact on developing individuals with holistic skills and capabilities. Consequently, we're all trained to become nuts and bolts of this giant social machine with one or two specialized skills and know very little of things outside of our specialty or field. If we're not a good bolt or nut, we will be sifted out and that's how the American society works. Mobility in career change could sometimes be limited since the lack of relative experience leads the employer to perceive an individual as unfit although he or she might be well educated.

The landscape of the Chinese society is quite different. China is undergoing rapid economical and social changes and literally the government is building cities like Las Vegas every few weeks over the vast mainland. This amazing speed and focus are due to the fact that China has a very powerful government with absolute central authority. Development and growth of domestic companies are also amazingly rapid. As a consequence, employers in China take on workers with diverse backgrounds, sometimes their background has nothing to do with the job requirement. The development in China presents many opportunities. They will be seized by those who are prepared and understand the Chinese market. Many believe the golden period of opportunities has passed in China. I personally don't think so. China is just barely scratching the surface. It is an exciting place nowadays... There are many many opportunities for success awaiting those who are able to see and pursue it. [123]

At the time this book goes through its first printing (2010), the U.S. economy is definitely in a recession. I, myself, am virtually unemployed. It can be very discouraging. For those of you who are perhaps feeling as down as I am, keep in mind that often growth is not possible without discomfort. There are possibilities that may never have crossed your mind were it not for the stark circumstances of today's economy.

---

[123] Dong to Andersen, "Re: American's career rigidity."

The Unemployment of Kong Sang

Back in the 1970s, the Hong Kong film industry had its own little bubble burst. There was a young man named Chan Kong Sang who began his career as a stunt double. This career demanded a great deal of risk and produced frequent and unusual injuries. They included everything from a sprained ankle to a dislocated cheekbone (yes, it can be done). His career wasn't without its thrills, though, including the pleasure of being kicked across the room by the legendary action star, Bruce Lee.

Kong Sang had trained his whole life to be a stunt man. From the age of five, he was raised in an eastern style boarding school to perform in the Hong Kong Opera. Hong Kong opera is different from traditional European opera. There is singing, to be sure, but the physical demands are strenuous, including on-stage stunts and complex choreographed sword fights.

The martial arts film industry was booming, catalyzed by Bruce Lee and driven forward by Hong Kong's major film studio Golden Harvest. As a daring stunt man, even by the standards of his trade, Kong Sang's career was on solid ground and his future looked bright.

It is said, "in life, change is the only constant." This proved true when Bruce Lee unexpectedly died, sending the Hong Kong action film industry into uncertainty and turmoil.

"What do you mean, there's no work?" Kong Sang said to his agent Samo, a friend since childhood.

"The studio isn't doing so well right now," said Samo. "Ever since Bruce died, well it hurt Golden Harvest more than anyone else. They just canceled a lot of projects, you know. The trend is moving away from action–it's all comedies now."

I repeat: he said "the trend is moving away from action. It's all comedies now."

What was Kong Sang supposed to do about that paradox? He was a martial arts stuntman, not a comedian. Was he supposed to start making action-comedy films and change his name to... Jackie Chan? Hah! Well, of course! What else? That is exactly what he did. [124] Yes, Chan Kong Sang is none other than Jackie Chan; possibly the most successful action star in world history.

If not for Bruce Lee's untimely and tragic death, who knows if Chan or his action/comedy routine would have been fully realized. It is doubtful that Lee's style of rather violent martial arts films would have ever found the kind of broad audience that flock to Jackie Chan films, where his combination of action and comedy result in less violence, more fun and ultimately more entertaining films.

Miracles are often thought of as physical events. But nothing is as miraculous as the discovery of a new idea. Often the best ideas are born of seemingly irreconcilable differences. I pray that we may keep the hope of such discoveries during this particularly jarring economic bump in the road.[125]

And so, I close with Victor Hugo:

> For many great deeds are accomplished in times of struggle. There is a kind of squalid, unrecognized courage, which in the lowest depths tenaciously resists the pressures of necessity and ill-doing; there are noble and obscure triumphs observed by no one, unacclaimed by any fanfare. Hardship, loneliness, and penury are a battlefield, which has its own heroes, sometimes greater than those lauded in history. Strong and rare characters are thus created; poverty, nearly always a foster-mother, may become a true mother; distress may be the nursemaid of pride, and misfortune the milk that nourishes great spirits.[126]

---

[124] Chan, *I Am Jackie Chan*, 186.
[125] Written: August 2010.
[126] Hugo, *Les Misérables*, 584.

CHAPTER 3

GREEN POLITICS

For it is expedient that I, the Lord, should make every man accountable, as a steward over earthly blessings, which I have made and prepared for my creatures.

D&C 104:13

We are both excited about this topic because, in many ways, it is a little more "up our alley." Both of us have some formal training in science, by way of a degree in Mechanical Engineering and work experience in civil engineering. This gives us a little more credibility in the realm of the sciences. And environmental studies encompasses a whole range of physical sciences; ranging from chemistry, biology and physics, as well as other tools like the scientific method, statistical analysis, and, yes, economics.

We both have some formal training in science, by way of a degree in mechanical engineering and work in the field of civil engineering.[127] That gives us a bit more credibility in the realm of the sciences.

Keep in mind that, even considering any slight advantages or extra tools we may have in analyzing environmental issues, we're far from experts on the topic. A slight disadvantage comes into play because we may be prone to thinking that this B.S. degree means we actually know what we're talking about. Truth is, our knowledge and training are but a mere sliver of what is out there. We are, like most readers, just doing our best to understand the world around us.

---

[127] What's the difference between these two fields of engineering? Mechanical engineers build weapons (aircraft, tanks, even bullets) and civil engineers build targets (buildings, bridges, gas lines). So, which one of us is the liberal?

Global Warming

Whether you call it "global warming" or "anthropogenic climate change", it is of some importance in public environmental discussions these days. Far too many people, in our view, see global warming as the keystone of environmental policy; insomuch that "global warming" and "environmentalism" are talked about almost as if they were synonymous. So, although we will not wholly avoid the subject, we have chosen to *not* make it part of our debate for the following reasons:

First, the media seems so overly saturated with global warming right now that we feel it is getting a little boring. There are plenty of other important and interesting environmental topics to cover.

Second, we admit that neither of us know much about the subject, although we have our opinions. Noah considers man-made global warming to be nothing more than hot air, the latest environmental fad. He considers the earth's climate to be far too complex for even the most confident experts to predict successfully. Dan, on the other hand, believes that man's influence on the climate is, to an extent, predictable and that we are influencing it. However, he has not sufficiently studied the mechanics of the science to confidently defend it. Most importantly, we do not want to put all of our environmental eggs in one basket. Not all environmental policies should hinge on the truth or falsehood of merely one environmental issue.

RIGHT

"There is Enough, and to Spare"
(Noah)

All my life I have heard the argument that the earth is over-populated... [Sustainable growth] is becoming increasingly popular. How cleverly Satan masked his evil designs with that phrase. Those who argue for sustainable growth lack vision and faith. The Lord said, "For the earth is full, and there is enough and to spare" (D&C 104:17). That settles the issue for me. It should settle the issue for all of us. The Lord has spoken. [128]

President James E. Faust

Conservatives like clean water and air. We like grass and trees and enjoy nature in its purest forms. We are aware of environmental problems. What separates us from liberals is not a difference in solutions, but a difference in how we prioritize them. Conservatives see a world of complex problems where solutions are so abundant that the prioritization of values (environmental or otherwise) is where the debate should center. Conservatives definitely identify with the following scripture:

> *For, behold, the beasts of the field and the fowls of the air, and that which cometh of the earth, is ordained for the use of man for food and for raiment, and that he might have in abundance. (D&C 49:19)*

---

[128] Faust, "BYU Speech: Trying to Serve the Lord Without Offending the Devil."

Environmentalism, as practiced by the left, seems contradictory to this principle, namely, that we should use the earth for our own purposes and enjoyment.

That may sound a little selfish in this politically correct era of superficial altruism. This does not mean that we are given license to rape the earth of all resources, treating the earth with the distain as a spoiled child with a day old toy, as many environmentalists would have you believe. No, we are stewards of this planet and we should treat it with the same kind of respect that we treat our own backyards or our own bodies.

This planet may be said to be "on lease" from God. When you lease a car, this does not mean that you do not use the car. As with any other gift that God has given us, "disuse is misuse", even if such use results in a bit of wear and tear. Wear and tear is as natural as life and death.

It is, of course, impossible to cover every disagreement that conservatives have with liberal environmentalists. I have tried to narrow things down and have grouped my problems with today's "liberal environmentalist movement" into three generalized topics: 1) "Secular Environmentalism" as Religion, 2) Failures of Environmentalism and 3) the Cynicism and Suspicion of Environmentalism.

PROBLEM 1: A NEW RELIGION

There is no such thing as a human being who does not have beliefs so deep-rooted that when they are challenged, it makes him or her extremely upset. And those who think they have no religion are the ones most apt to think that their beliefs are TRUTH rather than simply one way to believe.[129]

Orson Scott Card

Separation of Environmentalism and State

Liberals constantly tout the separation of church and state but never do they include the "religion of secular environmentalism." This is of greater danger than traditional religions because it is not recognized as the religion that it most certainly is.

---

[129] Card, "OSC Answers Questions."

Environmentalism is such a powerful state funded religion these days that you have trouble singing "Silent Night" in public schools but little trouble singing a hymn to Mother Earth. Earth Day is celebrated without the blink of an eye. Can you imagine the uproar if someone even suggested a Creator Day?

Secular environmentalists worship their god, the source of all goodness, namely the impersonal Mother Earth. Within this belief-system, there is even a fall from grace and a path to redemption. The fall from grace is seen as the industrial revolution or the rise of western civilization or even the invention of agriculture. Redemption, however, from the fall of mankind (and womankind) may be found through such absolutions as renewable energy, sustainable growth or the paying of oblations, via the purchase and trade of carbon credits. This religion has its set of Holy Scriptures as well, including *Walden Pond, Silent Spring* and, most recently, *An Inconvenient Truth*, not to mention its prophets, like Al Gore, who prophecy about the future, including the end of the world.

Secular environmentalism is a religion, pure and simple. My beef is with this state funded religion, not conservation in general.

The Doctrine of Anthropogenic Climate Change

I know that Dan and I have agreed not to debate the subject of global warming. As was said in the introduction to this chapter, I do not claim to know much about global warming. But I hear far more rhetoric and emotional fervor when it comes to global warming than actual scientific discussions. This is probably because real scientific discussion about climate change involves people who understand the behavior of non-linear fourth order equations and who know calculus better than they know grammar. Your average Hollywood star or politician, including Al Gore, does not fall into that category. So, how can they claim to really know? Answer: faith.

My purpose in discussing global warming is that it is currently the best example of religious zeal and fanatical dogmatism put forth by secular environmentalism.

Have you noticed that they used to call it "global warming" but now they call it "climate change." This shift in terminology to "climate change" is preferable for secular environmentalists because now, no matter which direction the climate goes, they can always be right. As a true believer once said to me, "global warming does cause global cooling." Well, there is no disproving that one, is there? If this is the claim, then in scientific terms, anthropogenic global warming is not falsifiable and, therefore, does not qualify as science.

I mentioned to a liberal LDS friend of mine, Anthony Coulter,[130] that this chapter on environmentalism would not include a discussion or debate on global warming. He immediately objected with emotional vigor. No other environmental issue seemed to matter to him, nor was it reasonable to discuss any other issue while ignoring this "keystone doctrine" of man-made global warming. He was so sure about it that I naturally assumed he had studied the issue and took the opportunity to ask a question on the subject: "If carbon dioxide levels have been rising for the past century," I said, "why did global temperatures drop between 1945 and 1970?"

Silence. His eventual answer was enlightening: "Well... I don't know... that... that's true." Only then, to his credit, did he admit that he had not studied the issue and he was just trying to pick a fight. I did not mind since I had obviously won.

There may very well be a quick and obvious answer to that question. However, the issue here is not global warming itself but, rather, his religious zeal by which he accepted it and defended it. My friend was as certain as most liberals that the earth's temperature would raise dramatically in the next century but he had no knowledge of the historical temperature patterns of the last century.

I quote Dennis Miller:

> Global warming is becoming like piercings or tattoos. I don't want to go down that road because I've seen how crazy people get when they get hooked and it spooks me. Global warm-

---

130 Read more of Anthony's opinions in an upcoming book on Iraq, Bush and the War on Terror..

ing is now a religion populated to a large degree by people who make fun of Christians for being too fervent![131]

We could be working together to improve the present environment. Instead, the secular environmentalists are excommunicating members (see below) and trying to convert people into believing their prophecies of the future.

Egg Shells First! Humans Last?

Despite impressions from the mass media, AIDS is not the number one killer disease in Africa. A bigger killer is malaria! But malaria was not always just an African affliction. It used to kill en mass right here in America. How did we, in the affluent United States, conquer this disease? Malaria was eradicated with the help of a simple pesticide that kills mosquitoes but is not at all carcinogenic to humans. In fact, we can eat the stuff![132] This wonderful chemical is none other than DDT (Dichlorodiphenyl-trichloroethane). The wide use of DDT resulted in the near eradication of mosquito born diseases in the United States such as malaria and yellow fever.

Somewhere along the way, it was "discovered" that there was a chance that DDT was responsible for thinning the eggshells of some bird species. And so, in a pattern that would so often repeat itself, after we made full use of DDT for our own uses, we not only banned its use in the United States (in 1972) but affluent, healthy, environmentally conscious, westerners pursued the banning of DDT in other countries as well. These countries include places where mosquito-borne illnesses, like Malaria, persist in killing millions today.

Some environmentalists will tell you that mosquitoes started developing resistance to DDT and that's the reason for the ban. The science of mosquito resistance to DDT and other pesticides certainly shouldn't be ignored, but it is too complex to discuss here. In any case, it wasn't mosquito resistance to DDT that mobilized support for banning it. It was banned in the United States for "ecological reasons" like the supposed thinning of

---

[131] Miller, "The Buck Starts Here from December 20, 2008."

[132] Cueto, Durham, and Hayes, "The effect of... repeated oral doses of... DDT in man."

eggshells of raptors (birds of prey). By the time this study came out, malaria was no longer a problem in the US. Now that human lives were no loner in danger, why not ban it for the sake of saving a few bird species?

As I said, the DDT issue is much more complex than what can be presented here. In fact, this issue is so thick with arguments, counter arguments and counter-counter arguments that we might go on forever–and that's without even being experts on the subject.

My point, however, is that one horrible aspect of secular environmentalism is that the lives of children on another continent are often sacrificed for the sake of thin egg shells! Even if the ban on DDT in the United States is responsible for the recovery of the bald eagle (as environmentalists claim but have not proven), I do not believe that even the bald eagle is worth the lives of millions of children a year.

Michael Crichton on DDT:

> DDT is not a carcinogen and did not cause birds to die and should never have been banned. I can tell you that the people who banned it knew that it wasn't carcinogenic and banned it anyway. I can tell you that the DDT ban has caused the deaths of tens of millions of poor people, mostly children, whose deaths are directly attributable to a callous, technologically advanced western society that promoted the new cause of environmentalism by pushing a fantasy about a pesticide, and thus irrevocably harmed the Third World. Banning DDT is one of the most disgraceful episodes in the twentieth century history of America. We knew better, and we did it anyway, and we let people around the world die and didn't give a damn.[133]

The Earth is for the Use of Man

Before further illustrating the skewed priorities of what I call "secular environmentalism," in order to underscore how it contrasts with the principles of the gospel, I quote the scriptures once again.

---

[133] Crichton, "Environmentalism as Religion."

Verily I say, that inasmuch as ye do this, the fullness of the earth is yours, the beasts of the field and the fowls of the air, and that which climbeth upon the trees and walketh upon the earth;

Yea, and the herb, and the good things which come of the earth, whether for food or for raiment, or for houses, or for barns, or for orchards, or for gardens, or for vineyards;

Yea, all things which come of the earth, in the season thereof, are made for the benefit and the use of man, both to please the eye and to gladden the heart;

Yea, for food and for raiment, for taste and for smell, to strengthen the body and to enliven the soul. (D&C 59:16-19)

The environmentalist movement, as it markets itself today, is openly contrary to the above scriptures. Environmentalists do come across as elitists, believing that the earth is here to enliven their souls in their way, while most of mankind is seen as an enemy of nature, "earth's cancer".

Words You Could Die For

In case you need a refresher on secular environmentalist enmity towards the human race, read the following quotes by environmental leaders and activists.

Dave Foreman, co-founder of Earth First

My three main goals would be to reduce human population to about 100 million worldwide, destroy the industrial infrastructure and see wilderness, with its full complement of species, returning throughout the world.

Maurice Strong, 1992 Rio Earth Summit

Current lifestyles and consumption patterns of the affluent middle class–involving high meat intake, use of fossil fuels, appliances, air-conditioning, and suburban housing–are not sustainable. A shift is necessary which will require a vast strengthening of the multilateral system, including the United Nations.

Club of Rome

The Earth has cancer and the cancer is Man.

Michael Fox, vice-president of The Humane Society

Mankind is the most dangerous, destructive, selfish and un-ethical animal on the earth.

Sir James Lovelock, Healing Gaia

Humans on the Earth behave in some ways like a pathogenic micro-organism, or like the cells of a tumor.

Prof Paul Ehrlich, The Population Bomb

The population explosion is an uncontrolled multiplication of people. We must shift our efforts from the treatment of the symptoms to the cutting out of the cancer. The operation will demand many apparently brutal and heartless decisions.

Prince Philip, Down to Earth

I don't claim to have any special interest in natural history, but as a boy, I was made aware of the annual fluctuations in the number of game animals and the need to adjust the cull to the size of the surplus population.

Ted Turner

A total population of 250-300 million people, a 95% decline from present levels, would be ideal.

Jacques Cousteau, UNESCO Courier (1991)

This is a terrible thing to say. In order to stabilize world population, we must eliminate 350,000 people per day. It is a horrible thing to say, but it's just as bad not to say it.

Prince Philip of Edinburgh of the World Wildlife Fund

If I were reincarnated I would wish to be returned to earth as a killer virus to lower human population levels.

John Davis, editor of Earth First! Journal

I suspect that eradicating small pox was wrong. It played an important part in balancing ecosystems.

Christopher Manes, Earth First

The extinction of the human species may not only be inevitable but a good thing.

David Brower, First Executive Director of the Sierra Club

Childbearing should be a punishable crime against society, unless the parents hold a government license. All potential parents should be required to use contraceptive chemicals, the government issuing antidotes to citizens chosen for child-bearing.

Can anyone doubt that most (if not all) of the folks quoted above are members of the Democratic Party, or would be if they were U.S. citizens?

Myth: Civilization vs. Eden

I would like to discuss, briefly, another doctrine of secular environmentalism: a fall from grace. Jared Diamond, the author of the Pulitzer Prize winning book *Guns, Germs and Steel* wrote the following in his first book *The Third Chimpanzee*:

> Given [the] widespread belief in a Golden Age, some recent discoveries by archeologists and paleontologists have come as a shock. It's now clear that preindustrial societies have been exterminating species, destroying habitats and undermining their own existence for thousands of years. Some of the best-documented examples involve Polynesians and American Indians, the very peoples most often cited as exemplars of environmentalism.[134]

And from Diamond's most recent book, *Collapse*:

> [E]very human colonization of a land mass formerly lacking humans–whether of Australia, North America, South America, Madagascar, the Mediterranean islands, or Hawaii and New Zealand and dozens of other Pacific islands–has been followed by a wave of extinction of rare animals... Any people can fall into the trap of overexploiting environmental resources, because... resources initially seem inexhaustibly abundant;
> Past peoples were neither ignorant bad managers... nor all-knowing conscientious environmentalists who solved problems that we can't solve today. They were people like us, facing problems broadly similar to those that we now face.[135]

PROBLEM 2: ENVIRO-FAILURES

We simply cannot... ignore it. We cannot risk inaction. Those scientists who say we are merely entering a period of climatic instability are acting irresponsibly. The indications that our cli-

---

[134] Diamond, *The Third Chimpanzee*, 319.
[135] Diamond, *Collapse*, 9-10.

mate can soon change for the worse are too strong to be reasonably ignored.[136]

Lowell Ponte

This is not a quote about global warming, at all. Lowell Ponte is referring to the global cooling scare of the 1970s! I own his book.

While this is a fine example of a failed prediction (for failed policies, keep reading), I do not fault environmentalists for making predictive mistakes. No field of science is free from mistaken hypotheses. What environmentalism needs is a little humility. I quote Michael Crichton:

> Unfortunately, it's not just one prediction. It's a whole slew of them. We are running out of oil. We are running out of all natural resources. Paul Ehrlich: 60 million Americans will die of starvation in the 1980s. Forty thousand species become extinct every year. Half of all species on the planet will be extinct by 2000. And on and on and on.
>
> With so many past failures, you might think that environmental predictions would become more cautious. But not if it's a religion. Remember, the nut on the sidewalk carrying the placard that predicts the end of the world doesn't quit when the world doesn't end on the day he expects. He just changes his placard, sets a new doomsday date, and goes back to walking the streets.[137]

Let's take a closer look at one of those bogus predictions, namely, the claim that we are running out of oil. I quote Sowell:

> There may be enough oil underground to last for centuries, but its present value determines how much it pays anyone to discover—and that may be no more than enough to last for a dozen or so years. A failure to understand this basic economic reality has led to numerous false predictions that we were "running out" of petroleum, coal, or some other natural resource.
>
> In 1960, for example, a best-selling book said that the United States had only a 13-year supply of domestic petroleum at the existing rate of usage. At that time, the known petroleum reserves of the United States were not quite 32 billion barrels. At the end of the 13 years, the known petroleum resources of the United States were more than 36 billion bar-

---

136 Ponte, *The Cooling,* 237.

137 Crichton, "Environmentalism as Religion."

rels. Yet the original statistics and the arithmetic based on them were accurate. Why then did we not run out of oil in 13 years? [138]

The answer is quite simple. All of the oil reserves in and throughout the earth's crust are made up of "known" oil reserves and "unknown" or undiscovered oil reserves. Therefore, "known oil reserves" are not a matter of how much physical stuff is in the ground. The amount of any natural resource that is known to exist depends on how much it costs to know. The costs of knowing include geological exploration costs, the drilling of "dry holes" as well as the opportunity cost of just keeping the money in the bank, which depends upon the current interest rate.

If environmentalists would learn more about the science of economics, such misunderstandings and fear mongering would be reduced. I say reduced but not eliminated because generating "crises" will always be in demand by politicians. In this case, if the average citizen understood basic economics, politicians would have less of a motive to scare the public with make believe "crises."

And now for the most well known transgression of the human race: our very existence (i.e. population). I quote President Faust:

> Few voices in the developed nations cry out in the wilderness against this coined phrase "sustainable growth." In Forbes magazine of September this year, a thoughtful editorial asserts that people are an asset, not a liability. It forthrightly declares as preposterous the broadly accepted premise that curbing population growth is essential for economic development. The editorial then states convincingly, that "free people don't 'exhaust resources.' They create them" (Forbes, 12 September 1994, pg 25).[139]

Michael Crichton, once again:

> Although the preachers of environmentalism have been yelling about population for fifty years, over the last decade world population seems to be taking an unexpected turn. Fertility

---

[138] Sowell, *Basic Economics (Hardcover)*, 187-188.
[139] Faust, "BYU Speech: Trying to Serve the Lord Without Offending the Devil."

rates are falling almost everywhere. There are some who think that world population will peak in 2050 and then start to decline. There are some who predict we will have fewer people in 2100 than we do today. Is this a reason to rejoice, to say halleluiah? Certainly not. Without a pause, we now hear about the coming crisis of world economy from a shrinking population. We hear about the impending crisis of an aging population. Nobody anywhere will say that the core fears expressed for most of my life have turned out not to be true.[140]

I believe that overpopulation, alone, is not the problem. Population multiplied by an over-indulgent consumer culture? Yes, that is a problem. I worry more about what our consumer culture does to our souls and less about what it does to the environment.

Backfire #1: "Shoot, Shovel and Shut Up"

What law, passed by Congress in the 1970s helped to accelerate the dissemination of certain endangered species? The Endangered Species Act, of course. Like so many utopian fantasy laws passed by liberals, this law created incentives that were detrimental to its intended goal.

How could that have possibly happened? The story is quite simple. If you are a farmer and some blue-toothed newt is on your land, anything you do to endanger the survival of that newt is now subject to penalties under the law. The list of activities that might endanger the survival of that species includes farming, grazing or any other way of living off the land. In other words, as a farmer, feeding your family means endangering the newt. Of course, that's only if the government actually finds out that there is a blue-toothed newt on your land. If you're a farmer and you'd rather not see your children starve, when you discover anything that resembles a blue-toothed newt, you've got a big incentive NOT to tell the government about it as well as an incentive to... ahem, get rid of all evidence. There is an actual term for this that farmers, ranchers and the like use: "shoot, shovel and shut up"!

When an endangered species on your land lowers the value of your land, that species is in far more danger than it was before.

---

140 Crichton, "Environmentalism as Religion."

This is not only a prime example of an environmental law that has backfired, it illustrates the broader point that just because you pass a law with a specific purpose in mind, that does not magically make the goal of that law come to pass.

But guess what? The environmentalists who lobbied for this law sure felt good about themselves. When that law passed, they all took a breath of fresh air, felt rejuvenated and marched on to the next "feel good" law, leaving it to others to actually deal with the incentives that the law created. For liberals, if the goal is just and motives are pure, reality can take a back seat to ideology.

Backfire #2: The Battery Powered Car

Here's another feel good concept. A battery powered car. Maybe it's a little less reliable than a gas-powered vehicle, but, like anything else powered with batteries, there are absolutely no carbon dioxide emissions, right? Wrong.

The energy created to charge up those batteries has to be generated somehow, somewhere. Electric power, the kind that lights up your house and powers your computer, microwave and television set, is generated at power plants. What kind of power plants?

Hydroelectric power plants: These are cardinal sins to environmentalists because they dam up rivers and disrupt the ecosystems of the river environment, even though they do not produce one speck of air pollution. In the southwest, hydroelectric power contributes a substantial amount of the power to the electric grid.

Nuclear power plants: The ultimate sign of human arrogance. No air pollution here; although nuclear power plants do pollute our streams and rivers with... warm water.

Then we have eco-friendly power generating stations such as wind powered turbines and solar power, which constitute next to nothing as far as the electrical grid goes.

So, what are we left with? Carbon powered plants; power plants that generate electricity by burning fossil fuels, such as hydrocarbons (gasoline) and pure carbon (coal). About 40% of the electrical power in the United States is generated by coal.

When you burn coal, no matter how efficient you are, you will always produce carbon dioxide as a by-product. That's simply how the chemical equation works: Carbon plus oxygen goes in; heat and carbon dioxide come out.

So, what is generated at a coal power plant is carbon dioxide and heat. That heat is converted to electrical power, which is sent into the electric grid. Energy is always lost when converting it from one form to another. But it doesn't stop there. Energy is also lost all the way down that electrical wire, all the way to your house and into your garage where it loses more energy as it is converted from electrical energy to chemical energy inside the batteries. Then, when it's finally time to move your car, more energy is lost in converting that chemical power to electrical power and then into mechanical power to turn the wheels.

The point is, a great deal of energy is lost (wasted) in using batteries as the power "source" for an automobile because the real source of power is a coal burning and carbon emitting power plant hundreds of miles away. Are you sure you are helping the environment by driving a battery-powered car?

In the case of gasoline, hydrocarbon and oxygen goes in; carbon dioxide, water and heat result. That heat converts quite directly into the power that moves your car. In short, using gasoline engines to get from A to B may actually result in much less carbon dioxide emissions than a battery-powered car.

The hybrid car is another story and is something that society should have far more hope in. Batteries in hybrid cars do not rely on power generated hundreds of miles away but from power that is generated when you put on the brakes and/or drive downhill. Hybrid cars take advantage of that wasted energy and utilize it to help power the car. It's exciting, really. I would like to get a hybrid myself, one day, and drive it around with an "I love George W. Bush" bumper sticker. The only reason I don't is that I've never bought a new car. Also, a hybrid is so expensive that even at today's high gas prices; the money it would save on gas would not make up for the high price of the hybrid.

For those of you who think that hybrid cars are a great way to "stick it to the man," think again. Perhaps you are using less fossil fuel, which upsets the oil guys, but the automobile manufacturer is probably getting your money for the car as well as some government subsidy, not to mention some nice free positive publicity. It is good business sense for them and they are happy to do business with you.

Backfire #3: Managing Yellowstone

The history of the environmental mismanagement of Yellowstone National Park is a humbling story. Actually, it's so bad, it's almost comical.

Soon after the park's inception, it was erroneously believed that elk were becoming extinct in Yellowstone Park. Park rangers concluded that eliminating or reducing the resident predators would save the elk. Soon, after the wolf, bear and coyote populations were virtually annihilated, studies began to show that the predators were not to blame for the elk shortage, but competing herbivores, such as deer and big horned sheep. Of course, with the predators out of the way, these overabundant herbivores soon decimate the parks flora, from grasses to tree bark (a particular favorite of the elk).

Aspen trees, for example, dwindled so severely that beavers could no longer make dams. And without beavers as part of their diet, wolves could not even be reintroduced. Without beaver dams, meadows dried hard in the summer. Big horn sheep began to disappear as well.

Bear-human interaction was once encouraged by park rangers but in the 1970s, it began to be a dangerous problem. Rangers did what they could, but soon the grizzlies were declared as endangered. One positive effect of this was that park rangers could no longer keep scientists from studying the bear population.

In 1988, yet another unwise park policy was exposed, namely, fire suppression. The Indians used to burn the forest regularly, causing fires every summer. But forty years of fire suppression had built up such a stock of tinder, that when 800,000 acres of Yellowstone (one-third of the park) finally burned, the fire was so hot that it all but sterilized the soil.

Author Michael Crichton summed up Yellowstone's fiasco:

> [I]t becomes impossible to overlook the cold truth that when
> it comes to managing 2.2 million acres of wilderness, nobody
> since the Indians has had the faintest idea how to do it. And
> nobody asked the Indians, because the Indians managed the
> land very intrusively...
>
> [E]everybody pretended that the Indians had never altered
> the landscape. These "pioneer ecologists," as Steward Udall
> called them, did not do anything to manipulate the land. But
> now academic opinion is shifting...[141]

For more on the environmental policies of Native Americans
before Columbus, I recommend the book *1491* by Charles C.
Mann. But neither Crichton nor Mann, recommend a do-
whatever-you-want approach as an environmental strategy.
Michael Crichton has lectured a great deal on the problems of
environmentalist hubris and Yellowstone is a classic example.
What he advocates, and what I would like to see, is more humility among environmentalists and a more forward-looking approach; rather than such an over-zealous quest to turn back the
clock and resurrect some past "golden age of eco-friendliness"
that never really existed.

I am not saying that there are no solutions. I am not saying
that we can just "eat, drink and be merry" and the earth will take
care of us. But environmentalism seems so clouded with religious zealotry and dogma that there is little room for science. A
scientific discussion is hard to come by among staunch environmentalists. That is my general impression from observing the
media, but I also speak from personal experience.

Backfire #4: Press Release Faux Pas

This one is an absolute classic. It's not exactly a "doctrinal" back-
firing like those last three, but it seems to be it's own kind of
backfire as far as policy goes. This faux pas should have had
much more attention than it got. I mean, I hadn't heard about it
until very recently. And when I did hear it, I instantly tracked
down a solid source because it sounded so outrageous.

In 2006, Greenpeace posted a serious statement on their website. It was a rejoinder to the, then recent promotion of nuclear

---

141 Crichton, "Complexity Theory and Environmental Management."

energy by President Bush. As you might expect, when anyone mentions nuclear power, the greens just chant "Chernobyl." It's a good bit of propaganda to use, of course. But, you've gotta at least have a full sentence about the Chernobyl disaster and how it relates to today's nuclear energy considerations to really be effective.

In a bit of a rush (obviously), here is exactly what Greenpeace posted on their website:

> In the twenty years since Chernobyl tragedy, the world's worst nuclear accident, there have been [FILL IN ALARMIST AND ARMAGEDDONIST FACTOID HERE]. [142]

Hah! That's so hilarious all by itself that I'll say nothing more. But uh… do tell your friends.

PROBLEM 3: "GREENLOCK"

Think about how to provide electrical power to a population and you run into what I call environmental "greenlock." That is, every option is an offense to the environment one way or another. Let's look at a few options:

Nuclear Power

While nuclear power is not strictly "renewable," the supply of uranium is virtually inexhaustible because it takes so little of it to generate power. There are generally two environmentalist objections to nuclear power. The first is, of course, nuclear waste that will be dangerously radioactive for the next 10,000 years. First, radioactive material must be encased in concrete. This is done on-site at nuclear power plants. The next step is much more difficult to accomplish, depending on where you are. The nuclear power industry in the southwestern U.S. would like to do something more with the radioactive material that is currently just sitting on the lot. The plan is to re-encase the radioactive waste into a more permanent concrete structure, located five miles deep into a mountain.

---

[142] Washington Post, "Greenpeace Just Kidding About Armageddon."

"What's the hold up?" you may ask. "Get that stuff off the pad and into the mountain as quick as possible! Who's responsible for holding things up?"

Take a guess. That's right, environmentalists and their red tape brigade. In their zealotry to stop nuclear power all together, they have managed to hedge up every way of making nuclear power safer and more efficient. This is why the newest nuclear power plant in the United States is 20 years old.

The environmentalists just can't leave well enough alone. They actually have another serious objection to nuclear power; yes, its only other waste product: hot water!

Fossil Fuels: Oil and Coal

As if I even need to say much about oil and its byproducts. Oil is the life-blood of our economy, but too much comes from across the seas. What other options do we have? Building a new oil field in the U.S. is a huge hassle, even in such remote places like arctic tundra.

As for coal, The United States has the largest coal reserves in the world. For global warming folks and aesthetic environmentalists, coal should be the last source of power on their list and for two reasons. First, the environmental impact of pumping oil is minuscule compared to the vast scars that are left behind when mining coal. Second, while it potentially produces less smog, coal produces the most carbon dioxide per unit of energy. Basic chemistry tells you that. Environmentalists only tout coal as alternative in the battle against "big oil."

Hydroelectric and Wind Power

Neither windmills, nor hydroelectric dams emit any pollution into the sky. They have no radioactive byproduct. They are clean and renewable. But even they have other offenses that make them near impossible to build in this country. Dams are not being built in this country anymore because of habitat destruction.

Windmills encroach on the landscape and they obstruct the beautiful view for aesthetic environmentalists. I must agree that the sight of thousands of windmills whizzing away is just plain ugly to me. Visual pollution is a problem, particularly if wind power is going up in your own backyard.

Don't windmills kill birds and bats? Good question. Read on.

PROBLEM 4: ENVIRONMENTAL CYNICISM

I have had close-up views of situations where big business found it in their interest to adopt environmental safeguards more draconian and effective than I've encountered even in national parks.[143]

Jared Diamond

(Dis)Missed Solution #1: Grown-ups!

In researching this chapter, I contacted Sam Enfield, one of the heads of the American Wind Energy Association to ask about bird and bat fatalities involving windmills.

By the way, doesn't American Wind Energy Association just sound a little bit like a government entity? It did to me, at first. I asked Mr. Enfield about that and–whew!–I've never heard someone say "no" faster than when I asked him if he worked for the government.

In any case, are windmills a serious danger to bats and birds? Well, it's relative. Windows, power lines, and lightening storms all kill substantial amounts of birds and bats each year. As for windmills, there was one incident in particular in which wind turbines were killing a number of bats and birds. In consultation with Bat Conservation International, the American Wind Energy Association did some redesigning. As a result, modern windmills turn at a much slower rate and Enfield's team is doing much more to make them safer.

When I asked Enfield who it was that blew the whistle in the first place, he gave a response that I will never forget:

"No one did," he said. "We're grown-ups."

Wait a second! You mean that they redesigned their windmills just for the sake of a bunch of little anonymous animals? Not because some animal rights activist blew the whistle? You

---

[143] Diamond, *Collapse*, 17.

mean they designed precautionary measures into their wind farms because they actually wanted to minimize impact on the environment and not because there was a government regulator looking over their shoulders!

Yep. That's right. No watchdog group. No regulations, even. These were just adults taking responsibility on their own. Imagine that. You won't hear stories like that from the environmentally dogmatic left. It wouldn't make their bulletin board because it doesn't fulfill their cynical vision of the business world.

But there's plenty of good news out there regarding the environment. Here's some more missed (or dismissed) good news.

(Dis)Missed Solution #2:
The Decarbonization Trend

Rejoice all ye who fear carbon when paired with dioxide, the combination of which creates a wonderful greenhouse gas, which secular environmentalists have declared a sign of the times. The developing world has been finding ways to burn less and less carbon, per unit of energy. While we are using more energy than ever before, the fuel is cleaner burning than ever before as we have shifted from wood, to coal, to gasoline and natural gas. Pure hydrogen is coming into play, as well; a fuel that burns without any emissions whatsoever.

For the past hundred years, the developed world has been decarbonizing and, for most of that time, we have done so without government mandates. There is every reason to believe that our society will continue to decarbonize.

To quote from a paper by Jesse H. Ausubel:

> Decarbonization began long before organized research and development in energy and has continued with its growth. Many ways to continue down the curve have been documented (Nakicenovic, 1992).
> During the 1970s and the 1980s the countries that reduced their carbon emissions were for the most part countries that expanded nuclear energy. The 150-year history suggests an ever-changing evolutionary envelope of opportunities.[144]

---

[144] Ausubel, "Climate Change: Some Ways to Lessen Worries."

(Dis)Missed Solution #3: The Science of Economics

It is incredibly annoying when environmentalists try to take economics out of the equation. The typical mantra is "there are non-economic values to consider." As I have said before, this demonstrates complete ignorance about what economics is really about. Actually, the cause of protecting the environment is nothing but an economic issue because economics is the study of limited resources with alternative uses. The environment is a limited resource, right? It has the alternative uses of either being left alone or being utilized by mankind in many alternative ways.

When most folks pit our economy against the environment, they simply mean human interests vs. the environment. Let me illustrate with this example: I am quite an animal lover. One might say that because I am human and love animals, animal wildlife is a human interest. But simply declaring animal wildlife or the environment as a priority gets us nowhere if we ignore economics.

Take dolphins, for example. Who doesn't love dolphins? No other wild animal says more about the power of a friendly face. They are probably a keystone species for the oceans. I am also a registered member of Bat Conservation International. I love bats. Fruit bats are actually as cute as a small dog without the constant yapping. But it's the smaller bats with those really ugly noses who are my heroes. Why? Let me put it to you this way: You don't need to love bats to wish they lived near you. You just have to hate mosquitoes.

I bring up dolphins and bats to demonstrate the importance of economics and, to help the reader think in terms of economics. "How many Mexican free-tailed bats are equal to the value of one common dolphin?" As Thomas Sowell said,

> Life does not ask what we want. It presents us with options. Economics is one of the ways of trying to make the most of those options.[145]

---

145 Sowell, *Basic Economics (Hardcover)*, 7.

(Dis)Missed Solution #4: Property Rights

Congressman Ron Paul comments on how property rights can lead to environmental protection:

> There is every reason to believe that the environment is better protected under private property rights. You just have to recognize that we, as property owners can't violate our neighbors' property. We can't pollute their air or their water and we can't dump our garbage on their property. So property rights are a very good way to protect the environment. Too often, conservatives and libertarians fall short on defending environmental concerns and they resort to saying "well let's turn it over to the EPA. The EPA will take care of us. And then we can divvy up the permits that allow you to pollute." I don't particularly like that method.[146]

Of course, the idea of private property is an offense to most liberals (reading glasses and clothing are the only things that qualify as true private property according to Hugh Nibley). But, using private property rights as a means of improving the environment? No doubt, liberals would consider the idea as nothing more than a ruse by conservatives and corrupt corporations and dismiss it out of hand.

Still, the worst polluting countries in the world are those with either undependable property rights laws or no property rights at all, namely China and Russia.

(Dis)Missed Solution #5: Potential Allies

"Michael Crichton is a quack!" said a co-worker one day.

One of the most frustrating aspects of secular environmentalism is the self-defeating practice of banishing people from the fold for their disbelief. The premier example is the late Michael Crichton author of several best selling books, including Jurassic Park and creator of the television show ER. He was certainly a liberal as well as an environmentalist by several measures, including his support for a carbon tax. However, many liberals consider Crichton a "quack," simply because he does not subscribe to "global warming" or "climate change."

---

[146] Paul, "Ron Paul on Dennis Miller Radio."

I am not challenging global warming. I am challenging Crichton's virtual excommunication from the liberal environmentalist religion simply because he does not subscribe to the typical global warming doctrine. Let's clarify what Michael Crichton *does* believe in regards to global warming. Crichton himself set the record straight in the appendix to his book *State of Fear*. Some of his conclusions are listed below:

- The earth is definitely getting warmer, somewhere around 0.7 degrees Celsius in the last 100 years.
- Humans have caused a 30% increase in carbon dioxide in the earth's atmosphere over the course of the last century.
- Carbon dioxide is a greenhouse gas and does have an effect on global temperature.
- Human land use also has an effect on the global temperature, such as cutting down rain forests and the heating effects of urbanization.
- Warming is occurring, humans are involved and temperatures will continue to rise probably another .8 degrees in the next 100 years.
- It is NOT likely that carbon dioxide will prove to be the primary driver of global warming.
- Decarbonization should be supported as well as a carbon tax.

In an interview with Charlie Rose,[147] Crichton underscored his support of a carbon tax by saying, "It should have been done 30 years ago."

"Then, what makes you different?" asked Charlie Rose.

Crichton answer was simple enough: "I'm not a catastrophist."

There it is. Yet, environmentalists and many liberals in general refuse to see him as an ally but rather view him as an enemy, an apostate, a "quack." Why? Because of his disbelief in that crucial bit of doctrine: that human action is the prime cause of global warming. He also puts a higher priority on stopping deforestation and preserving biodiversity.

---

[147] Crichton, "Michael Crichton on Charlie Rose (Feb 17, 2007)."

But what seems to push secular environmentalists over the top is the fact that he also argues for more money and effort to be spent here and now on problems like world hunger and the malaria epidemic (via DDT) rather than on trying to affect the average global temperature of the earth 100 years from now. Quite a quack, indeed!

Michael Crichton's harassment by groupthink environmentalism perfectly illustrates that today's liberals are far more concerned about bashing and banishing unbelievers than about losing potential and current allies who could be an asset to other noble causes, like putting an end to poverty!

(Dis)Missed Solution #6: Affluence

Lest you think that I only listen to those environmentalists who scoff at global warming, I will recommend a book whose authors completely buy into global warming as a crisis, believing that it fundamentally threatens human civilization. The book is called *Break Though: From the Death of Environmentalism to the Politics of Possibility.* I recommend this book because it proposes many new strategies on how to approach and solve environmental problems. The authors approach wealth and affluence a little differently than the traditional "get back to nature" environmentalism of the past 40 years. They make the claim that wealth is (get this) a *good* thing for the environment:

> Environmentalism and other progressive social movements of the 1960s were born of the prosperity of the postwar era and the widespread emergence of higher-order postmaterialist needs. As Americans became increasingly wealthy, secure, and optimistic, they started to care more about problems such as air and water pollution and the protection of the wilderness and open space. This powerful correlation between increasing affluence and the emergence of quality-of-life and fulfillment values has been documented in developed and undeveloped countries around the world
>
> [Environmentalists] have tended to view economic growth as the cause but not the solution to ecological crisis. Environmentalists like to emphasize the ways in which the economy

depends on ecology, but they often miss the ways in which thinking ecologically depends on prospering economically.[148]

Technology and affluence, in and of themselves, are not problems. They are potential solutions. Technology has afforded us access to an amazing amount of knowledge, including information about habitat destruction and a range of possible solutions. And affluence? Never has thee been such a maligned tool. Wealth, my fellow Americans, is the very thing that allows us the leisure time to lift our heads up, look around, and do something about environmental problems.

(Dis)Missed Solution #7: Big Businesses

Conservatives reject the mantra of blaming big business for all the world's problems, including environmental problems. The judgmental attitude of so many liberals and environmentalists toward businesses is, well, not only is it pompous and self-righteous, but it is simply unproductive. I quote from the unarguably pro-environment book *Collapse: How Societies Choose to Fail or Succeed* by Jared Diamond:

> It is easy and cheap for the rest of us to blame... But that blaming alone is unlikely to produce change. It ignores the fact that businesses are not non-profit charities but profit-making companies, and that publicly owned companies with shareholders are under obligation to those shareholders to maximize profits, provided that they do so by legal means.
>
> Our blaming of businesses also ignores the ultimate responsibility of the public... For instance, after the U.S. public became concerned about the spread of mad cow disease, and after the U.S. government's Food and Drug Administration introduced rules demanding that the meat industry abandon practices associated with the risk of spread, meat packers resisted for five years, claiming that the rules would be too expensive to obey. But when McDonald's Corporation then made the same demands after customer purchases of its hamburgers plummeted, the meat industry complied within weeks... The public's task is to identify which links in the supply chain are sensitive to public pressure: for instance, McDonald's, Home Depot, and Tiffany...

---

[148] Shellenberger and Nordhaus, *Break Through*, 5.

> To me, the conclusion that the public has the ultimate re-
> sponsibility for the behavior of even the biggest businesses is
> empowering and hopeful, rather than disappointing. My con-
> clusion is not a moralistic one about who is right or wrong,
> admirable or selfish, a good guy or a bad guy. My conclusion
> is instead a prediction, based on what I have seen happening
> in the past. Businesses have changed when the public came
> to expect and require different behavior... I predict that in the
> future, just as in the past, changes in public attitudes will be
> essential for changes in businesses' environmental prac-
> tices.[149]

Too many environmentalists prefer to pontificate about the sins
of big business rather than to hunker down, see the world as it is
and get things done.

Merlin Tuttle, another very successful conservationist put it
this way:

> Believe me, miners, loggers, oilmen, hunters–people who
> have so long been reviled by conservationists–are the prime
> targets for those who want to make real progress. There's no-
> body who feels better about finally being included in doing
> something good. All these people: They like clean environ-
> ments. They like wildlife.
>
> We like to pretend that they're just mean old greedy de-
> spoilers of the environment, that they do this just to get rich.
> But all these miners are supporting our lifestyles. How would
> we drive to work in the morning? How would we live in a com-
> fortable home if it wasn't for them?
>
> For far too long, we've reviled them unfairly as if the whole
> environmental problems of the world were because of them
> and we had no culpability at all. It's so unfair. From their
> standpoint, they can't imagine how we could be so mean.[150]

Does it occur to liberals that "thy neighbor" includes not only
Samaritans and convicts but business owners as well?

---

[149] Diamond, *Collapse*, 483-485.
[150] Tuttle, *The Incredible World of Bats (2002 Chautauqua Lecture)*.

CONCLUDING THOUGHTS

If environmentalists aren't willing to engage with big business, which are among the most powerful forces in the modern world, it won't be possible to solve the world's environmental problems.[151]

Jared Diamond

On one hand, conservatives like clean air and water and an environment of biodiversity just as much as the next person does. On the other hand, we definitely see the earth as a means to an end to be used respectfully. We put people first, by putting people's freedom first. One form of this is property rights. We also believe that human affluence and prosperity is ultimately beneficial to the environment. Conservatives are champions of the environment, along with many other worthy and necessary endeavors like education, healthcare, personal fitness. We simply reject the knee-jerk liberal solution to all problems: government. We also reject the automatic liberal tendency to blame affluence, businesses and the free-market for environmental problems.

I never said that wealthy private property owners are automatically the best stewards of the environment. I did quote the book *Break Through*, which says that affluent people have the time and money to care about the environment, particularly the environment that resides beyond their own backyards. I acknowledge that the wealthy have the potential of being the world's worst stewards of the environment. However, they might just be the best stewards because they have the leisure to do so. It does seem like a certain level of affluence is prerequisite becoming a more capable caretaker of the environment on a worldwide scale.

While writing this chapter, I worried that I was just complaining, just arguing against the foibles of the left. Where was I arguing *for* anything? What is *the* conservative position on the environmental issues?

---

[151] Diamond, *Collapse*, 18.

The True "Conservative" Position

I don't speak for all conservatives. No one does. I can only give my own position. At the start of this project, interestingly, I thought I was a little "greener" than the typical conservative was; or maybe a little less free-market oriented, when it comes to the environment, than most conservatives. So, is the "conservative environmental position" more *free-market* or less *enviro-dogma*? And if I was unsure about this, how could I possibly hope to convey the "conservative environmental view"?

I did the logical thing. I decided to poll a few of my fellow conservatives, particularly those that I considered the most dogmatically free-market oriented. Were they merely against wacko environmentalist dogma? Or were they completely free-market oriented?

They agreed with me that free-enterprise solutions were too often ignored. However, to my surprise, these free-marketeers felt that a measure of government regulation was necessary in protecting the environment. I then asked the following: "Would you rather see more of a free-market or less wild-eyed environmentalist dogma?" Resoundingly, most conservatives said that they would rather see less enviro-dogma. Then one friend, Aaron, pointed out that the question was a bit of a paradox. You see, we conservatives view the free-market as an efficient means of conveying the values of a society, whether those values are good or bad. So, the question of more free-market verses less enviro-dogma was like the choice between more freedom or less idiotic group-think.

Let me just punctuate the philosophy that the free-market reflects our values by answering the following question: What is the largest wildlife park in Papua New Guinea?

Answer: Chevron's Kutubu oil field. I should say that the Kutubu oil field *acts* like Papua New Guinea's largest wildlife park. Don't take my word for it. Read from a man who has been there, Jared Diamond:

> When I began bird watching in the Kutubu area, I anticipated that my main goal would be to determine how much less numerous these species were inside the area of Chevron's oil fields, facilities, and pipeline than outside it.

Instead, I discovered to my astonishment these species are much more numerous inside the Chevron area than anywhere else that I have visited on the island of New Guinea except for a few remote uninhabited areas. The only place that I have seen tree kangaroos in the wild in Papua New Guinea, in my 40 years there, is within a few miles of Chevron camps; elsewhere, they are the first mammal to become shot out by hunters, and those few surviving learn to be active only at night, but I saw them active during the day in the Kutubu area. Pesquet's Parrot, the New Guinea Harpy Eagle, birds of paradise, hornbills, and large pigeons are common in the immediate vicinity of the oil camps... In effect, the Kutubu oil field functions as by far the largest and most rigorously controlled national park in Papua New Guinea.[152]

---

[152] Ibid., 445-446.

Stewardship vs. Lootership
(Dan)

Mindlessly degrading the natural world the way we have been is no different than a bird degrading its own nest, a fox degrading its own den, a beaver degrading its own dam.

We can't keep doing that and assume that it is just happening "over there." [153]

Thomas Friedman

Anti-Global Warming is a Religion Too!

Although we agreed not to debate global warming, Noah managed to bring it up several times. While I understand his purposes in doing so, I just can't let him get away with so many comments without saying something. Noah has, perhaps correctly, shown that many liberals accept global warming as fact,, even though they know as little about it as I do. Noah goes so far as to call belief in global warming a keystone of "the religion of secular environmentalism". However, there exists an equally powerful assertion, on the conservation end of things, that global warming is NOT something to worry about.

The over-zealous dismissal of global warming is just as unfounded by conservatives who know nothing of climate science. I will go so far as to call this a key doctrine of the "conservative anti-environmentalism religion" or whatever label you want to give it. The dismissal of all things environmental is much too common among conservatives. The instant denial of global warming is as annoying to me as global warming believers are to Noah.

---

[153] Friedman, *Hot, Flat, and Crowded*, 153.

What Liberals Care About

While liberal environmentalists care deeply about the environment, we do consider people to be a part of that environment. We do not prioritize the environment above people. This earth is where we live and it is the only earth we have. Our concern for the environment is a concern for people, both of our current generation and for future generations.

Noah opened his comments on the environment with the following: "What separates us from liberals is not a difference in solutions, but a difference in how we prioritize them." I can agree with that. However, his next paragraph says that the conservative view is grounded in scripture. I hope he was not implying that the liberal view is not grounded in scripture. Then again, don't all sides believe their view is "grounded in scripture," modern or ancient? Isn't that part of what makes each issue in this book so much fun?

Let me quote just a few scriptures that support my views on the environment:

> It pleaseth God that he hath given all these things unto man; for unto this end were they made to be used, with judgment, not to excess, neither by extortion. (D&C 59:20)

This sums up the liberal view on the environment: that the earth should be treated with respect, "with judgment, not to excess."

Furthermore, we liberals believe that humans are, in fact, powerful enough to cause irreversible harm to the earth. History is rife with man-made environmental catastrophes (I will cover a few of them in this chapter). No doubt, much of it was in ignorance of the harm to the environment, although usually motivated by the usual: power, greed and idolatry.

But now, more than any other time in earth's history, we are capable of seeing the harm that we are causing and we are more capable of fixing our mistakes. Refusing not to do so is a sin and we will reap the consequences, regardless of how much homage we pay to the gods of capitalism and technology.

I just know there are conservatives who read that last sentence the wrong way. I considered re-phrasing it, but I'd rather make a point. First, let me say that I do not necessarily equate capitalism and technology with carved stone idols, in the sense that idols are inert and, essentially, useless. Capitalism and technology are tools and useful ones. So, what I said in that last paragraph was not just a typical liberal swipe at capitalism and technology. Well, maybe it was a bit of a swipe but it was more than that.

Let me put it this way: I do not believe in magic. And the only miracles I believe in, originate with God. It seems like conservatives often expect capitalism to work magic for them and expect miracles from technology. Technology does give me hope and capitalism (within certain constraints) is a powerful institution for the good of the majority. However, these are the institutions of men. And it appears to me, that conservatives put their faith, or rather, show their faith in science and/or capitalism. They allow themselves or others to "degrade the nest" and just expect capitalism and technology to magically clean up after them.

I believe we have to own up to our mistakes, whether economic or environmental. I have hope in God, in people and their institutions and cultures that give us such security right here and now. While I hope for the best, I do plan for the worst. If history has shown us anything, it is that we, as a species and as children of God, are powerful and capable of self-destruction. Still, history has also shown a few examples of cultures that had the foresight to realize their mistakes and avoided environmental catastrophe. There are even examples of victory within the last few decades. It's not all gloom and doom.

Environmentalism in the Scriptures

"The earth is full," says the conservative, quoting scripture, "...and there is enough and to spare..." (D&C 104:17). Case closed!

Case closed? No. Something is missing here. Quoting that scripture by itself like that is like quoting one of several scriptures in *The Book of Mormon* that proclaim that the Nephites "will prosper in the land." Well, despite that promise, the Nephites were utterly wiped out. How can that be? Because that's not the whole scripture. Every promise is predicated upon a principle of obedience. As most members know, the promise to the Nephites that they would prosper in the land was conditional *inasmuch as they keep the commandments.*

Likewise, God will fulfill his promise that "the earth is full" with "enough to spare," but only upon conditions of righteousness. In fact, the Lord gives some very specific conditions of righteousness in the very same section 104 of the Doctrine and Covenants. Let's find out what those conditions are and give verse 17 some context by reading D&C 104:14-18:

> *I, the Lord, stretched out the heavens, and built the earth, my very handiwork; and all things therein are mine.*
>
> *And it is my purpose to provide for my saints, for all things are mine.*
>
> *But it must needs be done in mine own way; and behold this is the way that I, the Lord, have decreed to provide for my saints, that the poor shall be exalted, in that the rich are made low.*
>
> *For the earth is full, and there is enough and to spare; yea, I prepared all things, and have given unto the children of men to be agents unto themselves.*
>
> *Therefore, if any man shall take of the abundance which I have made, and impart not his portion, according to the law of my gospel, unto the poor and the needy, he shall, with the wicked, lift up his eyes in hell, being in torment.*

Those are some serious conditions. I would imagine that capitalists are not only uninterested in such conditions, but more than likely repulsed by them. I mean, these conditions do sound a bit, dare I say it, *socialist* in practice.

RESPECT FOR THE EARTH, NOT WORSHIP

If a bird's nest chance to be before thee in the way in any tree, or on the ground... thou shalt... let the mother go, and take the young to thee; that it may be well with thee, and that thou mayest prolong thy days.

Deuteronomy 22:6-7

There are plenty of "earth worshiping environmentalists" out there. Clearly, members of the Church are not in that camp. We agreed, back in the economics chapter, that conservative views on economics and money do not necessarily equate to "worship of the dollar". Likewise, an environmentalist Mormon does not worship the earth. But, the earth is God's creation. We are stewards of this earth. The capitalist idea of an "ownership society," as President Bush touted, leads to the idea that we humans own the earth or at least parts of it (the parts that we consider useful to our own ambitions).

Let us look at a few examples of environmental degradation that have occurred in recent years. The following two examples deal mainly with the exploitation of the ocean. What is different about the earth's oceans is that we have not had the technology to harvest its vast resources until relatively recently, particularly the past 100 years, beginning with steam-powered vessels.

Blue Whales

Railroads and trains often come to mind when one thinks of steam engines. But, the greatest beneficiaries of the steam engine have been ocean-going vessels. Obviously, there was fishing and whaling before steam-powered vessels came along. But when they did, it was an entirely new ball game.

Before steam powered vessels, whaling ships were too slow to hunt down the two fastest sea animals that have ever lived, namely the blue whale and the fin whale.

Before steam powered vessels, whaling ships were never successful at even catching up to some animals in the ocean, much less hunting down the two fastest and largest sea animals that have ever lived, namely the blue whale and the fin whale.

With steam powered vessels, both of these creatures were finally within our grasp. During the early part of the 20th century, whalers mowed down the blue whale population as if it was inexhaustible. The numbers are staggering. Blue whales are now 0.1% of what they were a hundred years ago.[154]

It is ironic that the biggest factor that saved most whales from extinction was petroleum, which replaced whale oil. However, extinction may already be inevitable for most whale species.

---

[154] Fothergill, *Blue Planet*, 46-47.

While gray whales have made a complete comeback, they are the exception. Despite a ban on whaling, most whale species have not made any kind of comeback at all.[155]

Cod Fish

Codfish was, for many years, the target fish of the north Atlantic and is an example whose environmental impact is even more obvious. Cod are caught by dragging large nets along the bottom of the ocean. When it comes to mass netting, it takes four pounds of "catch" to provide one pound of food. In other words, when fishing boats haul up the line and sort through their findings, 75% of what they catch is commercially useless to them so they just throw it back, dead or alive.[156]

Today, there is no more cod fishing because populations have been decimated. That resource is gone, at least for now, but perhaps permanently, if we are not careful. This is bad news for us.

The conservative answer to the cod decimation is "the market will find a substitute." Well, the overlooked problem is the fact that the market will have to find more than just a substitute for cod but for other resources that depended on cod for their survival such as kelp forests and the myriad of other sea life that depend on kelp forests.

Kelp itself is a fast growing plant and has been used as a renewable resource by humans for centuries. One of kelp's most dangerous predators is the sea urchin, that spiky cousin of the starfish. What keeps the sea urchins in check? Codfish. Without a large cod population, the sea urchin population explodes and devours not only kelp forest but coral reefs as well. Cod are a long-lived species but they are also slow to reproduce. So, until their population recovers, kelp forests and coral populations will have difficulty in recovering.[157] The market must now find a substitute for a great deal more than just the codfish.

---

155 Maxeiner, *Life Counts*, 102-103.
156 Earle, *Sustainable Sea (2005 Chautauqua Lecture)*.
157 Kurlansky, *Cod.*

THE ECONOMICS OF ENVIRONMENTAL DEGRADATION

I do not intend to imply that the whalers or cod anglers should be demonized for their actions. They were not necessarily aware of the destructive consequences of their overfishing. They were exploiting resources they assumed were endless and probably didn't understand the power of their new fishing technology. It is now painfully obvious that these resources are not endless.

My point is not that we should stop utilizing the earth or the oceans. My point is simple: we should learn from our mistakes, realize that nature has its own economy and we, humans and children of God, should be just as concerned about an ecosystem crashing, as we are of the stock market crashing. But no. Instead, conservatives chant slogans like "The Market Will Find a Way". It's the same old Republican tactic: using economics as propaganda, holding it up as a magic device instead of a scientific tool.

There is no economic law that ensures that the market will always find the solution. The market is made up of people. And people, well, they can go either way, now, can't they?

The Market Will Find a Way!?

Still many conservatives answer to resource depletion is just an apathetic shrug. "Big deal," they say. "The earth is ours, saith the Lord. The market will find a way."

I do agree that the market will always find a way. But which way? What if the "market's way" is catastrophic? Water will find a way down hill. But when a river starts flowing through your back yard and finally wipes out your harvest, there's no comfort from the phrase "the water found a way."

You see, when a resource is at risk of extinction, us big government progressives are more than willing to call upon the power of government in order to... ahem... *force* the market (as a canal forces a river to change direction) in such a way as to avoid the complete extermination of a resource. I'm not talking pink newts here. I mean valuable resources "for the use of man". I am for government intervention for better management of the environment. Without a good "preemptive strike," aimed at protecting endangered recourses, the magical market is left to its own devices and has been known to wipe out some resources completely. And once a resource is gone, the choice will be forced.

An Unexpected Victim of Outsourcing

Now, a quick note on the other end of things. While resource depletion can be a serious problem, what we do with our waste products should be taken seriously as well.

Did you know that the U.S. pays China to take our garbage? Why not? Out of sight out of mind, right? Each year, millions of pounds of old computer parts, electronics, etc fill up their land, not ours. It's cheap. Why not have them take our garbage? At least we're not polluting America right? Wrong. We need to be concerned about polluting other countries as it still affects global pollution. What if we were to inherit China as our own land? We'd be in a big mess.

As mentioned previously, the United States has much concern over pollution, child slavery, environmental degradation, when it occurs on their land. However, it seems they have no problem outsourcing it to other countries. Once again from Jared Diamond's *Collapse*:

> In September 2002 a Chinese customs office in Zhejiang Province recorded a 400-ton shipment of "electronic garbage" originating from the U.S., and consisting of scrap electronic equipment and parts such as broken or obsolete color TV sets, computer monitors, photocopiers, and keyboards.[158]

TRUE STORIES OF ECOLOGICAL SUICIDE

Many factors have contributed to societal downfalls, but environmental collapse is often overlooked probably because it occurs simultaneously with economic collapse. And environmental degradation may even be the primary cause. Here are some historical cases of ecological suicide.

---

[158] Diamond, *Collapse*, 370.

Ancient American Desolation

The Book of Mormon confirms that environmental catastrophe is a historical fact. Specifically, during the time of Helaman:

> *Yea, and even they did spread forth into all parts of the land, into whatever parts it had not been rendered desolate and without timber, because of the many inhabitants who had before inherited the land.*
>
> *And now no part of the land was desolate, save it were for timber; but because of the greatness of the destruction of the people who had before inhabited the land it was called desolate.*
>
> *And there being but little timber upon the face of the land, nevertheless the people who went forth became exceedingly expert in the working of cement; therefore they did build houses of cement, in the which they did dwell.*
>
> *And the people who were in the land northward did dwell in tents, and in houses of cement, and they did suffer whatsoever tree should spring up upon the face of the land that it should grow up, that in time they might have timber to build their houses, yea, their cities, and their temples, and their synagogues, and their sanctuaries, and all manner of their buildings.*
>
> *And it came to pass as timber was exceedingly scarce in the land northward, they did send forth much by the way of shipping.* (Helaman 3:5-7, 9-10)

The desolation of the land is similar (perhaps identical) to the deforestation that archeologists have discovered among the Mayan civilization. The Mayans fell victim to what is known as "the tragedy of the commons," in which a multitude of groups, tribes, or individuals, while acting in their own self-interest, can needlessly destroy a shared resource.

Imagine the shepherd saying something like, "Someone's going to use that hill to graze their sheep, so it might as well be me." Without an entity such as government to protect a common resource, individuals or competing groups can easily destroy a resource and quickly. I have already cited blue whales and codfish as prime examples that illustrate "the commons dilemma."

Of course, when it comes to the Jaredites desolating the land northward, or warring bands of Mayans deforesting their lands, one could say that they got what was coming to them. Well, environmental awareness is not important in order to "save people from themselves" but rather for reasons that are, well, economic.

I remember an interview in which Thomas Sowell said, "I don't want people making decisions who don't pay the price of their decisions..."[159] When a company can make a profit by manufacturing something and one of the costs of manufacturing is polluting the environment (air, ground or water), they are not "paying the price of their decisions." They are skipping out on that cost and the public pays for it. A broader populace may reap the cost of air pollution, while a more narrow population close by may reap the costs of water pollution by being the unfortunate ones downstream.

This isn't the tragedy of the commons where everyone acts foolishly and everyone pays for it. This is passing the cost to others.

International Logging

It costs so much less to buy logs from countries with less regulation, especially when these countries do not require reforestation. Lumber is, of course, cheaper where you don't have to ensure that the forest recuperates. So that's where the international logging corporations go, as reported by Jared Diamond:

> In Southeast Asia and the Pacific islands, large-scale logging is carried out mainly by international logging companies. They operate by leasing logging rights on land still owned by local people, exporting unfinished logs, and not replanting. Much of the value of a log is added on by cutting up and processing it after it has been felled: that is, the unfinished timber sells for far more than the log from which it was cut. Hence exporting unfinished logs deprives local people and the national government of most of the potential value of their resource. Companies frequently obtain the required government logging permit by bribing government officials, and then proceeding

---

[159] Sowell, "1990 Booknotes Interview with Thomas Sowell."

to build roads and cut logs beyond the boundaries of the area actually leased.[160]

So, a logging ship is sent in and negotiations for logging rights start immediately. Local leaders are wined and dined. They are tempted with food, luxurious accommodations, and prostitutes until they sign. Logging commences and the resource is dispensed.

Irresponsible logging is not good for the US, nor is it good for the countries in which the logs come from; not to mention the environment and the resources we will lack in the future as supplies continue to dwindle without replenishment. It does make a good business for dishonest people, but their practices need to be publicized so things can change.[161]

There is, however, a bit of good news on this front. Some countries have resisted the temptations of large timber companies, eager to pay large sums for logging rights. Countries like Surinam, Georgia and Mongolia have seen value in biodiversity by setting aside large amounts of land as protected areas.[162]

Ethnic Cleansing or Ecological Collapse?

No one ever thinks of the Rwandan genocides of the early 1990s as the consequence of environmental collapse. But that's exactly the claim I am making. There are always other factors, of course. One thing is certain: the tragedy of the Rwandan genocide cannot simply be chalked up to ethnic cleansing.

In 1994, it was estimated that between 800,000 and one million people were killed in the Rwandan genocide. That is, 11% of the total population at the time. If you ask most people what caused the mass killings, the majority will say that it was ethnic hatred; Hutu's killing Tutsi's. However, one village had no Tutsi's in it and still lost 5% of its population to the genocide.[163] So, this doesn't appear to be a mere case of ethnic cleansing.

---

[160] Diamond, *Collapse*, 374.

[161] Ibid., 468-479.

[162] Maxeiner, *Life Counts*, 208-209.

[163] Diamond, *Collapse*, 319.

What if I were to say that the Rwandan genocide was the result of environmental collapse or overpopulation? While an assassination may have sparked the killings, the ultimate cause, the fuel that drove it, may have been the economic hardship and extreme pressure from a depleted and crowded environment, in short, an environmental collapse in the area.

Oddly enough, the people themselves saw a link between relative overpopulation and may have supported the genocide as a way of ridding the surplus of people. Even Rwandan's viewed it as a population issue, as Jared Diamond testified when he visited the country:

> It is not rare, even today, to hear Rwandans argue that a war is necessary to wipe out an excess of population and to bring numbers into line with the available land resources.
>
> [P]opulation pressure, human environmental impacts, and drought [were] ultimate causes, which make people chronically desperate and are like the gunpowder inside the powder keg.[164]

So here, we have a modern example in front of our very eyes, of a holocaust that was driven, not just by ethnic cleansing, but by severe economic pressure, which was driven by the environmental collapse. As I see it, there were two fundamental causes of an enviro-collapse:

First, whether you claim that there are too many people or too little resources, it comes down to the same thing: a bad person-to-resource ratio. And it's exactly what those wacky tree huggers have been screaming about for years.

Second, there's a scarcity-to-knowledge ratio. In other words, if you have the right technology and education, you can get far more from available resources. There are certain farming practices, how the rows are tilled, for example, that would have curbed erosion in Rwanda.

I don't claim to be any kind of expert on Rwanda, genocide, or environmental collapse… or farming techniques. I don't believe in simple causes for this kind of thing. But the cause of caring for and protecting the environment should not be as quickly dis-

---

164 Ibid., 326.

missed and religiously ignored as some conservatives seem to do.

In the end, environment protection is not about the protection of the blue-toothed newt. Rwanda attests to that. Now, the question is, how do we, as a society, go about protecting the environment?

Other Crashes

Deforestation also happened with the Anasazi in northwestern New Mexico. The forest that they cut down hundreds of years ago has never recovered.

The Mayan civilization heavily deforested their environment as well. However, their forests did come back. It just took several hundred years to do so.

One of the most catastrophic and overlooked examples of deforestation is the Fertile Crescent, that is, Iraq and Syria. We think of them and think "desert," but thousands of years ago, the land was much more lush. How else could it have been known as "the breadbasket of the world" and the cradle of humanity? This is where much of agriculture originated.

We are, indeed, capable of destroying resources forever. It may not affect us or our children or grandchildren. But, perhaps we could be environmentalists for the sake of our posterity beyond just a few generations.[165]

TWO KINDS OF STEWARDSHIP: "BOTTOM UP" AND "TOP DOWN"

I understand how conservatives might suffer some indigestion from the phrase "government can be a friend." I have found it useful to use the terminology from Jared Diamond's book *Collapse*. In dealing with environmental management (or mismanagement), Diamond uses the terms "bottom up" and "top down".

---

[165] I can hear it now, "Oh, the Second Coming will be along by then." Why don't you just run up your credit card and eat as much delicious trans-fatty foods as possible while you wait? Using the Lord's Second Coming is one of the worst excuses (if not outright blasphemous) for environmental mismanagement. But I actually hear arguments like that.

Top down refers to environmental management that comes from national governments or international institutions, which might include international corporations. The term bottom up simply means environmental management supervised by locals, often in the private sector. History is replete with successful and unsuccessful examples of both top down and bottom up management of the environment.

One successful example of bottom up (and long-term) management of the environment has been the small island of Tekopia, which has sustained a stable population for thousands of years.

Another example is the center of Papua New Guinea, where farmers have successfully cultivated the central highlands for an estimated 10,000 years.

As for top down, Noah actually brought up several instances of environmental good news brought about by top down management, such as environmental laws brought forth just a few decades ago that give us much cleaner air and water today.

Noah also claims that these good news stories are mostly dismissed by us on the left. This is untrue. Just because environmentalists and liberals are still fighting the good fight, we are not ignoring the good news. In fact, it is encouraging to know we are making some headway and that we are capable of repairing some of the damage that we have done to our own "nest."

However, while there is good news to be had, I still worry about the kind of environmental degradation that is more difficult to notice because the effects span generations. Easter Island offers a tragic example of mostly bottom-up environmental mismanagement by a relatively small population (more on that below).

One of the most conspicuous examples of short-term environmental mismanagement that continues at this very moment is the unsustainable logging of the rainforests of Indonesia, namely Borneo and Sumatra. Forces have driven this destruction from the top: aggressive and irresponsible international logging companies and a weak Indonesian government, which tolerates these logging corporations.[166]

We can also thank the Japanese Shogun for providing a wonderful historical example of successful implementation of top down management. This management turned the tide of deforestation, which was devastating their environment back in the 18th century. Today, despite the fact that Japan is one of the most densely populated countries in the world, they have one of the most forested countries in the world.[167]

Germany has a similar story. Their reforestation project started around the same time as Japan's. But what do those socialist Europeans know, with their centralize government environmental policies!? I am certain that "the market," as conservatives define it, would not have succeeded in paving the way to reforestation at these particular times and places. So, you see, government *can* be a friend. Government and freedom must be evaluated within context of time and place.

Let's wrap this up with my favorite success story of top down environmental management. It is my favorite, you see, because I am a beneficiary. Despite conservatives' dreams of a clean environment without government, today the air and water in the United States is cleaner than ever. And this is precisely because of legislation by the federal government over forty years ago through the Clean Air and Clean Water Acts.[168]

Perhaps the top down management of government can be a friend after all.

---

[166] Diamond, *Collapse*, 475.
[167] Ibid., 297-306.
[168] Easterbrook, *The Progress Paradox*, Intro.

CONCLUSION

As we peer into society's future, we–you and I, and our government–must avoid the impulse to live only for today, plundering, for our own ease and convenience, the precious resources of tomorrow. We cannot mortgage the material assets of our grandchildren without risking the loss also of their political and spiritual heritage. We want democracy to survive for all generations to come, not to become the insolvent phantom of tomorrow.[169]

President Eisenhower

The Tragedy of Easter Island

It was Easter Sunday of 1770 (hence the name) that a Dutch sailor, Jacob Roggeveen, first discovered Easter Island. It is, without hyperbole, the most unique island on the planet, on several accounts. For one thing, it is the most remote island in the world. Even though it is currently a territory of Chile, it is over 2000 miles from Chile's South American coastline. It is 1,200 miles away from the nearest habitable pacific island of Pitcairn.

However, when people think of Easter Island, the first thing that comes to mind is the enormous statues on the island: nearly 900 giant stone statues (Moai) mostly weighing around 10 to 12 tons. The average height of a statue was 13 feet high, while the tallest was 70 feet. How were they made? How were they propped up? There were no trees on the island higher than 12 feet.

One of the misconceptions today is that we still don't know how they were built, leading people to conjecture that aliens built them. But, in fact, the statues were constructed out of quarries of lava rock found near Easter's dormant volcanoes. But lava rock wasn't the only resource used. Giant palm trees were used to transport them to the location and to erect them.

Over the course of 600 years (from 900 to 1500 A.D), the deforestation of the island was so incremental that the inhabitants would have been unaware of it. Yet, by the time Roggeveen came upon the island, all trees were gone. Its stranded population had been decimated by civil war, disease and malnutrition.

---

169 Eisenhower, "Military-Industrial Complex Speech (1961)."

They had built these statues to honor their ancestors. In the end, the islanders cursed their ancestors, toppled their magnificent statues and degraded into cannibalism.

It is easy to see why people have viewed Easter Island as a warning of the kind of environmental catastrophe that may affect or entire planet. Conservatives often say that the market will provide. But no one has yet found a substitute for wood as demonstrated by the Easter Islanders.

The Lord did say "the earth is full with enough to spare..." but this is not a statement without conditions and does not absolve any civilization of the consequences of bad management of the environment.

Wrong Until They Were Right

Let me use a Michael Crichton quote and twist it around a bit so that it sounds like... well, right-wingers on Easter Island who lived back in the days when they were depleting their island of its resources:

> The population bomb, for one. Paul Ehrlich predicted mass starvation in the 1960s. Sixty million Americans starving to death. Didn't happen. Other scientists warned of mass species extinctions by the year 2000. Ehrlich himself predicted that half of all species would become extinct by 2000. Didn't happen. The Club of Rome told us we would run out of raw materials ranging from oil to copper by the 1990s. That didn't happen, either.
>
> It's no surprise that predictions frequently don't come true. But such big ones! And so many! All my life I worried about the decay of the environment, the tragic loss of species, the collapse of ecosystems. It never seemed to end.[170]

Now I'm going to do a bit of a parody by altering Crichton's rhetoric slightly so that it would have applied to Easter Island in, say, the year 1500 A.D., some 400 years after these Polynesians first colonized the island:

> Environmental prophets predicted mass starvation in the 1260s. Six thousand Long Ears starving to death. Didn't happen. Other prophets warned of mass species extinctions by

---

[170] Crichton, "Complexity Theory and Environmental Management."

the year 1300, including the prediction that half of all species would become extinct by 1250. Didn't happen. They also told us we would run out of raw materials ranging from palm oil to timber by the 1290s. That didn't happen, either. No. None of that happened to Easter Island by 1300. Nor did it happen by 1400 or 1500.

It's no surprise that predictions frequently don't come true. But such big ones! And so many! All my life I worried about the decay of the environment, the tragic loss of species, the collapse of ecosystems. It never seemed to end.[171]

Only it did end. And it ended horribly. And, as for the prediction that "half of the species would become extinct by 1250", that actually did happen. The Easter Islanders drove over half of the native animal species into extinction within just a couple hundred years.

If there were any doomsayers on Easter Island (and I believe there were) warning the people of environmental collapse, these party crashers would have been wrong for a good six hundred years... that is, until they were finally, devastatingly right.

Is Easter Island a fair analogy to draw regarding how we treat the earth as a whole? Some will doggedly say no. But keep in mind that, what Easter islanders could deforest with stone tools and 600 years time would take minutes with today's high power tools. We are more dangerous than ever because of our technology.

I conclude with one final warning from (who else?) Jared Diamond:

What has to be remembered is that it's always been hard for humans to know the rate at which they can safely harvest biological resources indefinitely, without depleting them.... Thus, preindustrial peoples who couldn't sustain their resources were guilty not of moral sins... Those failures were tragic, because they caused a collapse in life-style for the people themselves.

Tragic failures become moral sins only if one should have known better from the outset... The past was still a Golden Age, of ignorance, while the present is an Iron Age of willful blindness.

---

171 I'm spoofing the Michael Crichton quote above. Pay attention!

From this point of view it's beyond understanding to see modern societies repeating the past's suicidal ecological mismanagement, with much more powerful tools of destruction in the hands of far more people. It's as if we hadn't already run that particular film many times before in human history, and as if we didn't know the inevitable outcome.[172]

---

[172] Diamond, *The Third Chimpanzee*, 337.

JOINT

How to Win Friends & Influence the Environment

Tough decisions have to be made to protect animals and our economy, so, whenever possible, compromises are sought. The science of conservation should always be tempered by the art of compromise as we seek truly win-win, entrepreneurial environmental solutions.[173]

Newt Gingrich and Terry Maple

Agreements

First, Dan and Noah both agree that, from the fall of Adam, the human race has been practically as destructive as a meteor when it comes to the extinction of other species on this planet. In many cases, we have only recently learned the magnitude of our destructive capabilities. Now that understand our own history better, we should work together and be humble enough to learn from our mistakes. After all, both sides agree that our primary concern should be for our own species and that this must be done by showing respect for this planet and its other inhabitants.

It turns out that Dan and Noah actually agree quite a bit more on the environment than any other subject covered so far. They even agree with each other's boasts regarding their own side, as well as their criticisms toward the other. To put it simply, on the issue of the environment, both conservatives and liberals have serious problems as well as useful tools and solutions. We should listen to each other.

In the introduction, Dan and Noah both admitted to a great deal of ignorance on the subject of global warming. However, there is equal frustration with liberals who accept global warm-

---

[173] Gingrich and Maple, *A contract with the Earth*, 53.

ing with unquestioning zeal and conservatives who dismiss it with the same blind faith.

They found agreement with Michael Crichton regarding complexity theory and environmental management. Dan is as distressed as anyone with the mismanagement of Yellowstone National Park. Dealing with complex systems like the environment (or a teenager) requires the humility to be open to paradigm shifts, to change strategy and roll with the punches.

Noah conceded to the idea that government action may sometimes be the only feasible way to protect the public environment. Similarly, if the laws (or lack of laws) allow companies or individuals to gain by hurting the environment, in democratic societies, at least, the citizens are ultimately responsible. Both credit and blame belong to the citizens.

Both Dan and Noah agreed with the following statement from the book *Life Counts*, which concerns both economics and environmentalism:

> Still more encouraging are the efforts the poorest countries are making to protect their natural resources. [Unfortunately] ...many of these areas are still imperiled because their boundaries exist only on maps. Often it has not been possible to keep settlers, prospectors for raw materials, and poachers out of the parks. When protected areas are established, poorer countries, in particular often lack the means to manage them.
>
> But even so, we can maintain our resources worldwide with the funds currently available. "The impediment here is the lack of a political will to change the structure of governmental expenditures," says a team of economists and biologists at the universities of Cambridge and Sheffield. ... [T]hey noted that, worldwide, **between $950 billion and $1,450 billion are spent annually on subsidies that not only burden the public budget, but also harm nature. These "perverse subsidies" go, for example, to agriculture, fishing, and unnecessary transport, and keep prices artificially low—beneath actual market levels.** With only about a quarter of the money spent on these subsidies, the British researchers maintain, the planet's biodiversity could be stabi-

lized by establishing larger and more effectively protected reserves.[174] (emphasis added)

Dan and Noah also agree that a more positive strategy should be
undertaken to solving environmental problems through stories,
as exhibited by the following statement from the book *Break-
through*:

> Through their stories, institutions, and policies, environmen-
> talists constantly reinforce the sense that nature is something
> separate from, and victimized by, humans. This paradigm de-
> fines ecological problems as the inevitable consequence of
> humans violating nature. Think of the verbs associated with
> environmentalism and conservation: "stop," "restrict," "re-
> verse," "prevent," "regulate," and "constrain." All of them di-
> rect our thinking to stopping the bad, not creating the good.
> When environmentalists do speak in positive tones, it is usu-
> ally about things like clean air and water, or "preserving na-
> ture"— all concepts that define human activity as an intrusion
> on, or a contaminant of, a separate and once pure nature.[175]

Misunderstandings

Dan assumed that when conservatives talk of economic realities,
they just mean free-market capitalism. Some conservatives, ignorantly, do mean that. And plenty of liberals, when they hear the
word "economics" do, ignorantly, assume that. But, what economics is truly concerned about is that we must be aware of the
trade-offs and unseen costs of environmental policies (to people
and/or to the environment). Economics is a tool for measuring
one value against another.

On a similar note, environmentalists might be uncomfortable
with assigning dollar amounts ("price tags") to environmental
resources or species. But using the dollar as a measuring stick is
simply more useful than trying to figure out how many bats a
dolphin is worth.

Noah was mistaken in his assumption that environmentalists
care more about birds than they do about people. On the contrary, one motive for environmentalists is an intense consideration for people.

---

[174] Maxeiner, *Life Counts*, 208-209.
[175] Shellenberger and Nordhaus, *Break Through*, 6.

Agreeing to Disagree

We must agree to disagree on the role and the extent of government. We actually agree that (unlike redistribution of wealth, etc) the environment that we all share is one area where government has its place (even at the federal level). Not all conservatives would agree with Noah on this, but many do. However, it is the extent and timing of government intervention where we find disagreement.

Noah believes that power over the environment should remain in the hands of the people, that is, the private sector. That should be the default. If government intervention becomes necessary, disenfranchised landowners (for example) should be more than fully compensated. Even so, whatever the government intervention, it should be treated with caution (such as having a time limit). And whenever a free-market solution arises for a given environmental problem, government should step aside immediately.

On the other hand, Dan believes that the government should be proactive in spotting environmental problems and in acting before it is too late. Too many resources, once consumed, are gone forever. And that is a cost borne by everyone.

The Good News

There is plenty of good news about the environment. For example, most forms of air pollution (with the exception of carbon dioxide) have been going down over the past few decades. Our waterways are also cleaner than ever.[176]

Our collective concern about the environment is higher than ever. And the opportunity to learn from the mistakes of the past is more extensive than it ever has been.

Jane Goodall has spent much of her life in Africa, studying and living among chimpanzees. She has seen both the wonders and the horrors that the continent has to offer. She has traveled the world and has seen environmental destruction on a large scale and over the course of her long life. People have often

---

[176] Easterbrook, *The Progress Paradox*, 41.

asked her if she has any hope for the future, for chimpanzees, for the people of Africa, for the world at large. The environmental health of our planet is one of her greatest concerns, but she has, nevertheless, found reasons for hope. In her book, *Reasons for Hope*, she outlines four[177] such reasons:

- The human brain
- The resilience of nature
- The enthusiasm of young people worldwide
- The indomitable human spirit

If anyone has found reason to despair, it is Jane Goodall. So, if she retains hope, why can't we? Her book goes into detail about her reasons for hope as well as her reasons for concern. But, it does more than that: it offers the willing reader actual solutions. For that reason, above all, I recommend it.

We live during a marvelous time. So much information is available. Yet, so much of that information is irrelevant or useless. Wading through it all to sift the good information from the useless is time consuming. After a while, particularly when it comes to the environment, it all starts to sound the same.

So, by way of saving the reader some time and monotony, here are some other books on the environment that should offer something unique and unexpected. Each of these books has the potential to change the way the reader thinks about the world, regardless of whether you are a liberal or a conservative. At the very least, each book has the potential of offending conservatives and liberals alike; a sure sign of their relatively non-partisan nature. They all offer a paradigm shift (one of these books is actually waterproof) as well as practical advice.

- *Reasons for Hope: A Spiritual Journey*
  by Jane Goodall

- *Break Through: From the Death of
  Environmentalism to the Politics of Possibility*
  by Ted Nordhaus and Michael Shellenberger

---

[177] Goodall, *Reason for Hope*, 233.

- *Collapse: How Societies Choose to Fail or Succeed* by Jared Diamond
- *Cradle to Cradle: Remaking the Way We Make Things* by William McDonough and Michael Braungart

CONCLUSION: DEALING WITH DESPOLERS

[W]e should not set our sights on rebuilding an environment from the past but… on shaping a world to live in for the future.[178]

Charles C. Mann

There are many battlefronts in the fight to preserve the resources of the natural world for future generations. Working with allies to save dolphins or majestic snow leopards is one thing. Dealing with potential enemies, while trying to preserve the less popular species, is a whole different challenge; especially when it comes to less cute and lovable creatures like, for example, bats!

Actually, some bat species are quite attractive. In particular, the larger fruit bats have the look and temperament of a small dog or a fox with wings. And that's exactly why fruit bats are also called flying foxes. But most bat species are small and… not quite so cute. But they do have a virtue that is far too underappreciated.

"Kill as Many as You Can"

Many years ago, a bat biologist approached an old Tennessee farmer to ask permission to study the bat colony located in a cave on his property. The farmer replied with, "Sure. Kill as many as you can!"

The biologist refrained from saying anything, at least not until he had found the cave and properly completed his observations. When he had finished, he was eager to get back to that farmer. No doubt, this farmer had killed his share of bats whenever he got the chance. Most often, when people fear bats, it is due to superstition or misinformation, not from any actual harm the bats may have caused. On the contrary, bats can be tremen-

---

[178] Mann, *1491*, 366.

dously beneficial to people. But... have you ever tried to convince an old farmer to change his mind about anything lately?

This biologist knew exactly how he could get this farmer's attention: bat poo, what else? Okay, technically, poo isn't the right word. It's called *guano*. And to be truly accurate, it would be better to say that this guano consisted of indigestible remains of the bats' diet. With plenty of it on the floor of the cave, this scientist scooped up a handful of... droppings, ready to give this farmer a lesson he would never forget.

It could have been an uphill battle with this old Tennessee farmer, but this was no ordinary bat biologist. He was Dr. Merlin Tuttle, the founder of Bat Conservation International. And he had a unique and powerful philosophy when it came to dealing with despoilers of the environment, from poachers to ignorant farmers. He prefers never to describe anything he does as fighting. As Sun Tzu tells us in *The Art of War*, "The skillful leader subdues the enemy's troops without any fighting."

So, what did Dr. Tuttle do with this handful of bat guano? Well, he walked up to up to the farmer and said, "Excuse me, I'm trying to identify what kind of insects these bats are eating. Could you identify these remains?"

The farmer gazed at the wing cases and exoskeletons. His jaw dropped and his eyes widened in shock and amazement. This farmer was not trained in insect forensics, but he knew exactly what kind of insect remains he was looking at. They were the remains of his most notorious insect pests, among them, potato bugs!

The farmer let out a string of swear words before asking, "How many bugs do them suckers eat?"

"Well, this species can eat up to 1,000 insects in a single hour," said Dr. Tuttle. "But the actual number would vary depending on the size of the insect and the bat's reproductive cycle. Mothers with babies may eat twice as much as others."

"How many bats are there?" asked the farmer.

"Well, according to my measurements, the number of bats in that cave is close to 50,000."

Hmmm. 50,000 bats, multiplied by 1,000 insects per hour, multiplied by... how many hours per day? You know, there's really no need to crunch those numbers is there. This farmer was already sold! Merlin didn't need to say another word. There was no need to explain the bat life cycle and the ecology of the surrounding habitat. As for reciting the Endangered Species Act... what's that? From that day on, that Tennessee farmer would be protecting what he now referred to as *his* bat colony.[179]

Turned out not to be such an uphill battle, after all. Sun Tzu was right about winning without fighting. Sun Tzu also said, "What the ancients called a clever fighter is one who not only wins, but excels in winning with ease."

Merlin Tuttle may not like to describe anything he does as "fighting", but he sure knows how to win... with ease!

Overhunting of Samoan Flying Foxes

Several years ago, in American Samoa, the fruit bat population was being absolutely devastated by commercial hunting. Two species had already gone extinct in the South Pacific.

Some members of the Peace Corps were working in Samoa doing what they could to protect the local environment, among other things. One day they saw several Samoans coming back from a bat hunt. It looked as if the entire group of hunters had killed no more than three bats, far less than the year before. This was a sure sign that the bats' numbers were dwindling fast. Yet, these Samoan hunters continued to take hunting expeditions. These people were not starving but were, in fact, fairly well-to-do and simply enjoyed hunting. They sold the bats commercially to pay for their shotgun shells and beer.

The two Peace Corps volunteers–either very brave or very foolish–walked right up to the hunting party and gave them a good tongue-lashing for their careless overhunting. When they noticed a mainlander with these hunters, they were especially outraged. Since the Samoans paid them little attention, they chewed the mainlander out for being a part of such devastation. To their surprise, the very next day, the man who they assumed was part of the problem came to their door to formally introduce himself.

---

[179] Tuttle, "Multiple correspondences in 2010."

It was none other than, you guessed it, Dr. Merlin Tuttle. He told them that he was in American Samoa with a group of conservationists in order to do something about the plight of the flying foxes.

What kind of a conservationist tags along with commercial hunters while they continued to decimate a clearly endangered species? What was Dr Tuttle doing?

Merlin explained that he was hanging around with the hunters, and would be joining them for the next two nights as well, with the hope of finding a way to work with them to protect the bats. (It should be noted that, Merlin was not merely hanging out with these hunters for the sake of conservation. He did, in fact, enjoy their company as well.)

So, how does that help protect the bats?

Well, Merlin had already made some progress. The night before, they had only shot three bats and one of the hunters commented, "Oh, you're too late. You should have been here last year. We could have shot a hundred in a single hour."

"Really?" said Merlin. "What's the problem, do you think?"

"Oh," said one of the hunters. "Too many of us are shooting too many."

By the third night, Merlin had become great friends with these hunters. He mentioned to them that he and his friends would be meeting with the governor of American Samoa in the next few days. He asked the hunters if they would like him to say anything to the governor about game laws to ensure bats to hunt in the future.

Keep in mind that, at this point, Merlin hadn't mentioned that he and his friends were conservationists. He just talked about the need to ensure a viable bat population for future hunting. This tactic did not sit well with Merlin's fellow conservationists, but it was far better than not gaining hunter cooperation and thus potentially losing the bats.

So, Merlin and his associates were able to walk into the office of the Governor of Samoa with a proposal for game laws for flying foxes. Naturally, the governor's initial fears were that the hunters wouldn't stand for it. Imagine his surprise when he learned that this proposal actually *originated* with the hunters themselves. Legislation passed within 6 months.

The story doesn't end there. Once they became friends, with shared concerns, these hunters became instrumental in establishing a national park in American Samoa that went from the coral reefs to the cloud forest mountaintops. Regarding this sanctuary for wildlife, Merlin said,

> And guess what? There's not a snowball's chance in you-know-where that we could have ever had this park without some of my favorite friends, the former commercial hunters of Samoa.[180]

Not only that, these hunters eventually participated in a voluntary five-year moratorium on all bat hunting.

If the Peace Corps volunteers thought they were doing any good by chewing out those Samoans, they found out that there was a better way. This was the ingenious conservation strategy of Dr. Merlin Tuttle.

The Philosophy of Dr. Merlin Tuttle,

So what inspired Dr. Tuttle to use such friendly and effective methods of solving problems and working with enemies? In his own words:

> When I founded Bat Conservation International, bats weren't very popular. Just about everyone in the world was, at least, a potential enemy. And when you don't have any power, you learn to be an incredibly good diplomat. And when you don't have any friends, you learn how to make friends even if you have to go to your enemies.
>
> It's so easy to blame people for the past. There's not a one of us here today who hasn't done something that was environmentally damaging that we did in our ignorance at some time in the past that we'd be really embarrassed to have shown on TV right now.
>
> It's amazing how much we take such pleasure in whipping and beating people for past mistakes instead of giving them a chance to solve future problems.
>
> And believe me, miners, loggers, oilmen, hunters–people who have so long been reviled by conservationists–are the

---

180 Tuttle, *The Incredible World of Bats (2002 Chautauqua Lecture)*.

prime targets for those who want to make real progress. There's nobody who feels better [about] finally being included in doing something good.

But you know, in every group, in every group there are people who share our concerns. And if we assume that they are our enemy before we ask any questions, they'll always be our enemies![181]

Am I not destroying my enemies when I make them my friends?

Abraham Lincoln

---

[181] Ibid.

CHAPTER 4

MUSINGS OF A SCHIZOPHRENIC

By proving contraries, truth is made manifest.[182]

Joseph Smith

If you chose to skip the *Optional Introduction* and are otherwise unaware of the... you know, the method I used throughout Part I, it is time that you knew the truth: Dan the Democrat/progressive and Noah the Republican/conservative are both make believe. That's right. Imaginary. I created a couple of fictional characters to act as advocates for two sides of each issue. I call this *the schizophrenic method.* I spent the last 3 chapters utilizing this method to fulfill one of the primary goals of this book:

> Exhibit ways of understanding opposing viewpoints. In fact, this book demonstrates one specific and powerful tool for understanding opposing viewpoints.[183]

Besides being a convenient way of exploring the issues, this method turned out to be quite an adventure. It was certainly fun for me. But it was also one of the most educational experiences of my life.

Incidentally, if you think this is a weird and ridiculous practice, bear in mind that I got this idea from a General Authority. I refer you to the April 2006 General Conference talk by Elder Robert S. Wood:

> I recall that as a graduate student I wrote a critique of an important political philosopher. It was clear that I disagreed with him. My professor told me that my paper was good, but not good enough. Before you launch into your criticism, she said, you must first present the strongest case for the position you are opposing, one that the philosopher himself could accept. I redid the paper. I still had important differences with the philosopher, but I understood him better, and I saw the strengths

---

[182] Smith and Roberts, *History of the Church of Jesus Christ of Latter Day Saints*, 6:428.
[183] See goal #5 in the Prologue.

and virtues, as well as limitations, of his belief. I learned a lesson that I've applied across the spectrum of my life.[184]

What this professor was urging Elder Wood to do was a thought experiment: to taking upon yourself the opposite view, arguing from that perspective using arguments that the person with that view would accept, rather than building up a straw man.

In essence, the first three chapters are my own personal homage to that simple mental exercise recommended by Elder Wood and his professor.

THE DEVILCRAT'S ADVOCATE

If you can learn a simple trick, Scout, you'll get along a lot better with all kinds of folks. You never really understand a person until you consider things from his point of view... until you climb inside of his skin and walk around in it.[185]

Atticus Finch

Harper Lee, through one of the greatest heroes in fiction, gave this simple advice in the classic book *To Kill a Mockingbird*. Not only did Atticus recommend such empathy but he relentlessly practiced it over and over throughout the entire book. He applied it to everyone, even and especially those who despised him personally. Atticus was always doing his best to see the world from another person's point of view. And if there's one thing the book captured more than the movie version of *To Kill a Mockingbird* (still a fantastic movie), it was that this hyper-empathy had a softening effect on Atticus himself.

So it was with my own thought experiment, my schizophrenic exercise in Part I of this book. Not only did I learn that there is no better way to understand another point of view than joining their ranks and fighting their cause for a while, but doing so was actually spiritually enlightening. And I don't mean spiritual in some mystical top of the mountains way: I mean that it was a *pleasurable* experience (eventually, at least) because it lifted the burden of bitterness from my shoulders. It was a relief, literally.

184 Wood, "Instruments of the Lord's Peace."
185 Lee, *To Kill a Mockingbird*, 33.

But I had to establish and follow some firm ground rules, as follows:

Rule #1: Emotional Conviction

Someone once asked actor Robert Duvall what makes him a good actor. His answer: "What's good acting? It's what's real." So, what I am doing here is a bit like acting. And a great actor never wants to be caught "acting." While the camera is rolling, or while he is on the stage, he is not acting. He *is* the character.

To successfully portray these opinions faithfully, I have in fact invested my emotions first and then my intellect. On each issue, and for each side, I had to force myself to *feel* that I was right, with emotional conviction. *Then* I gathered facts and arguments that supported my opinion on the issue. Seems completely irrational, doesn't it? Decide on my opinion first and then build up the logic to back it up? Believe it or not, that is actually more how our brains work than we would like to admit.[186]

In fact, the human brain works far more efficiently with emotions, than in their absence. There have been cases of brain damage that result in a loss of emotion. Such individuals lose nothing in terms of IQ, but they are quite handicapped.[187] So goes a modernized version of a classic Jefferson Skelton quote:

> Were they truly purged from all emotion, Spock and the rest of those Vulcans would starve to death from the simple act of having to choose between chocolate and vanilla ice cream, endlessly debating the pros and cons of each flavor.

Investing emotionally in a particular side of an argument not only allowed me to defend that position with real vigor, it also drove me to discover new and better intellectual arguments in defense of that position. I cannot tell you how many times I discovered an argument that I had never before considered confronted or noticed. All of this was because I had literally manufactured an emotional conviction first. This was particularly the case with Dan's arguments in the economics chapter.

---

[186] Gazzaniga, *The Ethical Brain (2005 Chautauqua Lecture)*.
[187] Grandin, *Animals in Translation*, 198-199.

Rule #2: Intellectual Sincerity

Emotional conviction or not, I was determined that my characters (mostly Dan) could only make arguments that I, myself, could sincerely and honestly accept as reasonable argument, even if I did not agree entirely. With each topic, I asked myself one question: "How could I possibly hold such & such view?"

This was different from asking the question, "How could *somebody else* possibly hold this view?" The problem with thinking about it that way is that *somebody else* could just be an idiot. Either that or ignorant.

Indeed, one of the most difficult and frustrating things about dialogue with an opposing party is the assumption or worry that they do not yet know what you know, do not understand what you understand or have never read what you have read. But two people who disagree about an issue while having a similar intellectual background on that issue, should be able to have a meaningful discussion.

In the case of this book, Dan and Noah have been able to accomplish something that would be impossible if they were two distinct and real people. They have the benefit of having matching intellects (with Noah, perhaps, a tad bit ahead) and an identical knowledge base. For example, both Dan and Noah knew basic economics, so I couldn't very well have Dan make some typical lame bleeding-heart liberal argument against greedy price gouging. Dan may have issue with greed but he was also not ignorant of the dangers of price controls.

Now, that does not mean that I, Joe Andersen, agreed with everything Dan said. No. It just means that I needed to believe that every argument Dan made was reasonable.

I also did my best to avoid worthless name-dropping of sources and authorities that would mean little to the opposing perspective. That is why Dan quoted more from Milton Friedman and Adam Smith than the likes of Noam Chomsky or Naomi Klein. Along those lines, I did my best to stay away from brawny emotional rhetoric like the type used by politicians at a rally of supporters. As Hugh Nibley said,

Authority is not evidence and... name-dropping is as futile as name-calling. Sweeping statements and general impressions are sometimes useful in the process of getting one's bearings and taking up a position, but they cannot serve as evidence...[188]

Rule #3: Intellect Always Trumps Emotion (even at the risk of sounding too conservative)

Because of this rule and the fact that I, Joe Andersen, am a conservative Republican, Dan may have adopted a few (or several) perspectives that may not reflect the typical–if there is such a thing–view of most Democrats. In fact, I anticipate this book will be criticized, by both left and right, for not portraying a truly accurate Democrat/liberal/progressive view or for not being aggressive enough about it.

I can easily imagine a hard-line right-winger sympathizing with Dan's opinions and perspectives but then saying, "Yea, but he's not like most Democrats. Most of them are idiots." And, actually, I don't need to imagine a left-wing partisan Democrat criticizing Dan's arguments. That's already happened.

But, what am I to do. I am a conservative. So, the more conservative arguments are the ones that appeal to me.

HOW CAN I POSSIBLY

Imagination is more important than knowledge. For knowledge is limited to all we now know and understand, while imagination embraces the entire world, and all there ever will be to know and understand.

Albert Einstein

Volumes have been written on each of these topics covered in the first three chapters. Endless debates have preceded this book. So, the point-by-point arguments in this book are actually incidental. As useful and refreshing as it is to know and understand some of the particular arguments and counter-arguments of each of these issues, it was not my intention to offer up just one more debate.

---

[188] Nibley, *Since Cumorah*, xiii-xiv.

Of course, the main goal here was to help readers (mainly conservatives) to see that you *can be* a reasonable, intelligent, member of the Church in good standing and have political views that might seem contrary to what you consider to be the "true political perspective". In short, this book was written in the hopes of convincing the reader to adopt a better attitude.

You could say that this book was not even written to answer the question, "How can you possibly be a Mormon and a Democrat?" Rather, this book was written to encourage people *not* to ask that question rhetorically.

If there is one thing that Albert Einstein demonstrated, it is that a creative imagination is an indispensable part of discovering great truths. In the course or writing this book, I have been surprised at how much I have learned from my own imagination.

And so, I recommend that if you truly wish to understand the other side of an issue, then get out there, study the issue and dare to answer the question yourself! First, emotionally invest yourself in the opposing viewpoint. Pretend! Put yourself in their shoes, emotionally and then intellectually, and dare to answer your own hardest questions.

Yes, I am recommending the schizophrenic method. But it does, in my opinion, strongly mirror how God wishes us to understand his mind and will: "You took no thought, save it [were] to ask me. You must study it out in your mind...." (D&C 9:7)

Indeed, the most useful question actually begins with,

How Can I Possibly...

Part II

MARRIAGE[189] ... OF CHURCH AND STATE

---

[189] Get it!? As opposed to "Separation of Church and State". And the word *marriage* isn't here just for the pun of it either. Marriage is dealt with in completely different ways in both Chapter 5 and 6.

CHAPTER 5

POLITICS IN THE CHURCH

The Church's mission is to preach the gospel of Jesus Christ, not to elect politicians. The Church of Jesus Christ of Latter-day Saints is neutral in matters of party politics. This applies in all of the many nations in which it is established.

Newsroom.lds.org

The above statement is posted on the Church's website under the topic "Political Neutrality" and is followed by the following:

The Church does NOT:

- *Endorse, promote or oppose political parties, candidates or platforms.*
- *Allow its church buildings, membership lists or other resources to be used for partisan political purposes.*
- *Attempt to direct its members as to which candidate or party they should give their votes to. This policy applies whether or not a candidate for office is a member of The Church of Jesus Christ of Latter-day Saints.*
- *Attempt to direct or dictate to a government leader.*

The Church DOES:

- *Encourage its members to play a role as responsible citizens in their communities, including becoming informed about issues and voting in elections.*
- *Expect its members to engage in the political process in an informed and civil manner, respecting the fact that members of the Church come from a variety of backgrounds and experiences and may have differences of opinion in partisan political matters.*
- *Request candidates for office not to imply that their candidacy or platforms are endorsed by the Church.*
- *Reserve the right as an institution to address, in a nonpartisan way, issues that it believes have significant community or moral consequences or that directly affect the interests of the Church.*

Elected officials who are Latter-day Saints make their own decisions and may not necessarily be in agreement with one another or even with a publicly stated Church position. While the Church may communicate its views to them, as it may to any other elected official, it recognizes that these officials still must make their own choices based on their best judgment and with consideration of the constituencies whom they were elected to represent.

Modern scriptural references to the role of government: Doctrine and Covenants, Section 134.[190]

A list of items rushed into my mind as I read the above statements. Among them are the three topics dealt with in this chapter: gay marriage, political neutrality and... well, gratitude.

Yes, I know. Gratitude sounds awfully corny and potentially boring. I must admit that I would not have given that last sentence even a second thought if I were not writing a book on politics and the Church. I don't think I would have given it a first thought, even.

How about you? Quick! Without looking, which section in the D&C did it say?

[190] LDS Church, "Political Neutrality of the LDS Church,"
       http://newsroom.lds.org/ldsnewsroom/eng/public-issues/political-neutrality.

The Gift of Government

That our belief with regard to earthly governments and laws in general may not be misinterpreted nor misunderstood, we have thought proper to present at the close of this volume our opinion concerning the same.

Preamble to D&C 134

This declaration about governments was adopted by unanimous vote at a general assembly of the Church in August of 1835. The header summarizes the entire section this way:

- Governments should preserve freedom of conscience and worship.
- All men should uphold their governments, and owe respect and deference to the law.
- Religious societies should not exercise civil powers.
- Men are justified in defending themselves and their property.

In reading this section, I get the impression that one of its primary purposes, at the time it was introduced, was to assure the general public that we Mormons were not revolutionaries or anarchists. No doubt, over the years, this section also served to remind the members themselves to forget about any ideas they might have of becoming part of a grand LDS theocracy.

But looking at it right now, Section 134 reminds me of the U.S. Constitution in two specific ways. First, there's the *explicit way* in which it outlines the purposes of government. Second, and to me, far more interesting, is the *implicit way* this section reminds me of the Constitution, which is simply this: It settles nothing. The war goes on.

You see, every so often in these United States of America, the government is overthrown; a new clan moves in; a new dynasty begins. A revolution can happen every two to four years and it almost always happens without a single shot being fired.

That's the beauty of western civilization in general and of the Constitution in particular. The best governments do not stop the warring parties from fighting each other. They just change the turf, or rather, the terms of engagement: from violence to rhetoric. Instead of slings and stones, its mudslinging and bologna; from keen-edged swords to sharp tongues; from sharp shooting to pontification and press releases. So before you get too outraged at the news of the day, at relentless backstabbing and the endless maniacal drama of the 24-hour news cycle, take a moment and conjure up a little gratitude for how disputes are handled in this country at this time. Or rather, be thankful for the way disputes are *not* handled.

Some things never change, of course, such as cheating, low blows and shameful tactics. But just compare a low blow in a political debate to a shameful tactic in a war and you can begin to see why I believe that our battles are getting even better, even more "civilized" as time goes on.

If you are in doubt of this, let me illustrate the point with a couple of quotes from *both* sides of the political isle, starting with Barak Obama:

> When Democrats rush up to me at events and insist that we live in the worst of political times, that a creeping fascism is closing its grip around our throats, I may mention the internment of Japanese Americans under FDR, the Alien and Sedition Acts under John Adams, or a hundred years of lynching under several dozen administrations as having been possibly worse, and suggest we all take a deep breath. When people at dinner parties ask me how I can possibly operate in the current political environment, with all the negative campaigning and personal attacks, I may mention Nelson Mandela, Aleksandr Solzhenitsyn, or some guy in a Chinese or Egyptian prison somewhere. In truth, being called names is not such a bad deal.[191]

This reminds me of what Dennis Miller said of the controversial preaching of Reverend Jeremiah Wright:

> One thing he knows about America is it's a place where you can stand at a pulpit and say the government has injected

---

[191] Obama, *The Audacity of Hope*, 21-22.

members of your race with the AIDS virus and you don't have
to worry about the government coming in and injecting you
with the AIDS virus![192]

Now, this all comes back to Section 134.

It must be said, here and now, that it is *so* easy to drone
through the verses in Section 134. But do not fall for the temptation of seeing it as a mere obligatory dictionary definition, in-
serted into the *Doctrine and Covenants* because... you know, you
gotta have a section on government.

At the very least, do not overlook the very first sentence of the
first verse. Don't skim, skip or gloss over it, lest you misread it or
miss it altogether.

> *We believe that governments were instituted of God for the bene-
> fit of man; and that He holds men accountable for their acts in
> relation to them, both in making laws and administering them,
> for the good and safety of society. (D&C 134:1)*

Behold! There is a subtle and wonderful point to be made here.
Take it to its logical conclusion. This verse clearly states that
governments are "instituted of God for the benefit of man". In
other words, as corrupt and fallible as every government has
ever been, it is still...

A Gift from a Loving God to His Children

Now, it's easy to be thankful for the Constitution. It's quite another thing to be thankful for... well, for those damned two-
faced Washington politicians. Am I right? I mean, to actually be
thankful for those... punks in Washington, that's asking a little
much, isn't it? Is that what this section is really implying? I think
so.

Truly, I believe that when Section 134 refers to governments,
it is referring to the rules of the game as well as the players, to
the written declarations as well as the bureaucrats. Like it or not,
those living pen pushes are doing the work. Their existence is
"instituted of God" and we should be daily thankful for it.

---

[192] "Miller Time! on The Factor on April 2, 2008."

"What do you say to your Uncle Frank?"

If you're having trouble mustering up some daily gratitude, try looking at it this way:

Government is like a Christmas present from your ostensibly senile (so you think) Uncle Frank. However, old Uncle Frank was a kid too, believe it or not. He might have actually given you something pretty nifty, if you'd just take it out of the package. But even if you don't take it out, that's no excuse to withhold your thanks. It's a common courtesy to do so. But think about how discourteous it is to constantly complain about this gift every day. That's just... well, it's being a spoiled brat, isn't it?

Love Thy Bureaucrat as Thyself

Let's take things even further. You may have accepted the courtesy of being grateful and saying thank you for government officials in general. While loving thy neighbor as thyself is a quintessentially Christian principle, is there any reason or any benefit to having gratitude or good will toward a politician that you specifically know and despise?

There is indeed a very sensible reason for loving thy bureaucrat as thyself, according to C.S. Lewis:

> Suppose one reads a story of filthy atrocities in the paper. Then suppose that something turns up suggesting that the story might not be quite true, or not quite so bad as it was made out. Is one's first feeling, "Thank God, even they aren't quite so bad as that," or is it a feeling of disappointment, and even a determination to cling to the first story for the sheer pleasure of thinking your enemies as bad as possible? If it is the second then it is, I am afraid, the first step in a process which, if followed to the end, will make us into devils. You see, one is beginning to wish that black was a little blacker. If we give that wish its head, later on we shall wish to see grey as black, and then to see white itself as black. Finally, we shall insist on seeing everything-God and our friends and ourselves included-as bad, and not be able to stop doing it: we shall be fixed for ever in a universe of pure hatred.[193]

---

[193] Lewis, *Mere Christianity*, 106.

An Official Call for Diversity

I have never yet heard a Democrat make a political speech that I felt was fair to the Republicans.

President Heber J. Grant

On May 3, 1998, the *Salt Lake Tribune* published an article by Dan Harrie on politics. Here it is, in its entirety.

LDS Official Calls for More Political Diversity

The LDS Church, through a high-ranking leader, is making its strongest public statement to date about the need for political diversity among members, while expressing concerns the Republican Party is becoming the "church party."

"There is sort of a division along Mormon/non-Mormon, Republican/Democratic lines," says Elder Marlin Jensen, a member of the First Quorum of the Seventy. "We regret that more than anything— that there would become a church party and a non-church party. That would be the last thing that we would want to have happen."

Jensen said major national political parties may take stands that do not coincide with teachings of the 10 million-member Church of Jesus Christ of Latter-day Saints, but that should not put them out of bounds for members.

A former attorney and lifelong Democrat, Jensen was careful in his comments not to suggest an official LDS preference for any political party but to maintain the church's traditional stand of partisan neutrality.

The First Quorum of the Seventy is the third tier in LDS Church leadership after the Quorum of Twelve Apostles and the governing First Presidency.

Jensen for the past three years has been a member of the church's Public Affairs Committee. He was designated by church officials to respond to The Salt Lake Tribune's request for an interview on the topic of partisan imbalance in Utah and among LDS members.

The Tribune's inquiry came on the heels of two significant developments: Utah Democrats' unprecedented failure to field a candidate in a congressional race and a statement from the LDS First Presidency—read over pulpits in January—urging members to seek elective office.

In an hour-long interview at the church's worldwide headquarters in downtown Salt Lake City arranged and overseen by LDS media-relations director Mike Otterson, Jensen discussed leaders' views about the seeming demise of two-party politics among members. Among the concerns he aired:

- The LDS Church's reputation as a one-party monolith is damaging in the long run because of the seesaw fortunes of the national political parties.

- The overwhelming Republican bent of LDS members in Utah and the Intermountain West undermines the checks-and-balances principle of democratic government.

- Any notion that it is impossible to be a Democrat and a good Mormon is wrongheaded and should be "obliterated."

- Faithful LDS members have a moral obligation to actively participate in politics and civic affairs, a duty many have neglected.

"I am in shock," Utah Democratic Party Chairwoman Meghan Zanolli Holbrook said when told of Jensen's comments. "I have never heard anything like this in the years I've been here."

"That's an earth shaker," said Democrat Ted Wilson, head of the University of Utah's Hinckley Institute of Politics and a longtime critic of the close connection between the Mormon Church and Republican Party.

"Mormon Democrats have been praying for this," said Wilson, who is LDS. "This is more than seeking—we have beseeched the divinity over this."

Utah Republican Chairman Rob Bishop's reaction was less enthusiastic. "Any time a major player in the social fabric of the state, like the church, says something, it will have an impact."

"We obviously will not change," Bishop added. "If Mormons feel comfortable we welcome them. And if non-Mormons feel comfortable, we welcome them, too."

Jensen, who was called as a general authority in 1989, said high church officials lament the near-extinction of the Democratic Party in Utah and the perception—incorrect though it is—that the GOP enjoys official sanction of the church.

All five Congress members from Utah are Mormon and Republican, four of the five statewide offices are held by GOP officials and two-thirds of the state Legislature is Republican. Nearly 90 percent of state lawmakers are LDS. Democrats last held a majority in the state House in 1975, and in the Senate in 1977.

President Clinton finished third in balloting in Utah in 1992, the only state in which the Democrat finished behind Republican George Bush and independent Ross Perot. Utahns last voted for a Democrat for president in 1964, when they supported Lyndon B. Johnson.

Public-opinion polls show voters identifying themselves as Republican outnumber Democrats by a ratio of about 2-1.

However, a statewide survey taken in April by Valley Research, The Tribune's independent pollster, found the state equally divided when asked [if the] Republicans had too much power. Forty-six percent of the 502 respondents answered yes, 45 percent did not believe the GOP held too much sway and nine percent were unsure.

"One of the things that prompted this discussion in the first place was the regret that's felt about the decline of the Democratic Party [in Utah] and the notion that may prevail in some areas that you can't be a good Mormon and a good Democrat at the same time," Jensen said.

"There have been some awfully good men and women who have been both and are both today. So I think it would be a very healthy thing for the church—particularly the Utah church—if that notion could be obliterated."

The idea that Mormonism and Democratic Party affiliation are incompatible traces back to the early 1970s, when LDS general authority Ezra Taft Benson, who later became church president, was quoted in an Associated Press interview as saying it would be difficult for a faithful member to be a liberal Democrat.

Church officials later claimed the comment was taken out of context, although the AP stood by its account.

Jensen said concerns exist on two levels about the unofficial linkage of the Republican Party and Mormon Church.

One is the fear that by being closely identified with one political party, the church's national reputation and influence is subject to the roller-coaster turns and dips of that partisan organization. Also bothersome is that the uncontested dominance of the Republican Party in Utah deprives residents of the debate and competition of ideas that underlie good government.

"There is a feeling that even nationally as a church, it's not in our best interest to be known as a one-party church," Jensen said.

"The national fortunes of the parties ebb and flow. Whereas the Republicans may clearly have the upper hand today, in another 10 years they may not."

Closer to home, he pointed to the Democrats' precarious toehold in Utah—a circumstance highlighted by the dearth of minority-party officeholders and the current one-sided election in the 3rd Congressional District.

Republican Rep. Chris Cannon in 1996 defeated Bill Orton, a conservative Democrat and Mormon who had been the lone member of the minority party in Utah's delegation. This year, Cannon is seeking a second term without any challenge from a Democrat—a first in Utah history.

(In 1982, Democrat Henry Huish missed the filing deadline and had to run as an independent. Still, he had the backing of the Democratic Party.)

"The Democratic Party has in the last 20 years waned to the point where it really is almost not a factor in our political life," Jensen said. "There is a feeling that that is not healthy at all—that as a state we suffer in different ways. But certainly any time you don't have the dialogue and the give-and-take that the democratic process provides, you're going to be poorer for it in the long run."

There also are more immediate, tangible costs, he said.

Jensen blamed the Republican monopoly for contributing to Utah political leaders' inability or unwillingness to grapple with long-range planning issues. He pointed to the lack of state leadership on issues of open-space preservation and land-use planning.

He also pointed to the massive, catch-up highway-building binge that has disrupted Salt Lake County commuters and businesses. "One might say that the transportation crisis that we're in might have been averted had there been better balance in the parties and something was thrashed out 10 years ago, perhaps during Gov. Bangerter's time, rather than being allowed to wait until we reached a crisis situation.

"There are probably issues like that environmentally, educationally that we'd really benefit from if there were a more robust dialogue going on. But we've lacked that and I think we've suffered somewhat because of it."

Jensen's comments are bound to cause ripples among the 70 percent of Utahns who are counted as members of the LDS Church, as well as millions of faithful throughout the country, say political observers.

"This is the second dramatic time in the history of the state when forceful signals have been flashed from church headquarters calling on Mormons to choose up political sides more evenly," said J.D. Williams, retired University of Utah political scientist.

Williams compared Jensen's public pronouncements to the church's attempts in the 1890s to divide congregations up evenly among the two major political parties.

"Thus, wonder of wonders, theocracy was the mother of democracy in the territory of Utah," Williams said. "We achieved statehood five years later."

Jensen also referred to the 19th-century splitting of congregations along partisan lines, when the territorial People's and Liberal parties were abandoned in favor of national party affiliations.

He repeated an anecdote told by prominent LDS Democrat Oscar McConkie about his father's recollections of a church leader telling a congregation during a Sunday morning meeting to "sign up to be Republicans."

At that time, Mormons favored the Democratic Party because it was less stridently anti-polygamy than were Republicans.

When members of the flock returned for an afternoon session, the Republican sign-up sheet remained blank, Jensen said. "Brothers and sisters, you have misunderstood," said the church leader. "God needs Republicans."

"And Oscar said his father would wink and say, 'And you know, Oscar, those damned Republicans think they've had God on their side ever since,' " Jensen said.

"I don't know if you can make any use of that but it's a great story. And there's a little of that embedded in our culture, unfortunately," he said.

Elbert Peck, editor of Sunstone magazine, said it is noteworthy that it is not LDS President Gordon B. Hinckley or one of his counselors breaking the church's silence on political imbalance.

"It is not as official as if it was an apostle or a member of the First Presidency saying it," Peck said. "Still, the quotes are out there and people will use them. You can bet they'll be remembered and taken as a sign."

Peck, whose Salt Lake City-based independent journal publishes articles on historical and contemporary Mormonism, predicts similar comments will be made in other settings—church firesides and the like, because messages sent by LDS general authorities are repeated.

"Privately, I've heard reports of these opinions, but not publicly," Peck said. "The church leaders have been careful about saying anything publicly."

The tremendous growth of the Mormon Church worldwide has forced attention to its image as a good, trustworthy neighbor in the communities, states and countries where it is taking root, he said.

"We need to develop a tolerance—so we don't demonize people that we have a disagreement with," Peck said. "It really was the church leaders' position on abortion and the Equal Rights Amendment [in the 1970s] that was the death of the Utah Democratic Party, because it became a litmus test," he said.

Pro-choice and, more recently, gay-rights stands of the national Democratic Party have helped Republicans paint the donkey-symbol party as taboo.

Jensen said it is time for LDS members to take a broader view of political affiliation.

"We would probably hope that they wouldn't abandon a party necessarily because it has a philosophy or two that may not square with Mormonism. Because, as I say, [parties] in their philosophies ebb and flow," Jensen said.

"You know, the Republicans came very close last time to bringing a pro-abortion plank into their platform. That was maybe the biggest battle of their [1996 national] convention," he said. "Which shows that if you're a pure ideologue, eventually you're going to have trouble in either party."

"Everyone who is a good Latter-day Saint is going to have to pick and choose a little bit regardless of the party that they're in and that may be required a lot more in the future than it has been in the past. But I think there's room for that and the gospel leaves us lots of latitude.[194]

This section started with a quote by President Heber J. Grant, which may sound a little partisan, if quoted out of context, which it certainly was. For the right perspective, here is the second half of that quote:

Being a Democrat, I shall not say anything about what I think of the speeches of Republicans regarding Democrats.

President Heber J. Grant

---

[194] Harrie, "LDS Official Calls for More Political Diversity."

Thoughts on Proposition 8

Some people fancy that because we have the Presidency and Apostles of the Church that they will do the thinking for us. These are men and women so mentally lazy that they hardly think for themselves. To think calls for effort, which makes some men tired and wearies their souls. No man or woman can remain in this Church on borrowed light.[195]

Elder J. Golden Kimball
Conference Report, April 1904

Every so often, the Church does step into the political limelight, to take an official stand. The 2008 election year comes to mind. The Church broke its usual pattern of political neutrality by giving official and explicit support to propositions involving marriage in several states.[196]

However, even such action by the Church does not absolve members from the responsibility to study and pray about the issues of the day and to vote according to the dictates of their own conscience. As Brigham Young made clear:

> I am more afraid that this people have so much confidence in their leaders that they will not inquire for themselves of God whether they are led by him. I am fearful they settle down in a state of blind self-security. ... Let every man and woman know, by the whispering of the Spirit of God to themselves...[197]

Whether state level politics or ward level callings, the Church has always discouraged intellectual laziness and blind obedience. We have, after all, been asked to serve the Lord "with all of our heart, might, *mind* and strength."

In the U.S., during election season, it is customary for the Church to issue a letter to be read to all congregations. This letter

---

[195] Givens, *People of Paradox*, 17-18.

[196] In California, it was called Prop 8. Arizona's similar proposition was called Prop 102.

[197] Young, *Discourses of Brigham Young, sel. John A. Widtsoe [1941]*, 135.

encourages members to participate in the election process. There is a great emphasis on reminding us of our responsibility to make our own decisions, which result from serious study and prayer (and even fasting). From the heights of the federal government, all the way down (and over) to the level of ward callings, the principle of study, prayer and acting by the guidance of your own conscience should always apply.

When the ban on gay marriage was overturned by a federal court in August of 2010, a friend of mine posted on his Facebook page the kind of comment that you'd expect: "Just think of all the wasted tithing money..."

Someone responded with, "I wouldn't say a huge waste. But maybe its intent was revelation, and meant to start the end of days. Other than that, there is no reasonable justification for the Church to spend money on it."

As far as I have been able to find out, tithing money was *not* used. However, the fact remains that the Church certainly used its resources and lent official support for Proposition 8, etc. Now that the proposition has been overturned, however, people seem to be treating the Church's support as if the Brethren were making some sort of prediction about Prop 8. But the Church is not in the business of predicting the future.

Devine Guidance vs. "Divination"

Revelation (public or private) is not a matter of fortune telling. This kind of thing happens with Patriarchal blessings, too. People read theirs over and over as if they were gazing into a crystal ball, peering into the future. This really misses the point.

I recall a science fiction movie from a few years back where the main character received a kind of patriarchal blessing of sorts. The old sage predicted some bad news. But, more importantly, he was given a "heads-up" that, at some point soon, he was going to have to make a critical choice, which would end his own life. When the time came, this character looked death straight in the eye and charged ahead. Consequently, he found greater inner-strength than he thought possible. As a result, things started turning out much differently–and much better!– than he had expected. He had discovered his own tremendous inner strength. And since he wasn't dead (yet), he approached a wise friend and asked why the prediction had not come true. His friend replied with a grin, "You were told exactly what you needed to hear. That's all! There is a big difference between knowing the path and actually walking the path."

So, the old sage was not so much fortune telling, but rather, lighting the path and showing the way.

Our modern day prophets, seers and revelators are not there to "predict the path but to illuminate it," so to speak. Many members of the Church have a rather juvenile idea about what it means to follow the prophet and hearken to his words. They imagine the prophet telling us to do something and we go and pray about it and the Holy Ghost then confirms the truth and then we go and do the thing we are told to do. But this view is far too simplistic. So, let's drop the sci-fi parables and lit path analogies and just tackle the Church's very real support of Proposition 8.

My Experience

I was certainly leaning towards supporting these propositions. But when the Church came out in public support of these propositions, there was *more* to think about, not less. Now, there was no need for me, personally, to go and pray and confirm the truthfulness of the Church's support for the propositions, etc. I already sustain our General Authorities as prophets, seers and revelators. But that also doesn't mean the thinking has been done. On the contrary. For me at least, the tough thinking had only just started.

LDS.org states that the Church "*encourages* its members to play a role as responsible citizens in their communities..." and the Church "*expects* its members to engage in the political process in an informed and civil manner..." As I read that, the Church merely *encourages* us to engage with the community, but it *expects* us to do so in a civil manner. That is *not* a subtle difference.

Voting in the privacy of my own booth was the easy part. The hard part was engaging with the "opposition". You see, I have a friend, Phil (name change) who is gay. And he knows that I am

LDS. So this issue was no longer just a private matter between me and my ballot. And because I did not like the idea of an unspoken cloud hanging over our friendship, I knew I was going to have to talk to him about it.

I don't think it was coincidental that, at the time, I came across an article by Thomas F. Rogers. His words reflected my own dilemma:

> That old difficulty again: how to reach out to others with the certainty and conviction of our faith and values without counting on any personal acceptance or even respectful acknowledgement? But let's turn that question around: How willing are we to extend to "the other" equivalent respect and appreciation while not compromising what we call our" testimony" or standing at a comfortable remove from what may be our own energizing faith? Do we simply have to view the world's various religious philosophies and systems of belief as interchangeable and relatively the same? [198]

Well, that sums up the crux of the situation for me. Those are some tough questions. But the only real way to answer them is to engage in a dialogue, to take a chance. I know it's the right thing to do but that devil in the details makes me nervous. I mean, how do you start that conversation?

"Yo, Phil! I'm voting yes on Prop 8. Me and all my Church buddies! You cool with that?"

That would certainly be direct enough. But obviously that's not the way to go about it. One can be both direct and tactful. In the end, the phrase I planned to use was simply, "Phil. I voted for Prop 8. Are we still friends?"

That's not a joke. That was to be my opening line. And it is a fair enough reflection of my general comfort level with Phil. There will be disagreement, of course. And, the fact is, the issue affects him much more personally than me. Would taking a chance like this really be worth it? I suppose this conversation with Phil could strain our friendship a bit. But I wouldn't bet on it. He's such a pleasant person and we've always been open about our views and beliefs and such. I was certain that our

---

[198] Rogers, "InterConnections," 27.

conversation would be totally civil, respectful and educational for both of us.

Still, you may wonder what on earth I hope to accomplish. Did I hope to change his mind? Not at all. But I am reminded of some words by Elder Maxwell:

> Occasionally, even with full communication, we may continue to hold to differing points of view–but at least with increased appreciation of another's views... followed by a determination to make things better, which involves taking a loving initiative.[199]

How did it pan out?

I actually told my Elder's Quorum about my plans to talk to Phil about Prop 8. The majority responded with comments like, "Bad idea." or "I wouldn't recommend that." Boy, most of them were certain it would end in disaster. I couldn't wait to prove them wrong.

So, guess what happened? Nothing. Phil moved. He moved out of state! His old number didn't work. I even tried to find him on Facebook. No such luck. Now what?

"That's anti-climactic," you might say. "It practically negates everything you had to say."

No so fast! Luckily, I had a back up!

You see, Phil was not the only friend of mine who was gay. I had... well, at least one more friend that I knew was gay. (I could have 20 others that I do not know are gay, but I only know that I know of two.)

My other friend's name is Chris[200] and I have corresponded with him for over a decade. How do I expect him to respond? Actually, I am even more confident that a discussion about Prop 8 would not do a thing to damage our friendship.

So, when it came time to ask, I realized that it had been a good six months since I had heard from him. We mostly correspond by email and he had not returned any of my emails in the past six months. Ah, this gave me an even better way to pop the Prop

---

[199] Maxwell, *All These Things Shall Give Thee Experience*, 77.
[200] No name change. In fact, his full name is Chris Mathew Sciabarra.

8 question, and this is how I did it. I wrote an email to him. Here it is, word for word:

Chris,
　　Is it possible that you are not replying to the emails I've sent over the past few months because of, well, a lingering resentment over Prop 8?

Joe

Hehehehe. I chuckled when I sent it because I knew that such an email would certainly get his attention. I knew that he would simply NOT want me thinking, for a moment, that *he* thought like that.

So, that was my prediction. How did it turn out? First of all, his response was immediate, but that was mostly out of serendipity. Here is his actual response:

Joe,
　　I could not care LESS about Prop 8. ... So, by all means, wipe out of your mind even the HINT of resentment. I have so enjoyed our correspondence through the years, and hope we will continue.

Chris

Behold! His reaction was just as I predicted and was the opposite of how most members of my Elder's Quorum had assumed. Perhaps their opinions reflect those of most members of the Church, that is, you can't talk to gays about gay marriage. Perhaps that is the case and I have simply lucked out on having two very reasonable friends. Perhaps.

I followed up on this query by asking Chris if he knew of anything written from gays who were against gay marriage. He said the closest thing he could think of was a book called *Beyond Queer: Challenging the Gay Left Orthodoxy*, edited by Bruce

Bawer.[201] It is a collection of 38 articles. And although most of the articles are written by the alternate lifestyle crowd, they "attack the queer establishment and argue for a more moderate approach to lesbian and gay rights," as one reviewer phrased it.

I cannot wholly recommend this book because I have not read all of it. But, from what I have read, I can say that it is refreshing to know that not all homosexuals are leftists and many have much more complex views on marriage than is portrayed by either side of the political spectrum.

At the end of the day, when it comes to the issue of gay marriage and proposition 8, I learned much more by opening my mouth than I would have if I had just kept silent and had done nothing more than mark my ballet on Election Day.

In short, the Church's official support of Prop 8 was not wasted on me.

On the contrary, the Church, acting in an official and public capacity, galvanized me to do something that I may not have done on my own: engage in a real discussion about these issues. But this discussion with Chris was only possible because we were friends first! And friendship is, after all, "the grand fundamental purpose of Mormonism," as Joseph Smith himself proclaimed.[202]

---

[201] Bawer, *Beyond Queer.*
[202] Ehat and Cook, *The Words of Joseph Smith,* 234.

CHAPTER 6

WHAT'S WITH HARRY REID!?

I do not know Harry Reid. I have never met him. We've never talked. I have no connection with him professionally. With the exception of "The Open Secret" (at the end of this chapter), all information about Harry Reid has been obtained by reading books and articles and by listening to speeches and interviews online. They are sourced in the footnotes and bibliography.

I want to make it clear that I have no connection with Senator Reid. Why? As you can tell by reading this chapter and the abortion chapter, I have portrayed Harry Reid, or rather, revealed him in a *very* positive light. This is *not* because we are pals. This is because that is what I have simply discovered about him, all by myself. But I don't know him. And I don't owe him. So I've never had any reason to paint him with a positive brush, that is, other than my own desire to see the best in others, I guess.

Most members of the Church know little about Harry Reid. Conservative members know even less. I should know. I knew next to nothing about Reid before I started this project. Didn't even know he was pro-life and neither did any other Republicans that I knew. However, this lack of information didn't stop us all from having a strong and unfavorable opinion about him.

For my part, I remember being put off by Reid's comments a few years ago regarding Justice Clarence Thomas. Reid called him an "embarrassment to the Supreme Court". Now that absolutely ticked me off! Other than that, I suppose my own negative opinion was the result of simple groupthink. Kind of like the screeching diatribes I hear from liberals about Glenn Beck. They don't know a thing about Beck. I didn't know a thing about Reid. I've talked to a few of his staff over the phone. But that was simply to give them a heads up about this book.

I've learned a lot about Harry Reid lately. And, my opinion of him has improved. Would I ever vote for him? I'm afraid not.

But I would never expect Senator Reid to vote for me if I ever ran for office. We've got different political philosophies, especially regarding economics.

Quick Time-Line

Now, if I'm going to devote a whole chapter to Harry Reid, I probably ought to give you a quick bio of him first. What follows is just a brief timeline of events in his life.

- Reid grew up in the small ex-mining town of Searchlight, Nevada, where his mother made an income from what has to be the world's *third* oldest occupation: doing laundry for prostitutes, mainly.
- Reid was first introduced to the Church–or any form of religion at all–when he attended LDS seminary in high school in a town nearby.
- He eventually married his wife, Landra, who was from a strong Jewish heritage, at the objection of her parents. But, after the wedding, her parents told the newlyweds that, having done all they could to prevent the marriage, they would now do everything in their power to ensure their daughter's happiness, by supporting the young couple as best they could.
- Reid was a boxer! (So was Orin Hatch, by the way.)
- He was also a football player with enough skill to win him an athletic scholarship to Southern Utah University.
- His athletic dreams quickly ended with an injury.
- He received his bachelor's degree from Utah State in 1961.
- Reid graduated from George Washington University Law School with a J.D. while working for the United States Capitol Police. [203]
- His father committed suicide when Harry was 33.

---

[203] Reid, "Faith, Family and Public Service."

Glenn Beck vs. Harry Reid

"How can he even be a member of the Church?"

"He's a crook and—mark my words—he will go inactive some day."

"I am appalled that he is a Mormon."

"He will lose popularity and then he will leave the Church because he no longer will see a need for it."

Aren't these just the most pleasant statements? Each statement was made by an active member of *The Church of Jesus Christ of Latter-day Saints* about another member of the Church.

Which of these statements were made by a sophomoric college student? Which was made by someone near retirement who worked for the Church his whole life? Which of these did I hear at Church? In an email? At the in-laws? At the Bishop's storehouse? Which of these statements was said about Harry Reid and which was said about Glenn Beck?

Answer: all of the above, in every combination.

Oh, you've heard those kinds of comments too, haven't you? You might have even said them at one time in your life. To my own shame, I am pretty sure I have spewed the same nonsense about a fellow Church member at one time or another.

It's kind of a bummer, don't you think? These off-handed comments are so common in Zion… and so easily said. And to spew this kind of venom about a couple of converts seems a bit lacking in hospitality. It's doubly mean and callous when you ponder their backgrounds a bit. Each had a parent who committed suicide, apparently. Each of them joined the Church side-by-side with their spouse.

Why is it that, when it comes to public characters like Reid and Beck, we are so quick to justify our backbiting and gossip? I guess, if they can't take the heat, they shouldn't be in the business, right? Well, they are in that business 24-7, so they obviously can stand the heat. What concerns me is that we cannot stand them! Oh, it's not that we can't stand listening to them. Neither side seems to do that!

On the contrary, the way Mormons treat Reid and Beck reminds me of how too many critics treat LDS scripture:

> *The Book of Mormon* has **not** been universally considered by its critics as one of those books that must be read in order to have an opinion of it.[204] (emphasis added)

Back in 2009, I listened to about three hours (3 discs) of the audio version of *An Inconvenient Book* written and read/performed by Glenn Beck. Because I tend to avoid the media, this was actually one of my first exposures to Beck. My first impression was that he was just hilarious. In fact, I can honestly say that I never took Glenn Beck seriously until I discovered that he was so funny.

But, humor aside, I was surprised at how little he talked of politics. In fact, I was certain that even the most die-hard liberal member of the Church would agree with him on everything he said, but only as long as they didn't know it was him talking. He didn't bring up politics at all in the parts that I listened to (perhaps he does elsewhere).

Having learned quite a bit about Harry Reid lately, including reading much of his biography *The Good Fight*, I can testify that even though most conservatives in the Church cannot imagine how Reid could be LDS, they are totally unaware that he is pro-life, pro-gun and pro-death penalty!

At the end of the day, I have this to say about Glenn Beck and Harry Reid: Mormon Democrats don't listen to un-spliced Glenn Beck and Republican Mormon's don't know a thing about Harry Reid.

But, at least, we are all united in our frustration with Evangelical anti-Mormons for *their* willful ignorance!

We Cannot Stand Them!

We so easily justify our backbiting towards public characters like Reid and Beck. And, as I said, while they can stand the heat, we cannot stand them! And what really concerns me is that, if those

---

[204] O'Dea, *The Mormons*, 26.

opening quotes are an indicator, it is specifically their membership in the Church that we cannot stand.

And claims that they will leave the Church when their popularity goes down are just desperate comments, driven by emotion. It's not as if either of them touts their Mormonism on any regular basis. They are both somewhat reticent about it, in fact.

I wonder... don't all these salacious comments fall under the category of evil speaking of the Lord's anointed? We usually think of the "Lord's anointed" as leaders in the Church (local or general). But, like it or not, Harry Reid and Glenn Beck have both been found worthy by judges in Zion, baptized, confirmed and married in the temple, all done by those who hold the Lord's priesthood, that is, "the Lord's anointed".

As I see it, trash talking about Reid or Beck amounts to the same thing as evil speaking of the Lord's anointed, at least when it pertains to their membership or worthiness. Regardless, such negativity is in contradiction with the admonition by President George Albert Smith, "Whenever your politics cause you to speak unkindly of your brethren, know this, that you are upon dangerous ground."[205]

Shouldn't every member of the Church, from every political persuasion, welcome the membership of anyone, no matter their political persuasion. We should welcome the membership of the reddest communist, so long as he is willing to take His name upon them? If you haven't noticed, this kind of inclusivity does results in plenty of embarrassing moments on Fast Sunday. Not to mention that we have a leadership full of amateurs. But... who's in charge?

While we should certainly fight for what we believe is right in our homes as in the political arena, HIS Kingdom is not of this world.

"Would we hide that light?"

I found it interesting to learn that Harry Reid himself said that one of the people who was influential in his own conversion was a "crazy man" who lived next door to him and his wife:

---

[205] Smith, *Conference Report, April 1914*, 12.

He was expert in scripture, and referred to Satan as "Old Horns." A nice man, with a wonderful spirit, who, we later learned, had struggled with mental illness and had been in and out of institutions.[206]

There may have been times in this man's life when he would have been a feared outcast, thought of as too unsafe or unpredictable for anyone to allow them into their own home. But you're always welcome at Church. And yet here this man was an instrument in the Lord's hands for converting a young couple to the gospel.

Consider, carefully, the words of Elder Robert S. Wood:

We need, as the Lord counseled, to uphold honest, wise, and good men and women wherever they are found and to recognize that there are "among all sects, parties, and denominations" those who are "kept from the truth [of the gospel] because they know not where to find it." (D&C 123:12). Would we hide that light because we have entered into the culture of slander, of stereotyping, of giving and seeking offense? [207]

I must admit that the full impact of these words did not sink in to my mind until one ordinary day, while discussing politics with a friend. This friend was a co-worker who identified himself as a progressive. He was not a member of the Church and he had often expressed his displeasure (if not outright disdain) towards "conservative Christians" and "right-wing evangelicals". He viewed them as closed-minded and dogmatic. And, perhaps, he viewed Mormons in the same way. In any case, that day I had made a casual reference to the fact that Senator Harry Reid was a member of the Church.

"Harry Reid is a Mormon?!" came his response, quite obviously surprised.

"Uh, yea," I said in mild confusion. I thought he already knew.

He then furrowed his brow, said nothing for a moment. I could see the wheels turning: I was witnessing a paradigm shift, perhaps a minor one, perhaps much more. I can only guess as to

206 Reid, *The Good Fight*, 128.
207 Wood, "Instruments of the Lord's Peace."

what he was thinking but it is my belief that he was re-evaluating "those Mormons" a bit. Given his own political views (a lefty), I like to think that he saw the Church in a better light from that day forward.

Before that time, I had never viewed Reid's high-profile membership in the Democratic Party as an asset in spreading the gospel. I am sure that many non-member Democrats have viewed LDS churches as a place where liberals and Democrats would not feel welcome. But with Harry Reid at the helm of the Democratic Party, who knows what doors might be opened to our missionaries? Who knows what minds might remain open just long enough to consider the gospel or at least to take the Church more seriously?

This is one reason why I rejoice that Senator Harry Reid is a faithful member of *The Church of Jesus Christ of Latter-day Saints*. I feel the same way about Glenn Beck. They will open different doors to different people.

The Senator's TRUE Agenda

"So, you must be a fan of Harry Reid?" I asked.

"Reid?" said the BYU Professor. "Oh, he's way too conservative for me." [208]

My jaw dropped, not out of shock, but more from the entertainment I always get from a good paradigm shift. And although this was the first time that I heard anyone call Harry Reid "too conservative", it would not be the last.

What an astonishing statement. Senator Reid was "way too conservative"? I was under the impression (at the time) that Harry Reid was as far left as any member of the Church could get without... you know, without getting into trouble. However, this professor had a list of political views that would shock many conservative Church members. Well, gun control wouldn't be all that shocking. But some of the other issues raised my eyebrow.

Now, although these comments and opinions might be a bit repugnant to any self-respecting Republican, it does not come as a surprise that this was the opinion of an academic professor. It's hard to find a more liberal enclave than in the ivory tower of academia, right? In fact, it's hardly a surprise that this was a professor at Brigham Young University.

Of course, this professor's standing in the Church was beyond question. He was a lifelong faithful member, who had served in callings and leadership positions, which include serving as a member of the Stake Presidency. Now, this man did not use the pulpit to promote his politics, but in social and professional settings, he was as up front about his politics as anyone.

So, I had to ask the obvious: "Have any of the Brethren ever cautioned or admonished you regarding your political views?"

His answer was unforgettable: "On the contrary. I have received phone calls of support from General Authorities."

Keep in mind that when he said "support", in this case, did not mean agreement or endorsement of his politics. Rather, these

---

[208] A face-to-face conversation between the author and the professor (summer of 2008).

Brethren (including two Apostles) had simply called him to let him know that they had just had "an interesting discussion" where this professor's name came up. I got the impression that these conversations with general authorities were actually very casual, along the lines of, "someone came complaining again"… "thought I'd let you know"… "nothing to worry about"… "interesting conversation though"… "how's your family?"

Again, this man was a BYU professor, a member of the Stake Presidency and he had very liberal views on many issues. He had never been pressured to change or even apologize for his political views.

I felt like a reporter at a press conference with my next question: "Do you think the Brethren have failed to inform the general audience of the Church that there is such a wide spectrum of political views within the Church?"

"Well, the Brethren are in a difficult position," he said. He went on to explain that the agenda of the Church is a moral one, not political. They must ever be cautious about how the members and the public will interpret their statements.

Although the Church cannot and does not condone or support any immoral actions, from uncharitable resentment to murder, it is not the Church's place to dictate how the government should deal with these immoral actions of its citizens. Knowing that there are many members of the Church in good standing who are far far left of Harry Reid was an opportunity for me to look at Senator Reid in a new way.

Senator Reid, Too Conservative?!

First, is Senator Harry Reid truly a conservative in a way in which a true blue Republican could actually relate? Well, we know from Chapter 1 that he is certainly pro-life and always has been, as he himself explained at a 2007 BYU Devotional:

> On the topic of abortion, let me say I am pro-life and for the 25 years I have been in Congress have always been pro-life. Some say Democrats can't be pro-life, but I am proof that we can. During my first year in the Senate, there was an abortion issue that came up for a vote. It was a very close vote. My vote mattered; it could well have been the difference. In the

well of the Senate, Senators were explaining the importance of my vote and how important it was.

Senator Barbara Mikulski, at that time the only woman in the Senate and one of the nation's feminist leaders, told everyone to leave me alone, my vote was a matter of character. I have been left alone for more than two decades, but there are other Democratic senators who share my pro-life position.[209]

Kudos to Senator Mikulski! But what else might make Reid "too conservative"?

Well, back in 2005, when Reid first took the post of minority leader in the Senate, a headline[210] in *The New Yorker* read,

How a Pro-gun, Anti-abortion Nevadan leads the Senate's Democrats?

Given that this is *The New Yorker* talking here, I'm not inclined to simply take that headline at face value. So I figured I'd better do some of my own research: I checked out Project Vote Smart to see how he scored on gun-control issues.[211] On gun control issues in 2004, the NRA gave Harry Reid the grade of "B". But just knowing Reid's grade isn't enough for me. For all I know, 2004 may have been the year that everyone received roughly the same grade.

So, let's look at Reid in context, alongside a few peers from the same year:

Robert Bennet..... A
John McCain....... C+
Nancy Pelosi ...... F
Harry Reid......... B

If Pelosi get's an "F" and Reid scores higher than McCain, I think that places him squarely in the pro-gun camp.

What else? Well, there's one more position that seems to be a quintessentially conservative one: You may be surprised to learn that Harry Reid also supports the death penalty.[212]

---

209 Reid, "Faith, Family and Public Service."
210 Walsh, "How a pro-gun, anti-abortion Nevadan leads the Senate's Democrats."
211 Project Vote Smart, "National Rifle Association Rating."
212 sourcewatch.org, "Harry Reid on SourceWatch."

While his position on abortion, gun control and the death penalty are surprising, a couple other items are worth mentioning:

- Reid was the first Democratic Senator to support Desert Storm.[213]
- I was truly surprised to see that he spoke at the 2009 dedication of the statue of Ronald Reagan, [214] who Reid very much admired as a person and as the President. [215]
- Reid's always had good things to say about George Bush Sr., as well.[216]
- Most recently, regarding Israel, Senator Harry Reid publically opposed President Obama's suggested that the 1967 borders be used as a starting point for negotiations. Reid directly rebuffed this in his speech the American Israel Public Affairs Committee (AIPAC).[217]

Me and My Conservative Conclusion

I knew none of these things about Harry Reid before I started this book. But I'm glad to have made these discoveries. He's no longer two dimensional to me. At the very least, he's more interesting. At this point, I can't help but admire him for sticking to his guns.

How about you?

Or are you determined to disprove my conclusions on where Reid stands on these issues? Or, in spite of it all, are you still determined to think of him as a leftist pinko-commie, safe to denigrate and despise?

Tell you what. I'll make it easy on you by assuring you that he is, at least 90% leftist pinko-commie. And by that, I mean that, despite his conservative stance on the issues listed above, Reid still manages to vote along Democratic Party lines 90% of the time.

---

213 Reid, *The Good Fight*, 2.
214 Reid, "Reid Speaks at Dedication of Ronald Reagan Statue."
215 Reid, "Nevada NewsMakers Interview w/ Harry Reid."
216 Walsh, "How a pro-gun, anti-abortion Nevadan leads the Senate's Democrats."
217 Reid, "Harry Reid Speaks at AIPAC Annual Policy Conference (C-SPAN Video Library)."

Even so. It's still just politics. You know, there's nothing more American than disagreeing with a person and publically debating the issue. But there's nothing more unchristian than despising that person for those disagreements.

Post Script: Reid Campaigns for Romney... kind of

It is my opinion that during Mitt Romney's run for the 2008 Republican Presidential Candidacy, the Church, or members of the Church, were probably shielded from general criticism (by Democrats) perhaps because of Harry Reid.

You see, fairly early in the Republican primaries, the Reverend Al Sharpton made a tongue-in-cheek comment about Romney being a Mormon, saying "those that really believe in God will defeat him."[218]

At the time, I worried that this was but the first taste of the expected onslaught of Mormon bashing that would continue throughout the campaign, even while the primaries were still underway. However, it did not happen, at least not the way I expected, and not at all from Al Sharpton's camp or any Democrats in general. In fact, nothing like what I had expected came from the liberal side of the camp.

My theory is that, shortly after Sharpton made his comments, an advisor informed him that he had best not generalize about the Mormons since the current Senate Majority Leader was, in fact, a Mormon and a Democrat.

At the time, I remember my father commenting that perhaps Senator Reid's position in the government would actually increase Romney's chances of getting into the White House because Harry Reid, a leader of the Democratic party, would actually help shield Romney from much of the religiously based criticisms... at least, criticisms from Democrats. Instead, criticism of Romney's religion came from... Mike Huckabee.

---

[218] Hitchens and Sharpton, "A Debate: God is Not Great."

The Open Secret

The ultimate end of all activity in the Church is that a man and his wife and their children might be happy at home, protected by the principles and laws of the gospel, sealed safely in the covenants of the everlasting priesthood.[219]

President Boyd K. Packer

I am about to reveal something personal about Harry Reid's family. As stated in the first part of this chapter, this "open secret" is the only bit of information about Reid that I have obtained directly from the horse's mouth, so to speak, as opposed to reading it in some public or published source.

This "open secret", as I hope you shall see, is a most fitting way to conclude this book.

Normal or Exceptional?

I don't know how it is for others, but this is a time and a place in my life where it seems as if friends and family are dropping out of the Church in higher numbers than I had expected, not in droves, but with disturbing consistency. But there's nothing more consistent than the Nephite Pride Cycle, so I guess I shouldn't be too surprised.

In any case, it is hard to find a mature family (all children over 18), who does not have at least one who is openly unsatisfied with the Church or their membership in it. This got me wondering whether all of Harry Reid's children are currently active in the Church.

I thought I had remembered that all four of Reid's sons (he has one daughter) had served a mission. So, I contacted a reliable source, someone close enough to the family to verify this impression of mine: that all of his sons had served missions. And

---

[219] Packer, "The Power of the Priesthood."

that was just a springboard for asking if all of Reid's children were still active.

When I asked about the missions, I found out that Reid's youngest son did not serve a mission. Rather, he was offered an athletic scholarship and he chose that path instead of a mission. He went to nationals three years in a row. He also ended up getting married fairly young.

Ah, yes, I thought. There is the black sheep. There's always one, right?

But wait! Not so fast. I was then told that, while this son did not serve a mission, he had always remained faithful and active throughout college. He married quite young, but in did marry in the temple. And remains married to the same woman to this day.

If it is even my business to evaluate the lives of strangers, there seems to be no question that a temple marriage trumps serving a mission on the eternal scale.

So, I then asked if *all* of Reid's children were married in the temple.

"Yes," came the answer.

"Are they all currently active in the Church?"

Again, the answer was, "Yes."

"Are there any divorces?" I asked, growing bolder.

"Nope."

"None?"

"None."

Hmmm... So all five of Reid's children are, not only, active in the Church to this day, all five were temple marriages and (perhaps most amazing) all five marriages remain intact to this day.

These facts are actually quite astonishing and well worth pondering.

Halls of Fame vs. "the Real Record"

I remember, the story of a college football coach named Eddie Robinson, who retired back in 1994. He has had a lifetime of awards and accolades.[220]

At his retirement, at age 75, the press urged him to brag about his many accomplishments. His response was simple and humble:

> The real record I have set for over 50 years is the fact that I have had one job and one wife.

You know, marriage itself is a tough race with a high failure rate. But parenting is so intensely tricky, that you just can't pass judgment on parents whose children have strayed away. I mean, there's nothing that throws a wrench into *your* plans than trying raise a bunch of little sentient beings who all have plans of their own. The best men and women in history have scarcely figured out perfect parenting. From Lehi to Joseph Smith, from Alma to Corianton. Even God the Father lost a third of his own children.

So when I learned about Harry Reid's children, I was really excited! Extraordinary! Five children. All married in the temple. All still active in the Church. No divorces. You just cannot plan on such a thing!

The first person I called after I found out this simple little statistic about Reid's family was my father. He was, like me, not a Senator Reid fan, by any means. But I knew he would be excited to hear about this news. For he used to tell me:

> You cannot judge a parent if one or many of their children go astray. But if you find a family in which **all** of the children are married in the temple with no divorces and are fully active to this day... well, then you can probably pass one confident judgment about the parents: They are doing something right!

You might claim that there's a lot of luck involved. And you would be right. But with the youngest Reid child in his mid-30s, the family is showing a pretty strong trend here.

---

[220] NAIA Hall of Fame, Sugar Bowl Hall of Fame, Louisiana Sports Hall of Fame, Whitney M. Young Jr. Memorial Award, New York Urban League, Horatio Alger Award, Southwest Athletic Conference Hall of Fame and more.

As I said, there are those who are so cynical that they would attribute the fully-active status of Reid's children to keeping up appearances. (I guess it's all about whom to bribe for a temple recommend, isn't it?) That's a fair hypothesis, but only if you have a very low opinion of the Church.

You know, you can put on some ill-fitting fancy formal wear and look the part for a while. But at some point, either it rips or you just get tired of it. Being a Mormon is quite demanding on the heart, the mind, might and strength of any individual. And I don't care what your father does in the Federal government; sooner or later you get a Church calling that will tax your soul dry if you are not truly committed. There has to be a thousand other easier ways of gaining the façade of respectability than activity in *The Church of Jesus Christ of Latter-day Saints...* especially in Nevada.

I have told a few other members of the Church about the Reid family and it's interesting to see their reactions. One of the more interesting exchanges went something like this:

"Can you believe Reid is a Democrat and a member of the Church?"

"You know," I said. "I recently found out that all of Reid's children were married in the temple and they are all still active in the Church and yet he's still a Democrat."

"Yep," came the response, with a shake of the head. "It's just hypocritical, isn't it?"

"What?"

"Hypocritical..." Head still shaking. "...to be a Mormon Democrat."

Wow. I guess this shows that people really do hear just what they want to hear. The good news was completely missed.

(Bear in mind that, in this case, I have to bear a little responsibility for this reaction. I was the one who just swooped into this person's house, expecting an instant conversation about politics.)

I don't think this kind of thing will happen as easily in print. People have to slow down to read, particularly when they read books. That is, in part, why I wrote this book rather than just start a blog. I hope to encourage people to slow down for a moment, forget this Democrat-Republican thing, and recognize some of those other significant little details, which have far more eternal consequences. As Elder Maxwell said of the Prodigal Son,

> Whatever else happened on that particular day in that "far country"... one homeward-bound swineherd would scarcely have been noticed by the passersby, though things of eternal significance had happened to him.[221]

Check out Senator Reid's October 2007 BYU devotional. After my mother watched this devotional, she leaned back, breathed a seemingly sigh in relief. Then she simply stated, "Now, he is my brother." She had allowed the burden of bitterness to be lifted. The animosity went away. What a relief.

And yet, if she were a resident of Nevada, it's most likely that she would *not* vote for him. I've made it clear enough that my family is not politically supportive of Senator Reid. But that's beside the point. Or maybe that... *is* the point, that despite our political differences, as we strive together, we can rejoice, without hesitation, in the success of others.

Who Really Get's the Credit?

So, Reid's children are all still active in Church and have suffered no divorces. Not bad.

Now, that could all change tomorrow. Life offers no recess from... life. But even up to this point, they have certainly had a good streak going and have definitely beaten the odds. So, how did they do it?

As stated, I don't know Harry Reid's family. So, I can't make any real judgments about ways and means. I have no firsthand knowledge. But, in doing my research, I have gained just enough confidence to make a few suppositions (and that's all they are at this point) about why this family is the way it is.

I'm not about to give Harry Reid much credit for this phenomenon. Nope. I must give credit where credit is due, in this case, to Landra, the wife and mother. You see, in reading news about the Reids, I've detected a silent yet strong undercurrent, a

---

[221] Maxwell, "General Conference address: Care for the Life of the Soul."

foundation to the family, which is Landra Reid. For example, Reid is often assailed by opinionated people who chew him out. And yet, many of these ranters manage to include the side comment, "As much as I love your wife, I think you are..." and the rant continues. This top of the hat to Landra happens with curious and amusing frequency. I could be wrong about her. But, as I said, these are the musings of a complete outsider. I don't even know what Landra looks like.

However, I thought that the following interview excerpt was particularly enlightening, on many levels. This is Harry Reid being interviewed by Tom Daschle, a former Democratic Party leader and longtime friend:

Daschle: You've raised them particularly well despite incredible pressures of public life.

Reid: One of my pet peeves is when people leave public office and say, "Now I can spend time with my family." I don't say that. I've spent enough time with my family. I feel that I could have been practicing law... a businessman...

I think that people should understand that the mere fact that you've been in politics doesn't mean you can't be a good parent. Now, I hope I've been a good parent. But I wouldn't have been a better one if I had been doing something else.

Now, there's no question, Tom, that **my children are as good as they are mainly because of my wife.** She is a wonderful mother. Wonderful wife. But she would have been doing that if I had been doing something else. So I think that people should not hesitate going into politics because they're afraid it will hurt their family.

Daschle: Well, I can say–with some authority because I know them–that I think the test of a good parent is how good a parent your children become. And you've got children that are fantastic parents.[222]

Once again, I'll have to take Daschle's word for it. But, why not? It rings true to me. As I said, I may be wrong. I could emulate a few conservative friends by choosing to constantly think the worst of Reid.

---

[222] Reid, "Book TV interview with Harry Reid."

But, with limited time to spend on earth, I have no interest in spending it in the search for negativity. I have already been given guidance on how to spend my time: "If there is anything virtuous, lovely, or of good report or praiseworthy," I'll seek after those things.

So, at the end of the day, all I can say is that Senator Reid sure has my vote–uh, actually, no. Not literally. He doesn't literally have my vote. You know what I mean. Harry Reid seems like a great guy to me.

And, you know who else seems like a great guy? Glenn Beck. I await the day when a leftist Democrat writes a whole chapter praising Beck. I don't think that day will come. I can only hope to be proven wrong.

Opening the Door to the Treasure

I quote from Reid's recent biography *The Good Fight*, in which he describes his and his wife's conversion to the gospel. I will now quote that part more fully:

> We opened the door to our heavenly father. Yes, we were married, but now we would reconcile our disparate backgrounds in a union of spirit and understanding, and in a recognition that there was more to life—more to existence-—than what we could see. More than just us. It was as much choice as revelation. A simple act. And our choice was made so much easier by the people we'd met... even the crazy man who lived next door to the Birds. He was expert in scripture, and referred to Satan as "Old Horns." A nice man, with a wonderful spirit, who, we later learned, had struggled with mental illness and had been in and out of institutions. There were many others, who didn't so much speak their religion as live it. We would start a family soon. For my children, I would do anything to avoid the path that my parents had taken. This was to be a very different path.[223]

Their story reminds me of a talk by President Boyd K. Packer, in which he relates a parable about Celestial marriage:

> They made a covenant that together they would open the treasure and, as instructed, he would watch over the vault and protect it; she would watch over the treasure. ...his full

---

[223] Reid, *The Good Fight*, 128.

purpose was to see that she was safe as she watched over that which was most precious to them both.

With great joy they found that they could pass the treasure on to their children; each could receive a full measure, undiminished to the last generation.[224]

---

[224] Packer, "For Time and All Eternity," 21.

WHAT I REALLY THINK!

We probably wouldn't worry about what people think of us if we could know how seldom they do.

Olin Miller

There's a question, which people have said they wanted to ask all through those first three chapters, namely, "What does Joe really think about abortion, economics and the environment?"

You can find plenty of my own political sentiments in those joint conclusions. They were not, after all, true joint conclusions between different people. They were the joint opinions of two personalities of my own creation. As such, in case you hadn't noticed, the joint conclusions definitely have a conservative bend to them. Of course they do. They were written by me.

My own personal political views are not even as bipartisan as they might appear by reading the joint conclusions alone. I do *not* consider myself a moderate. I am much more comfortable calling myself a true blue conservative right wing Republican.

Of course, like any self-respecting Republican, I'm not at all pleased with the Republicans at the moment. These days, the choice between Democrats and Republicans is like choosing between communists and hypocrites. And it seems like it's always been like that. But I also don't think you can fault the politicians for that. I think Republican voters are pretty hypocritical when it comes to standing firm behind those free-market ideals. They want government out of their lives, but always with just that one exception that they directly benefit from. It's been my experience that conservatives are just as ignorant and reactionary as liberals when it comes to things like price gouging, for example.

But, by far the biggest topic that highlights Republican hypocrisy to date is... immigration. What's my thought on illegal immigration?

What do I Think of Immigration?

I hate the idea of illegal immigrants coming over here and living off welfare. But I also hate the idea of first generation *legal* immigrants living off welfare. And I don't like second generation immigrants living off welfare. Come think of it, I'm not a fan of anyone living off welfare. I'm not a fan of welfare.

You know what I am a fan of? Those two pillars of conservativism, namely, free-market economics and the rule of law. But there's a bit of a problem with that. What if a law gets passed that is in direct conflict with free-market economics? I call most of those laws... stupid. I'm not a fan of the stupid laws behind most welfare programs. But I'm practically an enemy of the state when it comes to laws that back subsidies, tariffs, trade restrictions or any other such protectionist laws. So, you see, the rule of law isn't a flag I like to march behind when so many laws are just plain stupid.

So, where do I come down on immigration? Well, it's quite simple: The only way to ensure that our borders are protected is to have far more open immigration. This is a free-market principle, folks. I don't want the government telling me I can't hire Poncho, even if he was born in Mexico. You know why I want to hire Poncho? Well, he's a harder worker than anyone I can find. Or maybe I just like his hair. Or maybe it's not really anyone's business why I want to hire him. I shouldn't have to justify my decision any more than I should have to explain why I prefer to buy vanilla ice cream.

We have a terribly restrictive immigration policy right now. These policies are trade restrictions and the results are what they always have been: bad. Conservatives usually get it when it comes to price controls or restrictive laws on commerce.

Conservatives should not be surprised that government restrictions on labor have created a black market for labor. Hence, the illegal immigration problem. It's a trade restriction problem, folks. Not an immigration problem.

Why aren't Republicans fighting to break down these trade restrictions on labor? If you allow the honest laborers to come through the port of entry, that allows us to keep track of them. We don't need to make them citizens. But they would, at least, be documented workers. As it is now, they're unaccounted for by the millions, with more trying to sneak across hundreds of miles of southern border. And they're running interference for the terrorists, drug dealers and smugglers.

So, let Poncho in. Keep track of him. Guest worker program. Whatever. Let Poncho and I trade our money and services without government interference. But Republicans are sounding so protectionist these days. It's embarrassing.

Okay, that about wraps up my own personal political diatribe. But that's not the end of this conversation. This is a fully formed opinion of mine, so fully formed, in fact, that I have outlined an entire book on the subject, which I intend to publish... soon. It's title?

How Can You Possibly
Protect the Borders with More Open Immigration?

As long as we're doing teasers for future book titles, the following titles are also in the works:

How Can You Possibly Respect those
Washington Politicians, Pundits or Pinko-Commies?

How Can You Possibly
be a Mormon and a Republican?

How Can You Possibly
be an LDS Proponent of Bush's Iraq War?

Though I am not entirely satisfied with the title of that last one, it is nearly finished. Look for it in stores some time during the Summer of 2011.

And that's what I really think!

BIBLIOGRAPHY

Amazon.com Customers. "Customer Reviews of The Shock Doctrine: The Rise of Disaster Capitalism by Naomi Klein." *Amazon.com*, n.d. www.amazon.com/review/RB0E7DDZKY828/ref=cm_cr_rdp_perm.

Ausubel, Jesse H. "Climate Change: Some Ways to Lessen Worries". Julian Simon Centre for Policy Research, October 2002. www.libertyindia.org/pdfs/Ausubel-ClimateChange2001.pdf.

Bawer, Bruce. *Beyond Queer: Challenging Gay Left Orthodoxy*. 1st ed. Free Press, 1996.

Benson, Ezra T. *An Enemy Hath Done This*. Paperback. Bookcraft Pubs, 1992.

Bestiat, Frederic. *Selected Essays on Political Economy*. Library of Economics and Liberty, 1995. www.econlib.org/library/Bastiat/basEss1.html.

— — —. *The Law (first published in 1850)*. Translated by Dean Russell. 2nd ed. Library of Economics and Liberty. Irvington-on-Hudson, NY: Foundation for Economic Education, Inc., 1998. www.econlib.org/library/Bastiat/basLaw1.html.

Block, Walter. "Rent Control." In *The Concise Encyclopedia of Economics*. Library of Economics and Liberty, 2002. www.econlib.org/library/Enc1/RentControl.html.

Blomberg, Craig L, and Steven E. Robinson. *How Wide the Divide?: A Mormon & an Evangelical in Conversation*. Paperback. InterVarsity Press, 1997.

Bowman, Alan K., Peter Garnsey, and Averil Cameron. *The Cambridge Ancient History*. 2nd ed. Cambridge University Press, 2005.

Buffett, Warren. "Warren Buffett and NBC's Tom Brokaw." Interview by Tom Brokaw. TV, November 9, 2007. www.cnbc.com/id/21553857.

Caplan, Bryan. *The Myth of the Rational Voter: Why Democracies Choose Bad Policies (New Edition)*. 1st ed. Princeton New Jersey: Princeton University Press, 2008.

Card, Orson Scott. "Government and the 'Free Market'." *The Rhinoceros Times*, January 13, 2003. www.ornery.org/essays/warwatch/2003-01-13-1.html.

— — —. "Student Research Area - OSC Answers Questions." *Hatrack River*, February 18, 2004. www.hatrack.com/research/questions/q0118.shtml.

— — —. "The Insanity of Parties." *The Rhinoceros Times, Greensboro, NC*, February 3, 2008. www.ornery.org/essays/warwatch/2008-02-03-1.html.

Carter, Jimmy. *Our Endangered Values: America's Moral Crisis*. Paperback. Simon & Schuster, 2006.

Chan, Jackie. *I Am Jackie Chan: My Life in Action*. Hardcover. Allen and Unwin, 1999.

LDS Church. "Embryonic Stem-cell Research - LDS Newsroom." *News Room of The Church of Jesus Christ of Latter-day Saints*, 2008. http://newsroom.lds.org/ldsnewsroom/eng/public-issues/embryonic-stem-cell-research.

— — —. "Political Neutrality - LDS Newsroom." *News Room of The Church of Jesus Christ of Latter-day Saints*, 2007. http://newsroom.lds.org/ldsnewsroom/eng/public-issues/political-neutrality.

Crichton, Michael. "Complexity Theory and Environmental Management" presented at the Washington Center for Complexity and Public Policy, Washington D.C., November 6, 2005. www.michaelcrichton.net/speech-complexity.html.

— — —. "Environmentalism as Religion" presented at the Commonwealth Club, San Francisco, CA, September 15, 2003. www.michaelcrichton.net/speech-environmentalismaseligion.html.

— — —. "Michael Crichton on Charlie Rose." Interview by Charlie Rose. TV, February 17, 2007. www.crichton-official.com/video-charlierose-2-17-07.html.

Crippen, Alex. "Warren Buffett's Fellow Billionaires Don't Bite on Million Dollar Tax Challenge." News. *CNBC*, November 9, 2007. www.cnbc.com/id/21708265/.

Cueto, C, W F Durham, and W J Hayes. "The effect of known repeated oral doses of chlorophenothane (DDT) in man." *Journal of the American Medical Association* 162, no. 9 (October 27, 1956): 890-897. www.ncbi.nlm.nih.gov/pubmed/13366680.

Democratic Party. "The 2004 Democratic National Platform for America", 2004. www.democrats.org/pdfs/2004platform.pdf.

Diamond, Jared M. *Collapse: How Societies Choose to Fail or Succeed.* 1st ed. Penguin (Non-Classics), 2005.

— — —. *The Third Chimpanzee: The Evolution and Future of the Human Animal.* 5th ed. New York: Harper Perennial, 2006.

Dille, Brian. Letter to Joe Andersen. "Abortion Update", January 6, 2010.

Dilorenzo, Thomas. *The Real Lincoln: A New Look at Abraham Lincoln, His Agenda, and an Unnecessary War.* Hardcover. Prima Lifestyles, 2002.

Dong, Jack (Haobo). Letter to Joe Andersen. "Re: American's career rigidity", June 3, 2010.

Earle, Sylvia. *Sustainable Sea.* Audio CD. The Great Lecture Library. Chautauqua, 2005. www.thegreatlecturelibrary.com.

Easterbrook, Gregg. *The Progress Paradox: How Life Gets Better While People Feel Worse.* Trade Paperback. Random House, 2004.

Ehat, Andrew F, and Lyndon W. Cook. *The Words of Joseph Smith: The contemporary accounts of the Nauvoo discourses of the Prophet Joseph.* 1st ed. Religious studies monograph series. Bookcraft, 1980. http://www3.librarything.com/work/1641637/book/63973628.

Eisenhower, Dwight. "Military-Industrial Complex Speech", January 17, 1961. http://coursesa.matrix.msu.edu/~hst306/documents/indust.html.

Ettlinger, Steve. *Twinkie, Deconstructed: My Journey to Discover How the Ingredients Found in Processed Foods Are Grown, Mined (Yes, Mined), and Manipulated Into What America Eats.* 1st ed. Hudson Street Press, 2007.

Faust, James E. "Trying to Serve the Lord Without Offending the Devil". Speech, BYU, November 15, 1995. http://speeches.byu.edu/reader/reader.php?id=7809.

Fothergill, Alastair. *Blue Planet: Seas of Life.* 1st ed. DK ADULT, 2002.

Friedman, Milton. "Charlie Rose Interview with Milton Friedman." Interview by Charlie Rose. Video, December 26, 2005. http://cafehayek.com/2005/12/milton_and_char.html.

— — —. "Commanding Heights : Milton Friedman Interview on PBS", October 1, 2000. www.pbs.org/wgbh/commandingheights/shared/minitext/int_miltonfriedman.html#4.

— — —. "The Open Mind: 'A Nobel Laureate on the American Economy'." Interview by Richard Heffner. TV, May 3, 1977. www.theopenmind.tv/searcharchive_episode_transcript.asp?id=493.

— — —. "The Pencil Story." *Free to Choose.* PBS, 1979. www.ideachannel.tv.

Friedman, Milton and Rose. *April 2003 Interview with Milton and Rose Friedman, by Bob Chitester (found on the bonus features of The Power of Choice: The Life and Ideas of Milton Friedman).* DVD. The Power of Choice: The Life and Ideas of Milton Friedman, 2003.

— — —. *Free to Choose: A Personal Statement.* Hardcover. Secker & Warburg, 1980.

Friedman, Thomas L. *Hot, Flat, and Crowded: Why We Need a Green Revolution and How It Can Renew America*. 1st ed. Farrar, Straus and Giroux, 2008.

Frontline. *The Secret History of the Credit Card*. Video. FRONTLINE PBS VIDEO, 2004. www.pbs.org/wgbh/pages/frontline/shows/credit/.

Galbraith, James. *The Predator State: How Conservatives Abandoned the Free Market and Why Liberals Should Too*. Paperback. Free Press, 2009.

Gazzaniga, Michael. *The Ethical Brain*. Audio CD. The Great Lecture Library. Chautauqua, 2005. www.thegreatlecturelibrary.com.

Gingrich, Newt, and Terry Maple. *A contract with the Earth*. JHU Press, 2007.

Givens, Terryl L. *People of Paradox: A History of Mormon Culture*. First Edition. Oxford University Press, USA, 2007.

Goodall, Jane. *Reason for Hope: A Spiritual Journey*. Hardcover. Grand Central Publishing, 1999.

Grandin, Temple. *Animals in Translation: Using the Mysteries of Autism to Decode Animal Behavior*. 1st ed. Scribner, 2004.

Harrie, Dan. "LDS Official Calls for More Political Diversity." *The Salt Lake City Tribune*, May 3, 1998. http://ldslivingonline.com/article.php?articleId=79643.

Hewitt, Hugh. *A Mormon in the White House?: 10 Things Every American Should Know about Mitt Romney*. Hardcover. Regnery Publishing, Inc., 2007.

Hitchens, Christopher, and Rev. Al Sharpton. "A Debate: God is Not Great with Al Sharpton and Christopher Hitchens", New York Public Library, May 7, 2007. http://fora.tv/2007/05/07/Al_Sharpton_and_Christopher_Hitchens.

Hugo, Victor. *Les Miserables*. Paperback. Penguin Classics, 1982.

Josephson, Matthew. *The Politicos*. First Hardcover. Quinn & Roden Co., Inc., 1938.

Kernaghan, Charles L. *Ending Child Labor and Sweatshop Abuses*. Audio CD. The Great Lecture Library. Chautauqua, 2005. www.thegreatlecturelibrary.com.

Kurlansky, Mark. *Cod: A Biography of the Fish That Changed the World*. Paperback. Penguin (Non-Classics), 1998.

Leamer, Edward E. *Macroeconomic Patterns and Stories: A Guide for MBAs*. Paperback. Springer Berlin Heidelberg, 2009.

Lee, Harper. *To Kill a Mockingbird*. 35th ed. HarperCollins, 1995.

Lewis, C. S. *Letters to an American Lady*. Wm. B. Eerdmans Publishing Company, 1978.

— — —. *Mere Christianity*. 1st ed. Touchstone Books, 1996.

Lewis, Stephen. *Munk Debates 2009: Foreign Aid Does More Harm Than Good*, 2009. www.youtube.com/watch?v=WClqi4Yr3Ys.

Mann, Charles C. *1491: New Revelations of the Americas Before Columbus*. Paperback. Vintage Press, 2006.

Maxeiner, Dirk. *Life Counts: Cataloging Life on Earth*. 1st ed. Atlantic Monthly Press, 2002.

Maxwell, Neal A. *All These Things Shall Give Thee Experience*. Paperback. Salt Lake City, UT: Deseret Book, 2007.

— — —. "Care for the Life of the Soul." *173rd Annual General Conference*. Salt Lake City, April 2003. http://lds.org/conference/talk/display/0,5232,23-1-353-23,00.html.

McCorvey, Norma, and Gary Thomas. "Roe v. McCorvey." *Leadership University*, July 13, 2002. www.leaderu.com/common/roev.html.

Memmott, Carol. "J.K. Rowling's fond look back at Harry Potter." *USA Today*, July 25, 2007. www.usatoday.com/life/books/news/2007-07-25-jk-rowling_N.htm.

"Miller Time segment on The O'Reilly Factor." Video. *The O'Reilly Factor*. Fox News, April 2, 2008. www.youtube.com/watch?v=7r_GChGHBqc.

Miller, Dennis. "Miller Time segment." Video. *The O'Reilly Factor*. Fox News, October 7, 2009. www.foxnews.com/story/0,2933,562565,00.html.

— — —. "The Buck Starts Here." Video. *The Half-Hour News Hour*. Fox News, December 20, 2008. www.youtube.com/watch?v=f21LmwI8MPk.

Myers, Dennis. "Prevent Pregnancy, Prevent Abortion." *News Review.com*, September 15, 2005. www.newsreview.com/reno/Content?oid=42381.

Nibley, Hugh. *Since Cumorah*. The Collected Works of Hugh Nibley, n.d.

Norberg, Johan. "Defaming Milton Friedman." *Reason Magazine*, 2008. http://reason.com/archives/2008/09/26/defaming-milton-friedman/print.

— — —. "The Klein Doctrine: The Rise of Disaster Polemics." *The Cato Institute*, May 14, 2008. www.cato.org/pub_display.php?pub_id=9384.

Oaks, Elder Dallin H. "Weightier Matters", BYU, February 9, 1999. http://speeches.byu.edu/reader/reader.php?id=6647.

"Obama Reverses 'Global Gag Rule'." *Medical News Today*, January 27, 2009. www.medicalnewstoday.com/articles/136755.php.

Obama, Barack. *The Audacity of Hope*. Later printing, Paperback. Three Rivers Press, 2006.

O'Dea, Thomas F. *The Mormons*. The University of Chicago Press, 1957.

O'Rourke, P.J. *Give War a Chance: Eyewitness Accounts of Mankind's Struggle Against Tyranny, Injustice, and Alcohol-Free Beer*. Paperback. Grove Press, 2003.

Packer, Boyd K. "For Time and All Eternity." *Ensign*, n.d. http://lds.org/ldsorg/v/index.jsp?hideNav=1&locale=0&sourceId=f51a425e0848b010VgnVCM1000004d82620a____&vgnextoid=2354fccf2b7db010VgnVCM1000004d82620aRCRD.

— — —. "The Power of the Priesthood." *Ensign*, May 2010. http://lds.org/ldsorg/v/index.jsp?hideNav=1&locale=0&sourceId=1ab5b73f64838210VgnVCM100000176f620a____&vgnextoid=2354fccf2b7db010VgnVCM1000004d82620aRCRD.

Paul, Ron. "Guest Ron Paul on The Dennis Miller Radio Show." Interview by Dennis Miller. Radio, May 2007. www.youtube.com/watch?v=MrACUZjNtDA.

Ponte, Lowell. *The Cooling: Has the Next Ice Age Already Begun?* Hardcover. Prentice-Hall, 1976.

Powell, Jim. *FDR's Folly: How Roosevelt and His New Deal Prolonged the Great Depression*. 1st ed. Crown Forum, 2003.

Project Vote Smart. "National Rifle Association Rating", n.d. www.votesmart.org/issue_rating_detail.php?r_id=2765.

Rand, Ayn. *Atlas Shrugged*. Paperback. Signet, 1959.

Reid, Senator Harry. "Faith, Family and Public Service" presented at the Devotionals/Forums, BYU, October 9, 2007. speeches.byu.edu.

— — —. "Nevada NewsMakers Interview with Harry Reid - 3 of 3." Interview by Sam Shad. TV, February 21, 2008. www.youtube.com/watch?v=jtG9NsRE2LA.

— — —. "Reid Speaks at Dedication of Ronald Reagan Statue", Washington D.C., June 4, 2009. www.youtube.com/watch?v=LM62D2-38i8.

— — —. "Sen. Harry Reid interviewed by Senator Tom Daschle | Book TV: After Words." Interview by Tom Daschle. TV, September 27, 2008. www.c-spanvideo.org/program/281299-1.

— — —. *The Good Fight*. Putnam Adult (2008), Hardcover, 304 pages, 2008.

Reid, Senator Harry. "Harry Reid Speaks at AIPAC Annual Policy Conference (C-SPAN Video Library)." *AIPAC Annual Policy Conference.* Washington D.C., May 23, 2001. www.c-spanvideo.org/program/ACAnn/start/207/stop/5136.

"Review of the book 'Freefall' by Joseph E. Stiglitz." *The New Yorker,* March 8, 2010. www.newyorker.com/arts/reviews/brieflynoted/2010/03/08/100308crbn_briefl ynoted1.

Ritchie, J. Bonner. *Sunstone Symposium: Pillars of My Faith.* Mp3. Vol. 52. Sunstone Symposium. Salt Lake City, UT, 1992. http://sunstoneonline.com/symposium/symp-mp3s.asp.

Roberts, Russ. *Brink Lindsey on The Age of Abundance.* EconTalk | Library of Economics and Liberty, n.d. www.econtalk.org/archives/2009/03/brink_lindsey_o.html.

— — —. *Caplan on the Myth of the Rational Voter.* EconTalk | Library of Economics and Liberty, n.d. www.econtalk.org/archives/2007/06/caplan_on_the_m.html.

— — —. "Is the Dismal Science Really a Science?" *wsj.com,* February 26, 2010, sec. Opinion. online.wsj.com/article/SB10001424052748704804204575069123218286094.html#art icleTabs=article.

Rogers, Thomas F. "InterConnections." *Sunstone,* no. 2009 (n.d.): 24-37.

Samuelsen, Eric. "A Federalist Candidate." *Deseret News.* Salt Lake City, UT, February 18, 2010, sec. A14. www.deseretnews.com/article/700010239/A-federalist-candidate.html.

Schuettinger, Robert Lindsay, and Eamonn Butler. *Forty Centuries of Wage and Price Controls.* Caroline House Publishers, 1979.

Seligman, Dan. "Keeping Up." *Fortune.* Journal of Commerce (February 27, 1989).

Shellenberger, Michael, and Ted Nordhaus. *Break Through: From the Death of Environmentalism to the Politics of Possibility.* 1st ed. Houghton Mifflin Co., 2007.

Shlaes, Amity. *The Forgotten Man: A New History of the Great Depression.* Paperback. Harper Perennial, 2008.

Smith, Adam. "Book Four, Chapter VIII, Article 2." In *An Inquiry into the Nature and Causes of the Wealth of Nations,* 1776. http://www.adamsmith.org/adam-smith-quotes/.

— — —. "Book One, Chapter VIII." In *An Inquiry into the Nature and Causes of the Wealth of Nations,* 1776. http://www.adamsmith.org/adam-smith-quotes/.

Smith, George A. *Conference Report, April 1914.* General Conference Report. Salt Lake City: The Church of Jesus Christ of Latter-day Saints, April 1914.

Smith, Joseph. "General Smith's Views of the Powers and Policy of the Government of The United States". John Taylor, 1844. http://olivercowdery.com/smithhome/1840s/1844Smit.htm.

Smith, Joseph, and B. H. Roberts. *History of the Church of Jesus Christ of Latter Day Saints.* Kessinger Publishing, 2004.

Sowell, Thomas. *A Conflict of Visions.* Paperback. Quill, 1988.

— — —. *A Personal Odyssey.* Simon and Schuster, 2000.

— — —. "At What Cost?" Web Magazine. *Jewish World Review,* July 30, 2002. www.jewishworldreview.com/cols/sowell073002.asp.

— — —. *Basic Economics 3rd Ed: A Common Sense Guide to the Economy.* Third (Hardcover). Basic Books, 2007.

— — —. *Basic Economics: a Citizen's Guide to the Economy.* 1st ed. Basic Books, 2000.

— — —. "My Platform." Web Magazine. *Jewish World Review,* March 30, 2004. www.jewishworldreview.com/cols/sowell033004.asp.

— — —. "Preferential Policies: An International Perspective (1990 Booknotes Interview)." Interview by Brian Lamb. CSPAN Video Library, May 24, 1990. www.c-spanarchives.org/program/12648-1.

— — —. "Q&A with Thomas Sowell." Interview by Brian Lamb. CSPAN Video Library, April 6, 2005. http://qanda.org/Transcript/?ProgramID=1019.

— — —. *The Housing Boom and Bust.* 1st ed. Basic Books, 2009.

— — —. "Uncommon Knowledge Interview of Thomas Sowell." Interview by Peter Robinson. TV, October 21, 2008. www.hoover.org/multimedia/uk/33647984.html.

Stein, Rob. "Abortions Hit Lowest Number Since 1976." *The Washington Post*, January 17, 2008, sec. A01. www.washingtonpost.com/wp-dyn/content/article/2008/01/16/AR2008011603624.html.

Stossel, John. "Crony Capitalism." Video/MP3. *John Stossel Show*. Fox Business Channel, March 1, 2010. http://acu.libsyn.com/rss.

Summers, Lawrence H. "The Great Liberator." *The New York Times*, November 19, 2006, sec. Opinion. http://www.nytimes.com/2006/11/19/opinion/19summers.html.

Taylor, John. *The Government of God.* S.W. Richards, 1852.

Thomas, Cal. "Mother Teresa has Anti-Abortion Answer." *The Salt Lake City Tribune*, February 15, 1994.

Tilly, Charles, Gabriel Ardant, and Social Science Research Council (U.S.). Committee on Comparative Politics. *The Formation of National States in Western Europe*, 1975.

Tuttle, Merlin. "Multiple Correspondences in 2010 between Merlin Tuttle and Joe Andersen." Interview by C. Joe Andersen. Email, phone, mail, November 2010.

— — —. *The Incredible World of Bats (Chautauqua Lecture).* Audio CD. The Great Lecture Library. Chautauqua, 2002. www.thegreatlecturelibrary.com.

WICKARD V. FILBURN, 317 U. S. 111 (1942) -- US Supreme Court Cases (Stone Court (1942-1943) 1942).

Wallis, Charles L. *Treasure Chest.* Deluxe Hardcover. HarperCollins, 1965. www.lds.org/library/display/0,4945,2044-1-4336-1,00.html.

Walsh, Elsa. "Annals of Politics: Minority Retort: How a pro-gun, anti-abortion Nevadan leads the Senate's Democrats." *The New Yorker*, August 8, 2005. www.newyorker.com/archive/2005/08/08/050808fa_fact?currentPage=all.

Washington Post. "Greenpeace Just Kidding About Armageddon", June 2, 2006. www.washingtonpost.com/wp-dyn/content/article/2006/06/01/AR2006060101884.html.

Williams, Walter. "Economics for the Citizen Series (Part 9 of 10)." Web Magazine. *Jewish World Review*, March 22, 2005. www.jewishworldreview.com/0305/williams_econ9.php3.

Wolfe, Alan. *The Future of Liberalism (Vintage).* Paperback. Vintage Press, 2010.

Wood, Elder Robert S. "Instruments of the Lord's Peace." *176th Annual General Conference.* Salt Lake City, April 2006. http://lds.org/conference/talk/display/0,5232,23-1-602-30,00.html.

Young, Brigham. *Discourses of Brigham Young, sel. John A. Widtsoe (referenced in 1997 Ensign Article "The Truth Shall Make You Free").* Edited by John A. Widtsoe, 1941.

ontheissues.org. "Harry Reid on Abortion." Political Voting Record. *On The Issues*, n.d. www.ontheissues.org/Social/Harry_Reid_Abortion.htm.

sourcewatch.org. "Harry Reid on SourceWatch", n.d. www.sourcewatch.org/index.php?title=Harry_Reid.

ACKNOWLEDGEMENTS

I must give special thanks to Brian Dille both for his work as an official editor and for the feedback and encouragement that he has provided in his spare time.

Thank you Karl Snow, Tom Bogle, Jorgi Andersen, Dr. Goodman, Peter Johnson, Rodney Jackson, David & Teressa Carr and others, plenty others, for your encouragement and feedback.

And I especially appreciate those of you who gave me not so nice feedback. Your feedback was perhaps the most valuable.

A special thanks to my mother (Janet) and my wife (Karen) for encouragement, feedback and emotional support.

Thank you Tom Rogers, Don Jarvis, Bonner Ritchie, Evans Farnsworth, Steve McFarland and Eric Samuelson. In particular, thank you for letting me call you "pinko-commies" now and then.

Thanks to the many editors, both volunteer and professional, namely, Cami Nuttal, Sonja Dahl, Cord Cooper, Carol Reynolds, Rachel Lyon and Larry Draughon.

And I must give praise and acknowledgement to the one person without whom this book would not have been written, my father Clint Andersen, for his life-long encouragement and his specific financial and spiritual support for this project. And, I will forever benefit from the answer that he gave me to so many of my questions: "I don't know. But I'm glad you're trying to figure it out."

ABOUT THE AUTHOR

Clinton "Joe" Andersen, Jr. spent two years in Russia as a missionary for the LDS Church. At age 19, he witnessed, firsthand, the devastation that Soviet communism had inflicted upon things like... customer service. That concept had been raped, pillaged and driven to extinction. There's nothing so strange as getting yelled at for not finding the sour cream on your own. It was no less strange for Joe to find himself, after two years, staring in complete awe and amazement at the cereal aisle of the grocery store. It was a formative experience, to say the least.

Upon his return, Joe met and married Karen, a woman with a special talent: a seemingly endless supply of patience with Joe's most eccentric undertakings, including a three-year venture into writing and publishing this very book. Before that, she endured a five-year construction project, which remained a constant eyesore out the back window. During construction, Karen gave birth to two children. When the project was complete, Clayton and Shereen had a life-sized hobbit hole to call their own.

The Andersen hobbit hole has appeared in print media, such as *The Mesa Tribune*, *The Los Angeles Times* and *Backyard Living* magazine. It has also appeared on HGTV's "Offbeat America" and local news. In fact, it was awarded 3TV's "Best Home Sweet Home of 2006".

These media clips can be seen on Joe's YouTube channel at **www.youtube.com/cjandersen**, which also showcases his knack for video editing. Also on the channel is a true classic in filmmaking: "Clayton's Backyard Documentary".

In the meantime, with a bachelors degree in mechanical engineering from ASU, Joe has found work in various and surprising engineering fields: from water treatment plants to designing multiple subdivisions, from aerospace solenoid valves to turbine engine parts. It's not rocket science, but its close. Besides, Joe also found work in the field of brain surgery as a neurosurgical image guidance engineer. Seriously.

(continued on next page)

So what could the future possibly hold for Joe and his family? Well, first there's... possibly publishing, as in *Possibly Publishing*, the publishing company launched by Joe for the purpose of developing the *How Can You Possibly*® book series. The book you hold in your hand is the first of that series. May it not be the last.

Another project on the horizon involves animal welfare. There is a long-overlooked behavioral problem, which mainly distresses zoo animals. In the industry, the affliction is called *stereotyping* and it could be described as "captivity-induced obsessive compulsive disorder". Stereotyping occurs when an animal (even captive-born) is not able to express its natural behavior.

Joe has envisioned a radical treatment strategy that would be both therapy for the animals and a self-sustaining enterprise that would pay for itself and more. This idea involves engineering interactive systems that facilitate game play between captive animals and people, but without any physical contact. We have the technology to do such things today.

This literally means playing sports with animals, but on *their* terms: not like rodeo or the circus, which evolved purely for human entertainment. On the contrary, the ultimate purpose of these games is to allow the animals to better express their natural and pleasurable instincts. By treating individual animals in this rather eccentric way, the hope is that these games attract public interest just like any other sport. If successful, it would lead to self-sustaining revenue and so benefit animals in and out of captivity worldwide.

By the way, Joe likes his steak cooked medium well.

11867769R0018

Made in the USA
Lexington, KY
06 November 2011